FOOD AND YOU

FOOD
AND
YOU

A Guide to
Healthy Habits
for Teens

Marjolijn Bijlefeld
and
Sharon K. Zoumbaris

Greenwood Press
Westport, Connecticut • London

Library of Congress Cataloging-in-Publication Data

Bijlefeld, Marjolijn, 1960–
    Food and you : a guide to healthy habits for teens / by Marjolijn Bijlefeld and Sharon
K. Zoumbaris.
        p.   cm.
    Includes bibliographical references and index.
    ISBN 0–313–31108–0 (alk. paper)
        1. Teenagers—Nutrition.   2. Teenagers—Health and hygiene.   3. Food.   I. Zoumbaris,
Sharon K., 1955–   II. Title.
    RA777.B554   2001
    613.7'043—dc21   00–061686

British Library Cataloguing in Publication Data is available.

Library of Congress Catalog Card Number: 00–061686
ISBN: 0–313–31108–0

First published in 2001

Greenwood Press, 88 Post Road West, Westport, CT 06881
An imprint of Greenwood Publishing Group, Inc.
www.greenwood.com

Printed in the United States of America

The paper used in this book complies with the
Permanent Paper Standard issued by the National
Information Standards Organization (Z39.48–1984).

10 9 8 7 6 5 4 3 2 1

Copyright Acknowledgments

The authors and publisher gratefully acknowledge permission for use of the following material:

Excerpts from authors' interviews with Anne Lehman; Christi R. Carver, Psychiatric Nurse Practitioner; Sue Snider from the Department of Animal and Food Sciences; Melanie Polk from the American Institute for Cancer Research; and Lawrence Lepisto.

Appendix B: "The Smart Snacker's Guide to Substitutions," Appendix F: "Pesticides," and portions of a press release dated December 1, 1999 on the history of nutrition courtesy of American Institute for Cancer Research.

CONTENTS

ACKNOWLEDGMENTS

The authors gratefully acknowledge the many people who generously provided their time and expertise to this volume, granting us interviews and steering us to other sources, published materials and web sites. Notably among them are: Christi Carver, Dun Gifford, Anne Lehman and her students at First Colonial High School in Virginia Beach, Virginia, Dr. Lawrence Lepisto, Chris OBrion, Melanie Polk, Sue Snider, and Scot Zoumbaris. A special thanks to Bob and Norm for taking over the cooking.

INTRODUCTION

Why do we eat? Obviously, there's the physical need to turn calories from food into energy. But that's not the only reason. Sometimes we eat when we're hungry, but many times, eating has little to do with actual hunger. We eat because our friends or family are eating. Eating together is a social occasion. We eat because we're sad or because we're celebrating. We eat because we're bored or lonely or anxious.

In other words, we eat out of habit just as much as we eat to satisfy a physical need. And many young Americans have unhealthy nutrition habits, eating too many fatty, high-calorie foods and not enough of a variety of foods including fruits and vegetables. The bad news is these less healthy habits have a direct effect on our overall health turning today's youth into overweight, sedentary couch potatoes.

Less healthy habits can be replaced by better habits. Our diets—the foods we choose to eat—should always be enjoyable, not an exercise in sacrifice. Healthier people eat a wide variety of foods—and enjoy it. Healthier people also balance their food consumption with physical activity. The two go hand in hand. Diet alone doesn't make one healthy; it's the combination of eating the right foods and performing enjoyable activities that strengthens muscles and endurance. The benefits of healthy nutritional habits can last a lifetime. Research continues to show the link of a varied and healthy diet and the decreased risk of developing serious diseases.

A goal should be good nutrition, not perfect nutrition. There is room in most people's diets for occasional indulgences like chocolate cake and ice cream. There's also room within healthy habits for occasional lazy afternoons spent lounging on the couch. However, for many people, indulgences and couch-potato afternoons aren't the occasional lapse but the routine. That's where the problems start. Just as the healthy cycle of good nutrition and physical activities go hand in hand, the flip side is true, too. Eat too much of the wrong foods and you feel tired, unwilling or unable to get moving. This results in weight gain and the overwhelming feeling that weight loss and physical activity are unachievable goals.

It doesn't have to be that way. Take steps now to improve your nutritional habits, and you'll begin seeing and feeling results soon. Make healthier choices now and they'll become habits for life. There are no tricks or magical treatments. It simply requires a decision to think about which foods to eat, to substitute healthier choices for less healthy ones, and to find ways to include physical activity into your daily schedule. This volume will help you become knowledgeable food consumers—by understanding the labels on food and what to look for and avoid. It contains suggestions on how to improve your diet step by step in a healthy way. It also explains why alternatives such as frequent restrictive dieting are less healthy in the long run and discusses some of the other damaging habits young people fall into.

Got ten minutes? Then you've got time to include some physical activity in your schedule. Find that amount of times three or so times a day and take a walk, skate, jump rope, dance, stretch and bend, climb some stairs. What you do, at least initially, is less important than sticking with it. As you explore some different types of activity, you'll find some you enjoy. And the more you do them, the easier they will become. When you first start, even climbing some stairs might leave you winded, but your body will respond to the new demands with increased strength and endurance—and you'll enjoy the activities even more. What started out as a chore, something you felt you had to do, becomes something you look forward to each day.

Ditto for the foods you eat. Primarily meat eaters who start sampling some other foods will find that a greater variety of foods on the plate is just as satisfying. Some people might reduce the amount of meat they eat; others might cut it out of their diets altogether. Plus, one of the easiest ways to try new foods is to start to cook. Cooking includes taking time to plan menus, to shop, and, above all else, to sit and enjoy the fruits of your labors when the cooking is done. With the wide variety of kitchen tools, fresh fruits and vegetables, and recipes available today it makes sense to eat less fast food and more fresh food.

Just as there's no one answer for everyone as to which exercise is best, there's no one answer for which specific diet is best. You're each individuals and your choice of foods and activities should be decided by you. The combination that makes you feel energetic and strong and supplies a full range of needed nutrients is the one that's right for you.

There are many ways to develop good nutritional habits. This volume will help you decide what works best for you. But the first step down the road is to decide that you're going to reward your body, for now and for the long term, by developing healthier habits.

1

MAKING
HEALTHY CHOICES

Americans are not taking good care of themselves. Study after study reveals some shortcomings in the way we, as a nation, eat and exercise. Maybe that applies to you, or maybe it doesn't. Either way, this volume is designed to lead you through the basics of nutrition and help you easily introduce more healthful options into your lifestyle. The book is not designed to turn you into a vegetarian triathlete—although that could happen. It is designed to help you understand what a healthy diet is and how exercise and the foods you eat affect the way you perform, and get you started on a lifelong process of living healthy.

A recent snapshot of the health of American youth was not encouraging. According to the National Association for Sport and Physical Education's Shape of the Nation 1997 survey, nearly half of young people ages 12 to 21, and more than one-third of high school students, do not participate in vigorous physical activity on a regular basis. Fourteen percent of children ages 6 to 11 are overweight and 12% of adolescents ages 12 to 17 are overweight. The percentage of young Americans who are overweight has more than doubled in the past 30 years. But inactivity is only part of the problem. (The NASPE website is www.aahperd.org/naspe.)

According to the federal Centers for Disease Control and Prevention

(CDC), the problem with the diet of most young Americans is that more than 84% of them eat too much fat, and more than 91% eat too much saturated fat. Only one in five young people eats the recommended five daily servings of fruits and vegetables. Fifty-one percent of children and adolescents eat less than one serving of fruit a day, and 29% eat less than one serving a day of vegetables that are not fried. The average calcium intake of adolescent girls is about 800 milligrams a day, considerably less than the recommended dietary allowance for adolescents of 1,200 milligrams of calcium a day. One in five students aged 15 to 18 regularly skips breakfast. Eight percent of high school girls take laxatives or vomit to lose or keep from gaining weight, and 9% take diet pills. Harmful weight-loss practices have been reported among girls as young as nine years old.

The results can be devastating. Researchers continually uncover links between diet and exercise and a myriad of diseases. Poor diet and inactivity cause at least 300,000 deaths among U.S. adults each year, according to the CDC. The number was reported in an October 27, 1999, issue of the *Journal of the American Medical Association* and by then Agriculture Secretary Don Glickman at a USDA Symposium on Childhood Obesity: Causes And Prevention. Researchers from the National Cancer Institute reported in April 2000 that women who eat healthy diets tend to live longer and healthier lives than women whose diets were less healthy. One of the authors of the report, which appeared in the *Journal of the American Medical Association*, Arthur Schatzkin, stated that the findings could point "to a very practical approach to making healthful dietary changes: eat more of the recommended foods, without concentrating on the exact nutrient content of the foods you eat." In a National Cancer Institute press release of February 25, 2000, announcing the research, he also stated that it's possible that people with healthy eating habits may have a more healthy lifestyle in general.

It's very likely that diet and health go hand in hand. People who do eat healthy foods, however, don't necessarily do it to minimize risk for cancer, heart disease, stroke, osteopororis, and diabetes. They do it because it makes them feel good and energetic and able to participate in a more active lifestyle. They enjoy the variety of tastes and textures in a well-balanced diet. In other words, good nutrition doesn't have to be a sacrifice. The fundamental basis of a good diet is to eat a wide variety of foods. That, in turn, makes eating more fun. And while we eat meals to satisfy hunger, we should also enjoy mealtimes.

NUTRITION AS A SCIENCE

One hundred years ago, nutrition as a science was a brand new concept. The American Institute for Cancer Research issued a December 1999 press release detailing the changes in American diets during the century that was ending. Melanie Polk, the director of nutrition education at the institute, asserted that the notion of a "balanced" diet was quite abstract. Families knew that they needed protein and "roughage." "They very likely knew that eating fruits and vegetables could keep you from getting sick, but that was probably about it."

The science of nutrition blossomed in 1914 when Casimir Funk, a Polish chemist, coined the term "vitamin," and scientists began to identify, isolate and synthesize these newly discovered nutrients. During the following half century, scientists began to better understand—and were able to correct—deficiency diseases such as scurvy, anemia or low iron, and rickets.

As research continues to explore the connection between nutrients and health, that knowledge is applied. For example, the list of recommended daily allowances of vitamins and minerals is updated every five years.

Researchers began examining the link between cholesterol and heart disease in the 1980s and studied possible substances called phytochemicals within fruits, vegetables, whole grains, and beans that seem to be active in preventing some cancers and other chronic diseases.

BUSY LIVES = QUICK FOODS

While researchers were studying foods, sociologists were studying the changes in American households. During the 1940s and 1950s, women began to enter the workplace. The food industry responded by developing prepackaged foods, allowing women strapped for time to put a quick meal on the table. Canned meats, presliced cheeses, canned tomato sauce, instant oatmeal, and frozen dinners appeared on grocery store shelves and refrigerated sections, fast food stores opened for business in many towns.

"The focus was on quick, simple meals," according to Polk. "At mid-century, ease of preparation was still paramount. It wasn't until the 60's and 70's, when nutritional research really began to gain the nation's attention, that food manufacturers started to offer options that were both quick and health-conscious."

That's when food manufacturers started adding vitamin-fortified cereals to their offerings. Many restaurants added salad bars and low-fat, nonfried food options. While those choices do allow people eating out to make healthier choices, there are still high-fat, high-calorie attractions on salad bars. Dressing, for example, can pack a caloric punch. The same is true for desserts often offered on salad bars.

Convenience isn't simply reserved for restaurants. The advent of the microwave oven in the mid-1960s also changed the way Americans ate. Today's frozen food sections in grocery stores offer numerous microwavable foods. These foods typically have high sodium contents, however, and while they are convenient—and provide a greater variety beyond burgers and fries—they are generally highly processed foods.

THE FITNESS CRAZE

In the late 1970s and early 1980s, Americans became concerned with their health. "It began with a few joggers in Southern California," pointed out Polk. "Before long, there were aerobics studios, racquetball clubs, fitness centers, exercise books, and workout videos. The number of diet books and weight-management clinics grew. The media, which had long offered up unrealistic ideals for women's bodies, started doing the same thing for men's bodies. Now everyone could feel inadequate."

In response, "diet" products hit the market in a huge way. Frozen low-calorie meals became available; poultry processors started packaging skinless, boneless chicken breasts. Polk noted that since 1970, per capita chicken consumption has seen a 39% increase, while beef consumption is down 19%.

So why aren't we healthier? It all comes down to the choices we make. You might opt for a bag of potato chips over an apple, a simple choice that results in more calories, more fat, more salt, less fiber, and fewer nutrients. You decide to order out for pizza and watch a movie rather than go bowling or dancing. You take a cab or hop in the car instead of walking a mile. You take the elevator instead of two flights of stairs. None of these choices is inherently wrong. An occasional bag of chips isn't going to go straight to your thighs. Pizza and a movie can be an enjoyable evening's entertainment. You might be in a hurry and need to take a cab or hop on an elevator.

It's the pattern of continually making the less healthy choice that results in a problem. When faced with choosing activity or another evening on the couch, what do you choose most of the time? When the choice is going into the kitchen to cook a fresh meal or picking up the phone and ordering out, which do you choose most of the time?

NUTRITIONAL KNOWLEDGE HELPS

The U.S. Department of Agriculture regularly summarizes American's diet quality in its Healthy Eating Index. The most recent report, 1996, shows that 71% of Americans eat a diet that needs improvement. Only 12% of Americans eat a good diet, and 17% eat a diet that is poor. The area where Americans typically need the most improvement is in eating more fruits and drinking more milk. Only 17% of people met the dietary recommendations for fruits, and only 26% met the recommendations for milk products. Areas where American diets fared better was in meeting cholesterol requirements, with 72% of people doing so, and in eating a variety of foods, with 53% of people doing so.

The federal department has been taking these measurements since 1989, when the average Healthy Eating Index score was 62 of 100. By 1996, the mean score—meaning half of the participants scored higher and half scored lower—was 64. There are many variations in these results. For example, young children ages 2 to 3 have the best overall scores of all age and gender groups (73), but by age 15 to 18, children's scores had dropped to an average 60 for males and 63 for females. Overall, women had an average score two points higher than men (65 to 63). Broken down by racial groupings, Asian/Pacific Islander Americans had the highest average score in 1996 (68), followed by whites (64), and African Americans (59). Regionally, Northeasterners had the highest score (66); Southerners had the lowest (61).

CHANGE DOESN'T HAVE TO BE HARD

Eating can be a habit—and good habits started earlier in life are easier to maintain. Yes, it will take some work and some self-control to make changes, but the rewards will be apparent for years to come. Is it worth it? Absolutely. Does a good diet guarantee an illness-free life? No. But the combination of a good diet and a good level of physical activity does reduce the risk of developing some diseases, and people who are in good health often recover more quickly from illnesses. There are also immediate benefits. If you're overweight, a balanced nutritional diet will help you lose weight. As a result, you'll be more active and feel better. That can provide the encouragement needed to continue to choose more active entertainment and healthier foods.

The same cycle works in reverse, too. Continue to choose the less healthy options and you don't have the energy to be involved in more active sports or activities. That's frustrating, so you turn to the comfort of foods—a box of chocolates, an ice cream, a burger and fries. As the weight continues to pile on, you feel even less inclined to participate in active events. The task of losing weight looms so monumental, you'd rather not try than try and fail.

The challenge is not to change overnight, but to change incrementally. Begin making healthy choices—eat a little better, become a little more active. Set realistic goals and work to accomplish those. Get off the subway or bus one stop earlier and walk. Take the stairs. Walk a little every day. Eat more fruit. Sit down with a cookbook and learn some new meals. Pack your own lunch. As you incorporate healthier options into your daily routine, they become the habits. In turn, it will become easier to add new healthy routines into the day.

A study, reported in the January 27, 1999, issue of the *Journal of the American Medical Association*, showed that small lifestyle changes that increase moderate-intensity physical activity are as effective as a structured exercise program in improving the health of your heart and lowering blood pressure.

Lack of physical activity is a major risk factor for heart disease and contributes to other illness. Heart disease is the leading cause of death for Americans. One of every two men and one of every three women aged 40 and under will develop coronary heart disease, the main form of heart disease.

Most Americans get too little physical activity. About one in four U.S. adults are sedentary and another third are not active enough to reach a healthy level of fitness, according to a January 26, 1999, press release issued by the federal National Heart, Lung and Blood Institute (NHLBI). The recommendation is that adults try to get at least 30 minutes of moderate-intensity physical activity on most, or preferably all, days.

Many people apparently feel that's an unachievable goal because they don't have the time, social support, or access to a fitness center or they simply don't like vigorous activity. Researchers at the Cooper Institute for Aerobics Research in Dallas, Texas, enrolled 235 sedentary men and women. None had cardiovascular disease but most were moderately overweight.

Participants were assigned to either the lifestyle group or a structured group. In the lifestyle group, participants were taught behavioral skills to help them gradually fit more physical activity into their daily routines. For example, they learned to track their inactivity and activity by writing down how much time they spent sitting and how many minutes of moderate activity. They were encouraged to lengthen those minutes of activity by walking more. The structured group used a fitness center for more vigorous activity, such as aerobics, swimming, stair climbing, and walking.

After six months, the structured group had greater results in terms of cardiorespiratory fitness, but that declined more dramatically after that time. By two years, both groups had significantly increased their physical activity and improved their cardiorespiratory fitness and blood pressure.

"People have more opportunities to add physical activity to their daily life than they might think. Anyone can sit down and think about what he or she does in the course of a day and then see how to work in more activity through a simple change or two," stated lead author of the study Andrea Dunn, according to the NHLBI's press release. The press statement emphasized that the recommended 30 minutes of activity don't have to occur all at once, but can be divided into periods of at least 10 minutes.

GETTING ACTIVE

In general, restoring physical activity to our daily routines is critical. According to surveys conducted in 1977–1978 and 1994–1996, reported daily caloric intakes increased from 2,239 calories to 2,455 calories in men and from 1,534 calories to 1,646 calories in women. Eating more frequently is encouraged by numerous environmental changes: a greater variety of foods—some with higher caloric content—the growth of the fast-food industry, the increased availability and marketing of snack foods, increased time for socializing, and a growing tendency to socialize with food and drink. At the same time, there are fewer opportunities in daily life to burn calories: children watch more television daily, many schools have done away with or cut back on physical education, many neighborhoods lack sidewalks for safe walking, the workplace has become increasingly automated, household chores are assisted by labor-saving machinery, and walking and cycling have been replaced by automobile travel for all but the shortest distances. According to Jeffrey P. Koplan, the director of the federal Centers for Disease Control and Prevention, the American lifestyle of convenience and inactivity has taken a devastating toll on every segment of society, particularly on children. Research shows that 60% of overweight 5- to 10-year-old children already have at least one risk factor for heart disease, including hyperlipidemia and elevated blood pressure or insulin levels. According to CDC research, published in the October 13, 1999, issue of the *Journal of the American Medical Association*, more than two-thirds of American adults are trying to lose weight or keep from gaining weight, but many do not follow guidelines recommending a combination of fewer calories and more physical activity.

Obesity and being overweight are considered some of the most important diet-related conditions in the United States today. And the situation has worsened. Between 1963 and 1991, the number of overweight children between 6 and 17 has doubled. By 1991, 10.9% of young children, ages 6 to 11 were overweight and 10.8% of adolescents, ages 12 to 19, were overweight, according to a 1998 fact sheet distributed by the Center for Nutrition Policy and Promotion. Being overweight during childhood and adolescence is associated with being overweight during adulthood.

Healthy People 2010, a federal initiative organized by the U.S. Department of Health and Human Services, considers obesity and being overweight to be one of the leading 10 health indicators—a measure by which the health of communities and Americans overall can be assessed. Healthy People goals are regularly updated and reviewed, and new goals for 2010 were introduced in January 2000. Among those are the reduction of adolescent and adult overweight and obesity rates.

HEALTHY HABITS AS A WAY OF LIFE

Young people have an advantage when it comes to switching unhealthy habits for healthier ones. The habits of young people are not as ingrained as those of older people. Many of you are now or will soon be setting off on your own, making more of these choices by yourself or with friends and roommates. Chapter 9 discusses what you'll need to set up a kitchen so you can start relying on yourself rather than on expensive restaurants.

Chances are you'll probably be spending at least $100 per week to

Figure 1.1
Overweight and Obesity, United States, 1988–1994

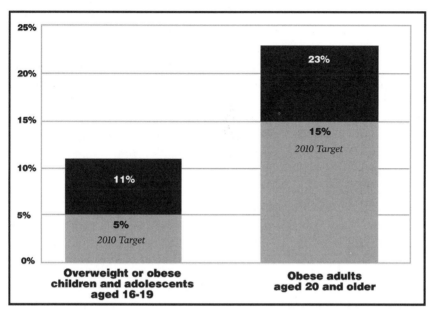

Source: Healthy People 2010.

feed yourself (that's what it costs your family to feed you). Making smart food choices and learning how to cook will be satisfying both nutritionally and financially. Begin paying more attention in grocery stores—if you haven't been to one for a while, take a field trip. If you're a meat eater, tally up how expensive it would be to cook meat every night. See how much you'd save if you reduced that amount by half. Look through cookbooks to find recipes that call for little or no meat. Read labels and see what you've been eating. If you're unhappy with the large amounts of fats or sodium in your favorite foods, start looking for other options.

Trying out a new variety of foods can be exciting—and it doesn't have to be expensive. Ethnic restaurants can offer menu items that are less expensive than American fare—often because the menu focuses more on less expensive vegetables than on meats. Libraries typically offer an Asian-to-vegetarian selection of cookbooks. If you're curious about foods from around the world or in experimenting with different flavors and food combinations, it's not difficult to satisfy that curiosity.

Those readers still living at home can begin to exert some influence and start practicing new skills. Offer to cook a meal once a week. Make suggestions on what the family shopping list should include. Make your own school lunches and after-school snacks.

College provides wonderful opportunities for meeting new people and trying new things. Make it a goal to try new foods. Most college-bound students have spent most of their lives eating foods prepared or purchased by parents or snacking on what's readily available in a vending machine or burger place. Enjoy the variety offered at college cafeterias and ask questions or sample the cuisines of new friends from other places.

The start of anything new, like college or a new job or even summer vacation or the first of a month, can be a starting point for a new, healthier lifestyle. Habits start a day at a time, so make this the month that you'll become more physically active. Make this the time that you'll begin reaching for fresh fruit instead of a high-calorie low-nutrition candy bar. Make this the time that you'll start treating your own body better. It will thank you—almost immediately—in terms of better performance and—in the long term—the reward of better health.

GUIDING PRINCIPLES

Keep in mind the basic philosophy of the dietary guidelines prepared by the government, with input from various health organizations. In May 2000, the USDA released its revised Dietary Guidelines for Americans. These guidelines are revised every five years, based on new evidence and findings. The fundamentals don't change drastically; it's more of a refinement. For example, in 1995, the seven dietary guidelines were as follows: eat a variety of foods; balance the foods you eat with physical activity—maintain or improve your weight; choose a diet with plenty of grain products, vegetables, and fruits; choose a diet low in fat, saturated fat, and cholesterol; choose a diet moderate in sugars; choose a diet moderate in salt and sodium; and if you drink alcoholic beverages, do so in moderation.

The 2000 guidelines are presented as A-B-C or "aim, build, choose" steps. A is to "aim for fitness" with the following two guidelines:

• Aim for a healthy weight.
• Be physically active each day.

B is to "build a healthy base" through the following:

- Let the Food Pyramid guide your food choices.
- Choose a variety of grains daily, especially whole grains.
- Choose a variety of fruits and vegetables daily.
- Keep food safe to eat.

And C is to "choose sensibly" through the following:

- Choose a diet that is low in saturated fat and cholesterol and moderate in total fat.
- Choose beverages and foods that limit your intake of sugars.
- Choose and prepare foods with less salt.
- If you drink alcoholic beverages, do so in moderation.

The most notable changes in the 2000 Dietary Guidelines include greater emphasis on limiting the intake of sugar and salt, a focus on a diet that is low in saturated fat and cholesterol, and a greater emphasis on physical activity than was evident in the 1995 guidelines.

Each of these guidelines—and more—is discussed in detail in this volume.

ADDITIONAL READING

Andersen, Ross E., Thomas A. Wadden, Susan J. Bartlett, Babette Zemel, Tony J. Verde, and Shawn C. Franckowiak. "Effects of Lifestyle Activity vs Structured Aerobic Exercise in Obese Women: A Randomized Trial." *Journal of the American Medical Association* 281, no. 4 (January 27, 1999): 335–40.

Allison, David B., Kevin R. Fontaine, JoAnn E. Manson, June Stevens and Theodore B. VanItallie. "Annual Deaths Attributable to Obesity in the United States." *Journal of the American Medical Association* 282, no. 16 (October 27, 2000): 1530–38.

Dunn, Andrea L., Bess H. Marcus, James B. Kampert, Melissa E. Garcia, Harold W. Kohl III, and Steven N. Blair. "Comparison of Lifestyle and Structured Interventions to Increase Physical Activity and Cardiorespiratory Fitness: A Randomized Trial." *Journal of the American Medical Association* 281, no. 4 (January 27, 1999): 327–34.

Herbert, Peter N., Michael Miller, Scott A. Lear, and Dean Ornish. "Effect of Lifestyle Changes on Coronary Heart Disease." *Journal of American Medical Association* 282, no. 2 (July 14, 1999): 130.

Jakicic, John M., Carena Winters, Wei Lang and Rena R. Wing. "Effect of

Intermittent Exercise and Use of Home Exercise Equipment on Adherence, Weight Loss, and Fitness in Overweight Women: A Randomized Trial." *Journal of the American Medical Association* 282, no. 16 (October 27, 1999): 1554–60.

Kant, Ashima K., Arthur Schatzkin, Barry I. Graubard, and Catherine Schairer. "A Prospective Study of Diet Quality and Mortality in Women." *Journal of the American Medical Association* 283, no. 16 (April 26, 2000): 2.

Ludwig, David S., Mark A. Pereira, Candyce H. Kroenke, Joan E. Hilner, Linda Van Horn, Martha L. Slattery, and David R. Jacobs, Jr. "Dietary Fiber, Weight Gain, and Cardiovascular Disease Risk Factors in Young Adults." *Journal of the American Medical Association* 282, no. 16 (October 27, 1999): 1539–46.

Mokdad, Ali H., Mary K. Serdula, William H. Dietz, Barbara A. Bowman, James S. Marks, and Jeffrey P. Koplan. "The Spread of the Obesity Epidemic in the United States, 1991–1998." *Journal of the American Medical Association* 282, no. 16 (October 27, 1999): 1519–22.

Must, Aviva, Jennifer Spadano, Eugenie H. Coakley, Alison E. Field, Graham Colditz and William H. Dietz. "The Disease Burden Associated With Overweight and Obesity." *Journal of the American Medical Association* 282, no. 16 (October 27, 1999): 1523–29.

Pratt, Michael. "Benefits of Lifestyle Activity vs Structure Exercise." *Journal of the American Medical Association* 281, no. 4 (January 27, 1999): 375.

Robinson, Thomas N. "Reducing Children's Television Viewing to Prevent Obesity: A Randomized Controlled Trial." *Journal of the American Medical Association* 282, no. 16 (October 27, 1999): 1561–67.

Wei, Ming, James B. Kampert, Carolyn E. Barlow, Milton Z. Nichaman, Larry W. Gibbons, Ralph S. Paffenbarger, Jr. and Steven N. Blair. "Relationship Between Low Cardiorespiratory Fitness and Mortality in Normal-Weight, Overweight, and Obese Men." *Journal of the American Medical Association* 282, no. 16 (October 27, 1999): 1547–53.

Winkleby, Marilyn A., Thomas N. Robinson, Jan Sundquist, and Helena C. Kraemer. "Ethnic Variation in Cardiovascular Disease Risk Factors Among Children and Young Adults: Findings From the Third National Health and Nutrition Examination Survey, 1988–1994." *Journal of the American Medical Association* 281, no. 11 (March 17, 1999): 1006.

2
THE BASICS

Imagine you just got a new computer—a state-of-the-art fast machine capable of an amazing number of processes—but the software you're running on it is slow and buggy. What happens? The computer is clearly not performing to its potential. It will be sluggish, and you'll probably experience frequent system crashes.

In a way, your body is like that computer because it also has incredible capabilities. The software you run on is what you put in—the food you eat. If that "software" is a lopsided diet of junk food, you'll have the same performance problem as the computer: sluggishness and system crashes in terms of frequent illnesses or lack of energy. Dangerous substances, such as tobacco, alcohol, and street drugs, are to your body what a computer virus is to an operating system: you risk serious failure.

And there's one more element. The greatest computer in the world is useless if it's not running. That's the analogy for "couch potatoes." Physical fitness is a combination of diet and exercise. It doesn't require you to run a four-minute mile or win a body-building competition, but it does require effort.

Unlike a computer, you cannot upgrade your body five years from now. The body you're in is the only one you'll be issued. The good news is that your body will respond to the changes you make. Improve your diet and add routine exercise and you'll begin to feel better. Research says you'll also do better in school or at work because you're not as tired and better able to focus. Furthermore, the steps you take toward developing a healthy lifestyle of good nutrition and exercise will affect you for the rest of your life. Diet plays a role in three of the leading causes of death: heart disease, cancer, and stroke.

WHAT IS GOOD NUTRITION?

No one item makes or breaks a good diet. For example, someone who eats a varied diet of healthy foods but occasionally buys a bag of potato chips is still following good nutritional principles. Conversely, the person whose diet consists primarily of hamburgers, French fries, and pizza is not a healthy eater just because he occasionally eats an apple. A varied diet provides the nutrients and other healthful substances needed each day. No single food provides them all. The appropriate balance of foods is shown in the food guide pyramid, which suggests the right number of foods to eat daily from each level. The foods at the bottom of the pyramid—breads and cereals, for example—should make up the bulk of your diet. The foods at the top—fats, oils, and sweets—should be eaten sparingly.

Again, variety is key for several reasons. Not all vegetables are the same. Some vegetables and fruits are good sources of Vitamin C, others are high in folate, and still others are a good source of calcium. The same is true of protein. Meats are high in protein, but also higher in fat. Varying the foods in each level of the food pyramid provides a greater nutritional balance and is also more satisfying. A cucumber salad, baked chicken breast, and boiled carrots might be a nutritionally balanced meal, but who would want to eat it night after night?

Meat products make up a significant part of the food pyramid; however, vegetarians can achieve healthy nutritional diets (see Chapter 3).

WHAT'S A SERVING?

Although the amount of a serving sometimes seems intuitive, the following list shows the actual amount considered a serving. Notice, for example, that a serving of bread is one slice. A sandwich, therefore, provides two servings from that category.

Figure 2.1
USDA Food Guide Pyramid

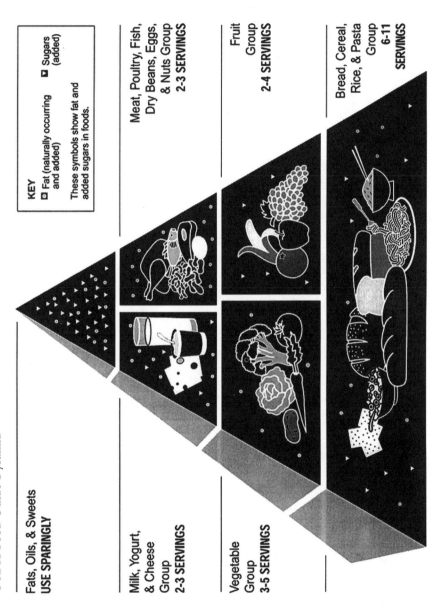

Fats, Oils, & Sweets
USE SPARINGLY

KEY
◨ Fat (naturally occurring and added)
◨ Sugars (added)

These symbols show fat and added sugars in foods.

Milk, Yogurt, & Cheese Group
2-3 SERVINGS

Meat, Poultry, Fish, Dry Beans, Eggs, & Nuts Group
2-3 SERVINGS

Vegetable Group
3-5 SERVINGS

Fruit Group
2-4 SERVINGS

Bread, Cereal, Rice, & Pasta Group
6-11 SERVINGS

Source: U.S. Department of Agriculture/U.S. Department of Health and Human Services.

Grain Products Group (bread, cereal, rice, and pasta)

- 1 slice of bread
- 1 ounce of ready-to-eat cereal
- ½ cup of cooked cereal, rice, or pasta

Vegetable Group

- 1 cup of raw, leafy vegetables
- ½ cup of other vegetables—cooked or chopped raw
- ¾ cup of vegetable juice

Fruit Group

- 1 medium apple, banana, or orange
- ½ cup of chopped, cooked, or canned fruit
- ¾ cup of fruit juice

Milk Group (milk, yogurt, and cheese)

- 1 cup of milk or yogurt
- 1-½ ounces of natural cheese
- 2 ounces of processed cheese

Meat and Beans Group (meat, poultry, fish, dry beans, eggs, and nuts)

- 2–3 ounces of cooked lean meat, poultry, or fish
- ½ cup of cooked dry beans; 1 egg counts as 1 ounce of lean meat; 2 table-spoons of peanut butter or ⅓ cup of nuts count as 1 ounce of meat.

The food pyramid provides a good guide for getting a varied diet, but there are other measurements that are important in eating healthy foods. These include the number of calories, carbohydrates, fiber, cholesterol, sodium, and vitamins and minerals found in food.

HOW DO I KNOW WHAT I'M EATING?

In 1990 the government passed the National Label Education Act, which requires that the manufacturers of food products put a uniform nutrition fact label on the package. The labels must contain the following:

Total calories

Calories from fat

Total fat

Saturated fat

Cholesterol

Sodium

Total carbohydrate

Dietary fiber

Sugar

Protein

Vitamin A

Vitamin C

Calcium

Iron.

These labels may contain more information, such as breaking down the fat counts to polyunsaturated fat and monounsaturated fat. They may also list other essential vitamins and minerals. Let's look at the required information.

Calories

A calorie is a measurement of heat needed to raise one kilogram of water one degree Centigrade. Since food "stokes the furnace" of our bodies, foods have assigned calorie values. Fat and alcohol are high in calories. Foods high in both sugars and fat contain many calories but often are low in vitamins, minerals, or fiber. Numerous calorie counters are readily available—on line and often in cookbooks. If you reduce your caloric intake, you'll lose weight. If you increase the amount of calories you consume, you'll gain weight. But that doesn't mean that a low-calorie diet is the best way to lose weight. That's how those awful grapefruit and black coffee diets originated. If you starve yourself for a week, of course you'll lose weight, but if you return to your old eating habits, you'll put the weight right back on again. Since a pound equals 3,500 calories, to lose a pound in, say a week, you'll either have to eat 3,500 calories less or burn off 3,500 calories in exercise or use some combination of the two.

Exercise burns calories. For example, walking briskly can burn off about 100 calories per mile. Bicycling for a half hour at nearly 10 mph will burn about 195 calories. The specific number is dependent on the person's weight and the intensity of the activity. A variety of interactive exercise counters are available on the Internet, which allow you to plug in your weight, age, and change variables such as the length of time and intensity of the activity (see Chapter 5 for more information on the benefits of activity).

The following formula will help you determine the approximate number of calories you need per day to maintain your body weight. Moderately active males should multiply their weight in pounds by 15. For example, if you weigh 170 pounds, you need about 2,500 calories per day. Moderately active females should multiply their weight by 12. A 130-pound female needs about 1,560 calories per day. However, the number of calories needed per day decreases as the level of activity decreases. Relatively inactive men should multiply their weight by 13, and women in that category should multiply their weight by 10: a 170-pound man who is relatively inactive needs only 2,210 calories, and a 130-pound inactive woman needs only 1,300 calories to maintain body weight.

The information on nutrition labels is based on a diet of 2,000 calories per day. Keep that in mind if your caloric intake is significantly higher or lower.

Calories from Fat

Numerous health and government authorities, including the U.S. Surgeon General, the National Academy of Sciences, the American Heart Association, and the American Dietetic Association, recommend reducing dietary fat to 30 percent or less of total calories. However, that doesn't mean you have to pass by all high-fat food products. For example, peanut butter with sugar added has 190 calories in a 2-tablespoon serving. Of those, 130 calories are from fat, or 68%. Add that peanut butter to two slices of whole wheat bread, which have 120 calories and 20 calories from fat, and the equation is different: now the fat is down to about 48%. It's still higher than the recommendation, but by adding a glass of skim milk and an apple, you start to bring it down to a healthy level.

Total Fat

Total fat is measured in grams. For someone eating a 2,000-calorie-per-day diet, daily fat intake should not exceed 65 grams. Fatty foods are always high in calories. Despite its bad image, though, fat isn't all bad. Some fat is needed because fats supply energy and help the body absorb fat-soluble Vitamins A, D, E, and K. Fats contain both saturated and unsaturated fatty acids. Saturated fat raises blood cholesterol more than other forms of fat. Limiting saturated fats to less than 10% of calories will help lower your blood cholesterol level. High levels of saturated fats and cholesterol in the diet are linked to increased blood cholesterol levels and a greater risk for heart disease.

Although polyunsaturated and monounsaturated fats might help lower blood cholesterol levels, the recommendation holds that total fat accounts for no more than 30% of the daily calorie intake.

Cholesterol

Your body makes cholesterol, but it is also obtained from food. Animal products, such as egg yolks, higher fat milk products, poultry, fish, and meat are high in cholesterol—and usually also in saturated fats. The daily value for cholesterol should be 300 milligrams. There are two kinds of cholesterol: LDL, the so-called bad cholesterol, and HDL, or good cholesterol. LDL stands for low-density lipoproteins. If there's too much LDL cholesterol in the bloodstream, it can build up within the walls of the arteries and contribute to the formation of plaque which ultimately can clog the arteries. That blockage could affect the flow of blood to the heart and cause a heart attack or to the brain and result in a stroke. Doctors can measure the level of LDL in the blood—ideally it should be below 130.

High-density lipoproteins (HDL) is the "good" cholesterol because experts believe HDLs can carry cholesterol away from the arteries and to the liver, where it's passed from the body. HDL levels typically range from 40 to 50 milligrams deciliter for men and 50 to 60 milligrams/dL for women. Levels below 35 milligrams/dL are abnormally low and form a risk factor for cardiac problems. Low HDL levels can be caused by cigarette smoking, obesity, and physical inactivity.

Sodium

Sodium is a trace mineral that helps maintain body fluid balance. Salt is an excellent source of sodium. One-quarter teaspoon, the typical serving, provides 540 milligrams of sodium, or 25% of the daily recommended allowance. Milk and processed foods are other sources. Sodium intake should stay below 2,400 milligrams. That might sound like a lot, but these sources add up quickly. A frozen turkey pot pie, single serving, contains about 29% of the recommended daily intake. Hot dogs typically have at least 21% of the daily total of sodium per hot dog. Even a tablespoon of ketchup has 190 milligrams of sodium, or 8% of the daily value. Lowering one's sodium intake can help people avoid or control high blood pressure—a risk factor in heart disease and strokes. If you eat many processed, packaged foods and are exceeding the sodium intake, start looking for ways to duplicate the foods you like while cooking them fresh. Many herbs and spices have no sodium and can add tremendous flavor to foods. These include garlic, basil, pepper, parsley, chives, vinegar, sage, cinnamon, nutmeg, and cloves.

Total Carbohydrates

Carbohydrates provide energy for the brain, central nervous system, and muscle cells. They are found largely in sugars, fruits, vegetables, and cereals and grains. Meats generally have no carbohydrates. There are simple carbohydrates, such as sugars, and complex carbohydrates, such as breads and pastas, which the body breaks down into sugars. Someone with a 2,000-calorie-per-day diet should limit carbohydrates to 300 grams. Someone with a 2,500-calorie-per-day diet can consume up to 375 grams of carbohydrates. A medium baked potato with skin has 51 grams of carbohydrates, an apple has about 21 grams, a tablespoon of sugar has 12 grams, and a slice of pie can contain 60 or more grams of carbohydrates.

Carbohydrates are divided into three kinds: monosaccharides or simple sugars, such as glucose and fructose; disaccharides—composed of two monosaccharides—such as maltose, sucrose, and lactose; and polysaccharides, which are starches and glycogen.

On the nutrition facts label, total carbohydrates are broken down into two categories: fiber and sugar.

Dietary Fiber

Fiber helps the body digest food. Soluble fiber, combined with a low-fat diet, may reduce levels of the bad cholesterol. The recommended dietary allowance for fiber is 25 grams. Generally, grains, such as oat, wheat, and rice products, are good sources of fiber, as are some vegetables. But some foods that might seem as though they would be high in fiber, such as cereals, in fact have very little. High-sugar cereals often have just 1 gram of fiber; a high-fiber hot wheat cereal could have 5 grams; and a 100% bran cereal could have 8 grams or more. Some fruits, such as an apple (3.5 grams), a banana (2.4 grams), three prunes (3 grams), and a half grapefruit (3.1 grams) also have high fiber content.

Sugar

Sugars in foods are the monosaccharides and disaccharides described above. In some foods, carbohydrate makeup is almost entirely sugar. For example, a tablespoon of fruit preserves, sweetened only with fruit juices, has 9 of its 10 grams of carbohydrates in sugar. Breads and pastas, on the other hand, have high polysaccharide contents. One pita bread, for example, has 2 grams of sugar out of its 24 grams of total carbohydrates. Looking at the nutrition facts label becomes especially important if you want to cut down on the simple sugars. Take breakfast cereals, for example. Let's look at two boxes of General Mills cereal designed to appeal to children. One is Kix; the other, Apple Cinnamon Cheerios. Both have 120 calories per serving and similar carbohydrate totals. But of the 25 carbohydrate grams in Apple Cinnamon Cheerios, 13 are sugar and 11 are "other" and there's 1 gram of dietary fiber. Of the 26 carbohydrate grams in Kix, only 3 are sugar and 22 are "other." There's also one gram of dietary fiber. Is that bad?

Is Sugar Bad for You?

The answer is it depends. By itself, one bowl of sweetened cereal isn't bad for you. But remember that sugars are at the top of the food pyramid. They are to be eaten sparingly and should not constitute the bulk of your daily diet. That's true for several reasons. First of all, consider your smile. Foods containing sugars and starches can promote tooth decay, especially if they stay in contact with your teeth for a long time. When you do eat or drink sugary foods, try to brush your teeth afterward. If you can't brush, at least rinse your mouth. That's also recommended after eating dried fruit.

Sugar is also at the top of the pyramid because it's high in calories and low in nutritional content. Taking in more calories without adding more physical activity will cause you to gain weight. If you fill up on sugary foods, you'll be less likely to eat a more balanced diet. For example, eat that candy bar a half hour before dinner and you'll probably eat less dinner—which should have much more essential nutrients than the candy bar did. You didn't "ruin your appetite" for good, of course, but you did miss the opportunity to stoke the furnace with a balanced meal and instead added "empty" calories to your day's diet.

Indeed, the new dietary guidelines released by the government in May 2000, and updated every five years, includes as one of the guidelines, "Choose beverages and foods to moderate your intake of sugars." The report states,

Foods containing added sugars provide calories, but may have few vitamins and minerals. In the United States, the number one source of added sugars is non-diet soft drinks (soda or pop). Sweets and candies, cakes and cookies, and fruit drinks and fruitades are also major sources of added sugars.

Intake of a lot of foods high in added sugars, like soft drinks, is of concern. Consuming excess calories from these foods may contribute to weight gain or lower consumption of more nutritious foods. ("Nutrition and Your Health: Dietary Guidelines for Your Family," Fifth Edition, May 2000. The guidelines can be downloaded at http://www.health.gov/dietaryguidelines/)

All carbohydrates eventually break down into sugars in your body. The difference is that complex carbohydrates do so more gradually, providing energy over a longer period of time. Complex carbohydrates also contain other nutrients not contained in simple sugars. That's particularly true of "empty" calories, such as soft drinks and candy.

Protein

Protein is actually a combination of 22 amino acids. Your body makes 13 of these amino acids on its own. These are called nonessential amino acids. Nine of the amino acids, however, the essential amino acids, must come from the foods you eat. Protein builds up and maintains the tissues in your body. Protein makes up much of your muscles, organs, and even some hormones. Protein also makes hemoglobin, the part of the red blood cells that carries oxygen around the body. Protein also makes antibodies to help fight off infections and disease. Protein is found in meat, chicken, fish, eggs, nuts, dairy products, and legumes.

Vitamins and Minerals

These are expressed on nutrition facts labels as the percentage of the recommended dietary allowance (RDA). If you're eating a varied diet most days, and not severely limiting your calories, you probably do not need additional vitamin or mineral supplements.

Some foods are enriched with additional nutrients. For example, enriched flour and bread contain added thiamine, riboflavin, niacin, and iron; skim milk, low-fat milk, and margarine are usually enriched with Vitamin A; and milk is usually enriched with Vitamins A and D. The ingredient list on the packaging will let you know which nutrients are contained in the food. In a nutshell, Vitamin A is found in fruits and dark green and deep yellow vegetables, such as carrots, pumpkins, and spinach. Vitamin A is important to vision and a healthy skin. Vitamin B actually refers to a group of vitamins—B1, B2, B6, B12, niacin, folic acid, biotin, and pantothenic acid. These vitamins play a role in making red blood cells, which carry oxygen to all the parts of the body. In other words, the B vitamins help with energy. Fish, beef, pork, chicken, whole wheat grains, green leafy vegetables, dried beans, and enriched breads and cereals are sources of Vitamin B. Vitamin C strengthens bones and muscles and also has some infection-fighting capabilities; however, large doses can result in kidney problems. Good natural sources of Vitamin C are citrus fruits, strawberries, melons, sweet potatoes, cabbage, broccoli, tomatoes, and peppers. Vitamin D contributes to strong healthy bones and teeth and it also helps the body absorb calcium. Vitamin D is found in fortified milk products, egg yolks, and fish. Another great source for Vitamin D is sunshine. Vitamin E helps form red blood cells, muscles, and other tissues throughout the body. Vitamin E also helps the body store Vitamin A. It's found in vegetable oils and dark green leafy vegetables, nuts, poultry and seafood, and wheat germ and fortified cereals. Vitamin K, essential for blood clotting, is also found in dark green vegetables, whole grains, potatoes, cabbage, and cheese.

Calcium

Calcium warrants special attention because new research is pointing to an even more crucial role than previously thought and because calcium requirements are highest for young people whose bones are developing. Calcium is used in building bone mass and also plays a role in the proper functioning of the heart, muscles, and nerves maintaining blood flow. Adequate calcium can also reduce the risk of osteoporosis, a weakening of the bones that can occur late in adulthood. Calcium is found naturally in dairy products and in dark, leafy green vegetables.

Bone mass is affected by much of what the body does. Weight-bearing exercise, such as dancing and running, affects bone mass and strength. Unhealthy activities, such as smoking, alcohol use, and a poor diet contribute to losing bone mass. Since calcium is lost through urine, caffeine increases the rate at which it is lost because it is a diuretic. Diets high in sodium increase losses in the urine, too.

According to the National Institute of Child Health and Human Development (NICHD), bones develop to maximum density if the calcium taken in is greater than the calcium lost throughout childhood, adolescence, and young adulthood. The teen years are the most important because of the rapid bone growth that occurs. By around age 17, approximately 90% of adult bone mass is established, and calcium loss from the bones begins at age 21.

Research sponsored by NICHD shows that supplementing the daily diets of girls, ages 12 to 16, with an extra 350 milligrams of calcium produced a 14% increase in bone density. Researchers say this is a striking difference because for every 5% increase in bone density, the risk of later bone fracture declines by 40%.

Adolescents and young adults, ages 9 to 18, should get about 1,300 milligrams of calcium per day, but few children and teens are drinking four or five glasses of low-fat milk per day. Nutrition surveys show that teenage girls average about 800 milligrams of calcium per day. Calcium requirements drop to 1,000 milligrams per day for adults over 19, but rise again for postmenopausal women. In the November 1999 issue of *Pediatrics*, the American Academy of Pediatrics revised its policy statement to read that preteens and adolescents should have from 1,200 to 1,500 milligrams per day of calcium. The policy also recommends exercise as an important component in achieving maximal peak bone mass and stresses that fat-reduced dairy products such as skim milk are not less nutritious for older children.

How do you get enough calcium? Consuming four or five glasses of low-fat milk per day is one way. Other milk products are also good sources of calcium. Green leafy vegetables, such as kale, collards, and beet and turnip tops, are also natural sources of calcium as are tofu, dried peas and beans, the soft bones of canned fish, and calcium-fortified orange juice. Many people find they can get enough calcium through a healthy diet, but calcium supplements are available for those who cannot or who are at particularly high risk for osteoporosis. Read the label of a calcium supplement carefully to find the amount of "elemental" calcium. There are different kinds of calcium supplements, including calcium citrate (generally the most easily absorbed), calcium carbonate, and calcium phosphate, which include other elements, such as Vitamin D, which help with absorption.

While more is generally better, too much is not good. Overdoses of calcium can interfere with the absorption of other nutrients, such as zinc and iron.

Recent studies have indicated that calcium may be far more important than previously thought. Calcium supplementation helped lower the blood pressure of African American teens tested over an eight-week period. Teens who normally ate a particularly low-calcium diet saw an overall greater drop in blood pressure. African Americans are more likely to have high blood pressure than Caucasian Americans, and dietary factors seem to be one of the contributing factors.

Iron

Iron is a trace mineral found in red meat, liver, fish, green leafy vegetables, enriched bread, and some dried fruits including prunes, apricots, and raisins. Recommended iron intake for young women is 15 milligrams per day; for boys aged 15 to 18, 12 milligrams per day, decreasing to 10 milligrams per day after age 19. The level of iron required for women stays the same until menopause. Blood loss, such as menstrual cycles, is a major cause of iron deficiency. Low iron levels can result in iron-deficiency anemia. Iron supplements can be taken, and foods higher in iron content can be eaten. Vitamin C can help iron absorption, but coffee, tea, wheat bran, eggs, and soy inhibit iron absorption. Medications such as antacids, for example, can also interfere with iron absorption.

Iron demands are typically highest for pregnant women. The requirement for iron doubles in the second trimester and triples in the third as blood volume increases and the fetus grows dramatically.

ANTIOXIDANTS AND THE ROLE THEY PLAY

Antioxidants are substances that counteract the harmful free radicals created by oxidation. Oxidation, for example, can rust cars. Some oxidation in the body is good because it produces energy and kills bacterial invaders, but in excess, it can damage tissues. Antioxidants are found naturally in many foods, primarily fruits and vegetables. Vitamins with antioxidant properties include Vitamins E, C, and A as beta carotene. Some minerals, such as selenium, are also considered to have antioxidant properties. There are claims that antioxidants in large quantities can help prevent or reduce the effects of a variety of diseases, including cardiovascular disease, diabetes, Alzheimer's, and various forms of cancer. Antioxidant supplements are widely available in groceries and health food stores, but whether they are helpful is the subject of ongoing research. On April 10, 2000, a panel of the Institute of Medicine of the National Academies of Science reported that megadoses of antioxidants haven't yet been proven to be helpful and might in fact be dangerous. "A direct connection between the intake of antioxidants and the prevention of chronic disease has yet to be adequately established," stated Norman I. Krinsky, chair of the study's Panel on Dietary Antioxidants and Related Compounds and a professor of biochemistry at Tufts University School of Medicine in Boston. "We do know, however, that dietary antioxidants can in some cases prevent or counteract cell damage that stems from exposure to oxidants, which are agents that affect a cell's molecular composition. But much more research is needed to determine whether dietary antioxidants can actually stave off chronic disease."

The panel established the following recommendations for dietary supplementation of antioxidants. It increased the recommended intake levels of Vitamin C to 75 milligrams per day for women and 90 milligrams per day for men. Smokers, who are more likely to be impacted from cell-damaging biological processes and deplete more Vitamin C, need an additional 35 milligrams per day. The report set the upper intake level for Vitamin C, from both food and supplements, at 2,000 milligrams per day for adults, noting that intakes above this amount may cause diarrhea. Food sources for Vitamin C include citrus fruit, potatoes, strawberries, broccoli, and leafy green vegetables.

Vitamin E recommendations were also increased: men and women should consume 15 milligrams of Vitamin E daily from food. Food sources for this vitamin are vegetable oils, nuts, seeds, liver, and leafy green vegetables. Synthetic Vitamin E from vitamin supplements should not exceed 1,000 milligrams of alpha-tocopherol per day for adults. Alpha-tocopherol is the only type of Vitamin E that human blood can maintain and transfer to cells when needed. People who consume more than this amount place themselves at greater risk of hemorrhagic damage because the nutrient can act as an anticoagulant, according to the report.

The report also states that men and women need 55 micrograms of selenium per day. Food sources include seafood, liver, meat, and grains. The upper level of selenium, including natural and supplement sources, should be less than 400 micrograms per day. More could result in selenosis, a toxic reaction that can cause hair loss and nail sloughing.

The report did not set a recommended daily intake or upper intake level for beta-carotene and other carotenoids, which are found naturally in dark green and deep yellow vegetables. However, it cautioned against high doses, recommending supplementation only for the prevention and control of Vitamin A deficiency.

The report stressed that a balanced and varied diet will provide adequate amounts of these vitamins and minerals without requiring supplements. The American Heart Association concurs in a February 1999 Science Advisory. "Antioxidant Consumption and Risk of Coronary Heart Disease: Emphasis on Vitamin C, Vitamin E, and Beta-carotene" concluded,

The most prudent and scientifically supportable recommendation for the general population is to consume a balanced diet with emphasis on antioxidant-rich fruits and vegetables and whole grains. This advice, which is consistent with the current dietary guidelines of the American Heart Association, considers the role of the total diet in influencing disease risk. Although diet alone may not provide the levels of vitamin E intake that have been associated with the lowest risk in a few observational studies, the absence of efficacy and safety data from randomized trials trails precludes the establishment of population-wide recommendations regarding vitamin E supplementation.

HOW'S MY WEIGHT?

A healthy diet is part of maintaining a healthy weight. If you're overweight, you're increasing your risk of developing a number of diseases, including heart disease and Type II diabetes. If you're underweight, you may be depriving yourself of essential nutrients and energy.

Researchers developed the body mass index (BMI) to help people gauge a healthy weight range for their age. The BMI is less reliable as a measure for children who have not reached full height. Here's how to calculate it:

#1. Multiply your weight in pounds by 703

#2. Multiply your height in inches by your height in inches*

Divide answer to #1 by answer to #2

*If you're 5'5", your height in inches would be 65 inches.

If your BMI is	your risk level is
19–24	minimal to low
25–26	low to moderate
27–29	moderate to high
30–34	high to very high
35–39	very high to extremely high
40+	extremely high

Using this formula, let's calculate the BMI of two people.

One is 5'4" and weighs 130 pounds.

#1. $130 \times 703 = 91,390$

#2. $64 \times 64 = 4,096$

BMI = 91,390 divided by 4,096 = 22.3

Look at the chart above. That figure is within the range of minimal to low risk.

Now let's look at another person who is 5'9" and weighs 210 pounds.

#1. $210 \times 703 = 147,630$

#2. $69 \times 69 = 4,761$

BMI = 147,630 divided by 4,761 = 31

That person is in the range of high to very high risk and needs to put some serious effort into losing weight.

SIMPLE CHANGES TO MAKE TODAY

It might seem difficult to change your eating habits now, but you might be surprised at the relatively simple steps you can take to start eating better—and feeling better—today. Good nutrition is a goal for life, and efforts made now will pay off for many years to come.

This is the message that Melanie Polk, director of nutrition education for the American Institute for Cancer Research (AICR), wants to get across. She knows that teens and young adults are typically focused on the here and now and it's difficult to look years down the road. But she encourages young people to look at their family health history. Many people know of someone in the family who was diagnosed with cancer or another disease or condition in which nutrition might have played a role. "Realize that there are some things you can do to help decrease the likelihood that will happen to you, too," she suggests.

The guidelines developed by the AICR reflect the thinking of nutritionists and health organizations. Choose a diet rich in a variety of plant-based foods. Eat plenty of vegetables and fruits. Maintain a healthy weight and be physically active. Drink alcohol only in moderation, if at all. Select foods low in fat and salt, prepare and store food safely, and don't use tobacco.

Here are some of Polk's recommendations for developing healthier eating habits. If you're living at home, ask that a wide variety of healthy foods be available. If it's as easy to reach for fruit as it is for chips or cookies, it greatly improves the chances you'll make the healthy choice. Consider this: the AICR says Americans' snack food intake has tripled in the last 20 years. An average American now consumes 16 to 20 pounds of snack food, or 40,000 snack calories, a year. "Discuss with your parents the foods you'd like to try or emphasizing more vegetables, fruits, beans and grains. You're at an age where you have a right to make some decision about the foods you'll be eating."

She stressed that many of these changes are very simple. For example, rather than eat an ounce of potato chips, opt for an ounce of whole wheat pretzels. You can save 60 calories and 11 grams of fat. Or instead of two cups of regular microwave popcorn, go with a light variety and save 80 calories and 5 grams of fat. For a whopping difference, make some changes in your sandwiches. For example, a sandwich with three ounces of bologna, one ounce of regular cheese, and two teaspoons of regular mayonnaise has 320 more calories and 36 more grams of fat than a sandwich filled with one ounce of turkey, one ounce of low-fat cheese, one teaspoon of mustard, leafy lettuce, and a tomato slice.

Go to the grocery store so you can learn more about foods. Look at the vegetables and fruit you've never tried before. Flip through cookbooks and magazines to get some ideas. "Food is not only for good nutrition, but meals fill a variety of needs: social time, satisfying hunger and sensory needs for taste and texture. There are lots of great reasons to enjoy food and learn the options," Polk said.

Try cooking. Even if you're starting off with different kinds of salads, be adventuresome and create.

Polk added some special advice for college students, many of whom are new to taking responsibility for their food choices. There's the tendency to skip breakfast because you're rushed for class, or to grab a meal and eat it on the run. "Even if that's your approach, it doesn't have to mean it's unhealthy. There are wonderful things you can grab in a hurry—yogurt, fruit, bagels. Many dining halls even offer salads that are prepackaged."

Polk also recommended that food can be part of an educational and philosophical awakening for college students and young adults. "The college years are times to experience new things—make new friends, study new subjects, explore new interests. It can also be used as a time to experience those foods mom never made. Food can be a way of enhancing a cultural background—try eating Asian, Ethiopian or Indian foods, for example."

Polk and other nutritionists speak of food as enjoyment. "It's important not to let food define you," she said. "Don't say, 'I was bad today because I ate two pieces of chocolate cake.' That doesn't make you good or bad."

Realize that nutrition is part of a process toward a healthier lifestyle. Another part of that is physical activity. An increased level of activity can offset some of the excesses of an indulgent day of eating.

There are great reasons for eating—and some not so good ones. Polk distinguished between hunger and appetite. "Hunger is physiological. Appetite is when you want to eat because you see someone else eating something that looks good or because you walk past the bakery and it smells good. Appetite can be stimulated by some external event." It becomes a problem when you give in to the appetite so routinely that you've essentially turned off the signal for hunger. It never has a chance to surface. "When the clock says to eat, we eat what's on the plate. What we should be listening for is when our bodies tell us we're hungry, and for when our bodies have had enough."

ADDITIONAL READING

"Adolescents Need More Calcium to Grow." *USA Today*, February 1999, vol. 127, issue 2645: 13.

Anderson, Jean, and Barbara Deskins. *The Nutrition Bible: A Comprehensive Nonsense Guide to Foods, Nutrients, Additives, Preservatives, Pollutants and Everything Else We Eat and Drink.* New York: William Morrow, 1995.

Carroll, L. "Calcium Lowers Blood Pressure in Black Teens," Medical Tribune News Service, September 8, 1998.

Chicoye, Lorena S., Marc S. Jacobson, Gregory L. Landry, and Cynthia Starr. "Getting Teens Fit and Well Nourished: Shaping the Future." *Patient Care*, July 15, 1997, vol. 31, no. 12: 72–83.

Cousens, Gabriel. *Conscious Eating.* Berkeley, Calif.: North Atlantic Books, 1998.

Diet & Nutrition Sourcebook: Basic Information About Nutrition, Including the Dietary Guidelines. Detroit: Omnigraphics, 1996.

Duyff, Roberta Larson. *American Dietetic Association's Complete Food & Nutrition Guide.* Minneapolis: Chronimed, 1998.

Dwyer, J. H., et al. "Dietary Calcium, Calcium Supplementation, and Blood Pressure in African American Adolescents." *American Journal of Clinical Nutrition* 68, no. 3 (September 1998): 648–55.

Farley, Dixie. "Bone Builders: Support Your Bones with Healthy Habits." *FDA Consumer*, September/October 1997, vol. 31, no. 6: 27–31.

Feder, David. "Food Facts and Fables." *Better Homes and Gardens*, January 1997, vol. 75, no. 1: 58–61.

Haas, Elson M. *Staying Healthy with the Seasons.* Berkeley, Calif.: Celestial Arts, 1995.

Herbert, Victor, and Genell J. Subak-Sharpe, eds. *Total Nutrition: The Only Guide You'll Ever Need.* New York: St. Martin's Press, 1995.

Jaret, Peter. "Nutrition in America: Only 5 a Day." *Health*, May/June 1998, vol. 12, no. 4: 78–85.

Kant, Ashirma K., Arthur Schatzkin, Barry I. Graubard and Catherine Schairer. "A Prospective Study of Diet Quality and Mortality in Women." *Journal of the American Medical Association* 283, no. 16 (April 26, 2000): 2109–15.

Maynard, Cindy. "How Does Your Diet Rate?" *Current Health.* March 1999, vol. 25, issue 7:6–7.

McCarthy, Alice R. *Healthy Teens: Facing the Challenges of Young Lives.* Birmingham, Mich.: Bridge Communications, 1999.

Murphy, Sallyann J. *The Zen of Food: A Philosophy of Nourishment.* Berkeley, Calif.: Putnam, 1998.

Roberts, Paul. "How Americans Eat: The New Food Anxiety." *Psychology Today*, March/April 1998, vol. 31, no. 2: 30–40.

Ronzio, Robert A. *The Encyclopedia of Nutrition and Good Health*. New York: Facts on File, 1997.

Shape of the Nation. Reston, Va.: National Association of Sports and Physical Education, 1997.

Sommers, Annie Leah. *Everything You Need to Know About Looking and Feeling Your Best: A Girl's Guide*. New York: Rosen Publishing, 1999.

Whelan, Elizabeth M., and Fredrick J. Stare. *Fad Free Nutrition*. Alameda, Calif.: Hunter House, 1998.

3

GOING VEG!

Vegetarian eating is moving into the American mainstream as more and more young adults say no to meat, poultry, and fish. According to a 1998 Cornell University news release, titled, "The Promise of Plant-Based Nutrition," an estimated 14 million Americans already consider themselves vegetarians and about 1 million people adopt a vegetarian diet every year. Teenage Research Unlimited, a marketing-research firm based in Illinois, found in their *Spring 2000/Wave 35 Teenage Marketing and Lifestyle Study*, that about 4% of all U.S. teens now follow a vegetarian diet. Those statistics don't surprise nutritionists and doctors who acknowledge the health benefits of a plant-based diet when compared to a meat-based diet high in cholesterol and saturated fat. Research shows vegetarians on the whole eat better than nonvegetarians and consume about two to three times as much fiber as their meat-eating counterparts. A diet high in fiber can actually lower the chances of developing certain cancers, particularly colon cancer, according to the National Cancer Institute.

In fact, the National Cancer Institute, the American Dietetic Association (ADA), the American Heart Association, and the U.S. Department of Health and Human Services now support a well-planned vegetarian diet and its associated health benefits. The ADA stated in a

1997 position paper, titled "Vegetarian Diets," "Approximately planned vegetarian diets are healthful, are nutritionally adequate, and provide health benefits in the prevention and treatment of certain diseases." The paper also stated that vegetarian diets have been used successfully to reverse severe coronary artery disease as well as offer protective benefits from hypertension and some cancers.

But health concerns are not the only reason that young adults give for changing their diets. Some make the choice out of concern for animal rights. When faced with the statistic that some 90% of animals raised as food live in confinement, many teens give up meat to protest those conditions. Others turn to vegetarianism to support the environment. Meat production uses vast amounts of water, land, grain, and energy and creates problems with animal waste and subsequent pollution. EarthSave, an organization founded in 1988 to educate people about the environmental benefits of a plant-based diet noted in an August 1998 press release titled, "Down on the Factory Farm," that the scale and concentration of modern farming operations is taking a huge toll on our environment. The press release quoted U.S. Senator Tom Harkin, "Animal waste is a national problem and current Federal regulations are an inadequate solution." According to Harkin, animal agriculture now generates an estimated five tons of manure for every man, woman and child in the United States every year. That manure is often held in pools or lagoons, which can leak and pollute groundwater or seep into underground aquifers. Whatever the reason you choose to become a vegetarian your choice brings with it questions from parents about your health and nutrition. By becoming an educated vegetarian you can achieve good nutrition, support a more humane and ecological world, and do your part to reduce global hunger.

IT'S TASTY, TOO

Bland, brown, and boring is what many people think when you say vegetarianism. Don't worry, meatless cuisine is much more than rice and beans. The plant kingdom is a multicolored world of crunchy, chewy, creamy, and meaty textures. From portabello mushrooms to polenta, from summer corn to seitan, there are wonderful tastes to try. In fact, you are probably already familiar with many basic and classic meatless dishes: eggplant parmesan, spaghetti with marinara sauce, pasta with pesto sauce, bean burritos, stuffed peppers, split pea soup, vegetable lasagna, and baked potatoes with broccoli and cheese sauce. Gourmet cuisine is also part of the vegetarian experience with foods like roasted pepper and tomato soup; fassolada, a Greek bean soup; and mango raita, a fruity yogurt sauce. Or maybe you would prefer your fresh mango in a couscous salad or fajita wraps with salsa verde and chocolate rum cake. Many Italian dishes are vegetarian naturals, and pasta in its myriad forms is the basis of numerous meatless meals. Mexican cooking is often meatless as well, using tortillas, beans, and cheese. Other ethnic cuisines have made a culinary art out of vegetables, like the Greek spinach dish spanakopita. Asian stir-fries are another example of delicious meatless cooking as are Indian curries and Ethiopian dishes of assorted vegetables and beans. Overall, a vegetarian diet can be an indulgence in good food and in good health.

HISTORICAL MORSELS

If you're a vegetarian you're in good company. Since ancient times the vegetarian community has included many important figures: Leonardo da Vinci, Albert Einstein, Benjamin Franklin, Charles Darwin, Thomas Edison, Leo Tolstoy, Henry David Thoreau, Mahatma Gandhi, and Clara Barton all abstained from eating meat. Today's famous vegetarians include Chelsea Clinton, Brad Pitt, Madonna, and Beatle Paul McCartney. According to British vegetarian Colin Spencer, whose book *The Heretic's Feast, a History of Vegetarianism* traces vegetarianism back to early human evolution, vegetarianism originated as far back as our hominid ancestors. Another prominent vegetarian, Greek philosopher Pythagoras who lived toward the end of the sixth century B.C., believed, along with Socrates and Plato, that a diet without meat was natural and sensible. Vegetarianism has also been practiced for centuries in Asia, where people of the Hindu religion comprise the largest concentration of vegetarians in the world. Hindus in India historically have believed that a diet without meat brings with it a longer, healthier, and more spiritual life. Closer to home, Americans like Benjamin Franklin were influenced by writer and teacher Thomas Tryon, a prominent seventeenth-century vegetarian who recommended a vegetable diet and refused to eat the flesh of what he called fellow animals.

According to Spencer, the term vegetarian was actually coined in 1847 during the first meeting of the Vegetarian Society held at Ramsgate, an English seaside town. In the early 1880s membership in the Vegetarian Society climbed until it reached over 2,000 with branches established in Manchester and London. In the twentieth century, how-

ever, vegetarianism became associated with pacifism, which created a
negative backlash in Europe and America following the outbreak of
World War I.

More recently, Frances Moore Lappé refocused American public interest on vegetarianism with the 1971 publication of her book *Diet for
a Small Planet*. Lappé criticized the inefficiency of a diet based on animal
foods, calling beef cattle "a protein factory in reserve" because cattle
consume much more protein than they ever provide as meat. She raised
the discussion to a global level by addressing the environmental effects
of food production like the destruction of the rain forests and the politics
of world hunger. She called for a large-scale move to a plant-based diet:
"What we eat is within our control, yet the act ties us to the economic,
political and ecological order of the whole planet. Even an apparently
small change, consciously choosing a diet that is good for both our bodies and for the earth, can lead to a series of choices that transform our
whole lives" (p. 8).

Another major influence on modern vegetarianism followed Lappé's
book. The publication of exposé's, horror stories, and photographs de-
picting slaughterhouse conditions focused public attention on animal
cruelty issues. This public relations campaign led by the group People
for the Ethical Treatment of Animals (PETA) encouraged vegetarianism
for humane reasons and attacked everything from fur coats to chicken
farms. Formed in 1980, PETA continues to work through a combination
of advocacy, public relations, and advertising to expose the American
people in sensational and graphic terms to what PETA terms the in-
humanity of animal agriculture.

WHERE DOES THE PROTEIN COME FROM?

If you have considered this multitude of reasons for saying no to meat
and have decided to give vegetarianism a try, what next? If you're like
many people you have followed the traditional basic four food groups to
eat a balanced diet. Without meat, however, how can your eating match
the U.S. Department of Agriculture's (USDA) food guide pyramid? The
pyramid lists servings-per-day requirements and promotes meat, fish, and
poultry as the primary sources of protein.

In 1998 an alternative to the USDA pyramid, a vegetarian pyramid,
was unveiled at the International Conference on Vegetarian Diets.
That pyramid, which promotes protein from soy, legumes, dairy, nuts,
and seeds, emphasizes a wide base of foods to be eaten at every meal

Figure 3.1
Vegetarian Diet Pyramid

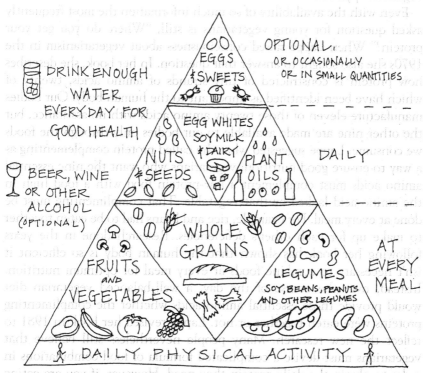

OO
EGGS
½ SWEETS

OPTIONAL
OR OCCASIONALLY
OR IN SMALL QUANTITIES

DRINK ENOUGH
WATER
EVERY DAY FOR
GOOD HEALTH

EGG WHITES
SOY MILK
½ DAIRY

NUTS
½ SEEDS

PLANT
OILS

DAILY

BEER, WINE
OR OTHER
ALCOHOL
(OPTIONAL)

WHOLE
GRAINS

FRUITS
and
VEGETABLES

LEGUMES
SOY, BEANS, PEANUTS
AND OTHER LEGUMES

AT
EVERY
MEAL

DAILY PHYSICAL ACTIVITY

Source: Oldways Preservation and Exchange Trust, 1997. Used with permission.

including fruits and vegetables, whole grains, and legumes. The middle band of the pyramid, to be eaten from daily, includes nuts and seeds, egg whites, dairy and soy cheese, milk, and plant oils. The pyramid top shows optional foods or foods that should be eaten in small quantities, including eggs and sweets. The vegetarian diet pyramid was developed by nutrition scientists and medical specialists from the Cornell-China-Oxford Project on Nutrition, Health and Environment; the Harvard School of Public Health; and the Oldways Preservation and Exchange Trust. Oldways is a Massachusetts-based, nonprofit organization devoted to preserving food traditions and promoting healthy, environmentally sustainable, and multicultural foods. The vegetarian pyramid is the fourth in a series of Oldways pyramids that include diets from Asia, the Mediterranean, and Latin American. Oldways is not the only option either; the Nutrition Council of the Seventh-day

Adventist Church, which advocates a vegetarian diet, also has its own vegetarian pyramid.

Even with the availability of so much information the most frequently asked question for young vegetarians is still, "Where do you get your protein?" When Lappé raised consciousness about vegetarianism in the 1970s she also sought to answer that question. In her book, she describes how protein is constructed of tiny strands of amino acids, twenty of which have been identified as important to the human body. Our bodies manufacture eleven of those twenty amino acids with no assistance, but the other nine are made available to our bodies only through the foods we consume. Lappé suggested what she called protein complementing as a way to ensure good nutrition; vegetarians who want the nine essential amino acids must complement a low-protein food with a food high in the amino acid lacked by that vegetable. That complimenting must be done at every meal. For example, rice and beans had to be eaten together to make up for each other's deficiencies. Research done in the years following her book has shown that the human body is so efficient it isn't necessary to combine foods at every meal for optimum nutrition. Instead, over the course of the day, a well-balanced vegetarian diet would provide those essential amino acids whether the complimenting proteins were eaten together or not. Lappé revised her book in 1981 to reflect the new research. Many people nevertheless still believe that vegetarians must devise a complicated formula of food combinations in order to obtain the daily protein they need. However, if you are eating enough calories in a day in a varied diet, you are getting enough protein. This is because every food, with the exception of fat, sugar, and fruit, has protein in it.

Since Lappé's revised book, the idea of balance, especially where it concerns diet, has been analyzed by more and more nutritionists and scientists. T. Colin Campbell, Cornell professor of nutritional biochemistry, is among the scientists who have studied the effects of diet on health. He is also the director of the Cornell-China-Oxford Project, a massive diet, lifestyle, and disease survey of more than 10,000 Chinese and Taiwanese families. Campbell's project investigated more diseases and dietary characteristics than any other study has to date. The study's research findings showed that eating even small amounts of animal-based foods was linked, at least for many Chinese and Taiwanese individuals, to significantly higher rates of cancers and cardiovascular diseases like those typically found in the United States. Campbell suggested in a Cornell University press release that Americans would reduce their rates of cancers, cardiovascular diseases, and other chronic, degenerative diseases if they shifted away from animal-based foods to plant-based foods. That shift will not be an easy one for many people to make when you consider the classic American diet contains easily 50 to 100 percent more protein than individuals can use. Protein deficiency in this country is so rare that many doctors and nutritionists would be surprised by the symptoms if faced with them. Yet while our protein intake in this country is high based on a meat-centered diet, nutritionists are making it clear that meat is no longer thought to be the best source of dietary protein because of its artery-clogging fat. So just how much protein does a teen vegetarian need and what foods are the best choices? The recommended dietary allowance (RDA) for a young man between the ages of 15 and 24 years is from 58 to 59 grams of protein per day, yet the average intake can be as high as 90 grams per day. The RDA for a young woman in that same age range is from 44 to 46 grams per day, but the average woman in this category often eats up to 65 grams of protein per day. To reach 45 grams, consider a simple pasta dinner: a cup and a half of pasta alone contains 11 grams of protein. Add in a cup of broccoli and a half cup of tomato sauce, and the protein tally is now at 20 grams, or almost half of the day's requirement in dinner alone.

If the protein comes primarily from calorie-rich meats, any leftover protein that isn't burned for fuel will be stored as fat. Luckily your body sees no difference in the protein found in one-half cup of soybeans or in five ounces of steak which brings with it four times as many calories and fat grams. Tofu plus a variety of nuts, whole grains, legumes, and beans give you plenty of protein without the high amounts of saturated fat. So, the answer to the question of how best to get dietary protein is by following a varied diet with a mixture of plants, grains, fruits, and vegetables. Take heart, you don't need to be a rocket scientist to maintain good health and to understand protein. It's important to know that protein helps you think and see, fight infections, regulate hormones and enzymes, and repair muscle and bone, but it doesn't make you feel energetic—carbohydrates provide energy. Protein doesn't build muscle; exercise is responsible for that.

VITAMINS AND MINERALS

Beyond protein, key areas for vegetarians to watch include intake of calcium, iron, and Vitamin B12. Calcium is an important part of the diet because bone density is largely determined in adolescence and young adulthood. In fact, calcium's main roles are to promote the healthy development of teeth and bones, to maintain bone mass, and to minimize bone loss. Because of these different jobs, your calcium needs change and adapt with age. The RDA of calcium for adolescents is four servings per day or 1200 milligrams per day. That can be obtained easily with a varied diet rich in leafy greens, kale and broccoli, sesame seeds, soymilk, and tofu made with calcium sulfate. What about milk? Milk has long been considered the best dietary source of calcium, but guess again. Researchers are starting to look at whether the body can absorb calcium better from plant sources, and, although nothing conclusive has been determined, milk has increasingly come under fire since the 1980s. At that time scientific studies found traces of the antibiotic drugs given to dairy cows in milk. Although the traces were small, it is important to remember that the U.S. Food and Drug Administration's (FDA) National Drug Milk Monitoring Program tests for only 12 of the 64 drugs commonly administered to dairy cows. In late 1994 controversy developed again over FDA approval of a new synthetic growth hormone known as bovine somatotropin, or bovine growth hormone (BGH). The controversy centered on the BGH and whether it caused mastitis in dairy cows. Mastitis is an infection commonly treated with antibiotics. Although there is no hard evidence, many people now worry that drinking milk containing increasing levels of antibiotics may eventually cause them to develop resistance to prescription antibiotics.

Dairy products are also under fire because of their high saturated fat and cholesterol content. Just one cup of 1% milk has 100 calories, 10 grams of cholesterol, and 10 percent of your recommended daily saturated fat intake. There is also some debate about calcium retention and absorption. Nutritionists have found the amino acids in milk protein make the kidneys excrete calcium and displace potassium bicarbonate, a calcium-friendly compound in plant food. The result is that people who consume the most dairy products ingest plenty of calcium but they also heavily excrete it and ultimately may be more at risk for calcium deficiency.

Iron requirements of teenagers, like calcium, are higher than at other times in life. The human body needs iron for energy production; too little leaves you tired and at risk for iron-deficiency anemia. Iron is especially important for teenage girls who are menstruating, since iron is essential for the expansion of blood volume. The highest incidence of iron deficiency occurs in adolescent girls. However, the incidence of iron-deficiency anemia in vegetarians is not significantly different from that in omnivores, according to the American Society for Clinical Nutrition. Foods high in iron include spinach, broccoli, raisins, chickpeas, pinto beans, whole grains, and blackstrap molasses. In fact, calorie for calorie, spinach has 14 times the iron of sirloin steak. However, as with calcium, absorption of iron is also affected by diet, and iron from plant foods is not as easily absorbed as iron from animal foods. For that reason, vegetarians should eat foods rich in Vitamin C to help to increase how much iron the body can absorb. Citrus fruits and juices, tomatoes, and broccoli are all good sources of Vitamin C.

You rarely hear about Vitamin B12 deficiencies unless you're a vegetarian, particularly a vegan, because this vitamin is readily available in meat, dairy products, and eggs but not from plant foods unless they are fortified. Veggie burgers, soy products, and many breakfast cereals are fortified with B12. Although it is found in seaweed, tempeh, and miso, that B12 is an inactive analog, not the active form our bodies can use. Even though we don't need much of it, B12 plays an important role in our bodies by helping make red blood cells and keeping the nervous system operating. Deficiencies can lead to anemia, and long-term deficiencies can cause nerve damage. Because we only need 1 microgram of this vitamin per day, according to the World Health Organization, taking a multivitamin with Vitamin B12 is the safest way to ensure you are getting enough.

WATCH OUT FOR THE FAT

Remember that a vegetarian diet is not automatically healthier or lower in calories than a meat-based diet if you fill up on high-fat foods. Nutritionists say the biggest mistake new converts make is to fill up on fattening foods such as cheese, French fries, pizza, avocados, and nuts. The best diet is rich in fiber and complex carbohydrates and low in fat. With the demands of school and outside activities, many teenagers say they don't have enough time to plan or eat nutritious meals. There are choices, often found in fast food restaurants, that are healthy. Plus, other choices from home require little or no preparation: apples, oranges, bananas, bagels, popcorn, pretzels, bean tacos or burritos, salads, frozen juice bars, smoothies, rice cakes, or sandwiches. Other good meal choices include soups and salads. Even traditional breakfast menus can become excellent suppers with potato or zucchini pancakes and soy sausages. But stay away from highly refined foods such as white bread and granulated sugar and choose whole grain breads and complex carbohydrates for energy rather than cookies or candy for empty calories. If you choose to continue eating dairy products look for low-fat or skim varieties and use monounsaturated fats, such as olive oil or canola oil. A diet of junk food that contains no meat or milk does not make you any kind of a vegetarian.

CAMOUFLAGING EATING DISORDERS?

Misuse of vegetarian eating has also been associated with eating disorders like anorexia and bulimia. Teens who choose to be vegetarian should be doing it correctly and with the right motivation rather than trying to camouflage an eating disorder. A report published in the *Archives of Pediatric and Adolescent Medicine* in August 1997 looked at how some teens hid eating disorders behind the healthy facade of vegetarianism. The study reported that although vegetarian teens ate more fruits and vegetables than their meat-eating peers, they were twice as likely to diet frequently. The meatless teens were also four times as likely to diet intensively and eight times as likely to abuse laxatives. According to the study, this was the first population-based look at eating disorders and their connections to vegetarianism. The authors suggested that due to the increased social acceptance of vegetarian diets, teens who adopt a meatless diet should be evaluated carefully by their parents and health care professionals. Excessive dieting, binge eating, intentional vomiting, and laxative abuse are more obvious red-flag behaviors associated with anorexia and bulimia, and teens may try to hide them by changing to a vegetarian diet.

The National Association of Anorexia and Associated Disorders estimates that more than 8 million Americans suffer from full-blown eating disorders and that 86 percent of them develop the problem before age 20. While anorexia, the pathological fear of weight gain, is rare, its consequences can be deadly. According to the Harvard Eating Disorders Center (HEDC), anorexia has the highest mortality rate among eating disorders. The HEDC is a national, nonprofit organization that provides research, education, and treatment of eating disorders (see Chapter 10). This is not to say that every teen who decides to go veg is going to develop an eating disorder, but when it is pursued to extremes there is potential for serious problems. Starving yourself by eating only lettuce or carrots does not make you a vegetarian.

A VEGETARIAN BY MANY NAMES

Now it's time to answer the important question, "Exactly what kind of vegetarian am I?" Vegetarian is the blanket term meaning a person whose diet omits "anything with a face." But what does that really mean? There are many definitions used to fit a variety of lifestyles and categories from the stringent to the most lenient.

The lacto-ovo-vegetarian is one whose diet includes milk, cheese, yogurt, and eggs. This form is easiest in terms of menu planning and facilitates making good food choices in most restaurants and fast-food restaurants.

Those who eat dairy but not eggs are called lacto-vegetarians. The reverse of this, if you eat eggs but no dairy, is called an ovo-vegetarian. Those who choose to eat no animal products at all are called vegans. Vegan diets are based on vegetables, fruits, grains, legumes, nuts, and seeds and exclude all meat, fish, poultry, dairy, and eggs. Many vegans are also philosophically opposed to animal products such as wool, leather, honey, cosmetics, and soaps made from animal products. A raw foodist eats uncooked nuts, fruits, vegetables, and sprouted seeds. Fruitarians are people who eat only raw fruits, nuts, and berries. A pollo-vegetarian eats a diet similar to lacto-ovo but incorporates poultry. A pesca-vegetarian eats fish and seafood along with the lacto-ovo diet. Whatever you call yourself, you need to make sure your style includes a variety of foods that supply the essential nutrients.

WHICH AISLE IS THE AGAR-AGAR IN?

When you come right down to it, vegetarianism is about common sense and about eating a variety of wholesome foods, but you still might need some help in decoding many of the food items you will find in meatless recipes. Agar-agar is a vegetarian gelatin substitute, derived from red algae. It is sold in sticks or flakes and you can use it like ordinary gelatin to thicken foods or set like a pudding. Balsamic vinegar is a dark brown vinegar made from grapes with a high sugar content. Its sweet and sour taste makes a flavorful dressing, or it is delicious just splashed over grilled vegetables. Basmati rice is a special variety of long-grain rice with a fluffy texture and a nutty taste. Carob powder is a sweet powder made from the seedpods of a Mediterranean tree with a flavor similar to chocolate but with less fat and no caffeine.

Chutney is a sweet, spicy relish used in Indian cuisine. Cilantro, the name for the leaves of fresh coriander, is used as a garnish like parsley or in sauces or salsas in Mexican and Indian cooking. Kelp, part of the family of brown sea vegetables, can be eaten fresh or dried. Miso is the beef bouillon of vegetarian cooking. This is a salty, fermented soybean paste used for flavoring soup bases. It can also be used to replace salt in many recipes. Phyllo, paper-thin sheets of flaky pastry dough, can be found frozen in supermarkets and ethnic groceries. If you've ever had spanakopita, the Greek pastry filled with spinach and feta cheese, you've had phyllo. Seitan is a chewy, high-protein food made from wheat gluten. With its meatlike texture, seitan is often used as a meat substitute in dishes. Shiitake is a chewy mushroom with a brown cap used in traditional Japanese cuisine. It has a rich flavor and can be purchased fresh or dried.

Soy milk is a milky beverage made from soybeans and water. It can be used like dairy milk but lacks the high cholesterol and lactose of cow's milk. It is usually aseptically packaged and once opened can keep for several weeks in the refrigerator. Tahini, a thick paste made of raw, hulled, and ground sesame seeds, is used as a spread, dressing, or sauce for Middle Eastern food. Tamari, a byproduct of miso, is a naturally brewed soy sauce that contains no wheat. Tempeh is also made from soybeans but unlike tofu it must be cooked before it is eaten. It has a firm, chewy texture and mild taste and is often used to replace meat in recipes.

Tofu, also called bean curd, is a white, bland, easily digestible food made from soybeans. It is made in a process similar to cheese making. Tofu, which is high in protein and contains no cholesterol, can be used as a meat substitute because it readily picks up the flavors of whatever it is cooked with. Several varieties of tofu are available—from soft and silken types to firmer styles that hold up well in casseroles and stir-fries. There are primarily two kinds of tofu: the type packaged in water and refrigerated and the tofu aseptically packaged in cardboard without water needing no refrigeration. Different degrees of firmness range from silken and soft to firm and extra firm. Soft is good for blending into dressings, sauces, dips or custards. Medium texture works well for puddings, pies, and fillings. Firm or extra firm tofu is suitable for grilling, broiling, stir-fry, or kebabs.

Finally, the little known food item wild rice, although not technically a grain, is used like one and triples in volume when cooked. It is expensive and has a strong nutty taste. The dark brown seeds are actually a grass native to the Great Lakes region.

Don't be put off by the unfamiliar names of these foods and others you may encounter in vegetarian recipes. Instead, enjoy the adventure whether you are making eating vegetarian a full-time commitment or are adding a few meatless meals as a way to include variety and better nutrition in your weekly menus.

ADDITIONAL READING

Atlas, Nava. *Vegetariana: A Rich Harvest of Wit, Lore and Recipes*. New York: Little Brown, 1984.

Bode, Janet. *Food Fight: A Guide to Eating Disorders for Pre-Teens and Their Parents*. New York: Simon and Schuster, 1997.

David, Marc. *Nourishing Wisdom: A New Understanding of Eating*. New York: Random House, 1994.

Harel, Zeev. "Adolescents and Calcium: What They Do and Do Not Know and How Much They Consume." *Journal of the American Medical Association* 279, no. 21 (June 3, 1998): 1678F.

Katzen, Mollie. *Vegetable Heaven*. New York: Hyperion, 1997.

Krizmanic, Judy. *A Teen's Guide to Going Vegetarian*. New York: Viking and Puffin Books, 1994.

———. *The Teen's Vegetarian Cookbook*. New York: Viking and Puffin Books, 1999.

Lappé, Frances Moore. *Diet for a Small Planet*. 20th anniv. ed. New York: Ballantine Books, 1991.

Lemlin, Jeanne. *Quick Vegetarian Pleasures*. New York: HarperCollins, 1992.

Maradino, Cristin. "The Pyramids Go Veg: New Food Guide." *Vegetarian Times*, January 1998, no. 245: 18.

Messina, Virginia, and Mark Messina. *The Vegetarian Way: Total Health for You and Your Family*. New York: Crown, 1996.

Neumark-Sztainer, Dianne, Mary Story, Michael D. Resnick, and Robert W. Blum. "Adolescent Vegetarians: A Behavioral Profile of a School-based Population in Minnesota." *Archives of Pediatrics and Adolescent Medicine* 151, no. 8 (August 1997): 833.

Newman, Judith. "Little Girls Who Won't Eat: The Alarming New Epidemic of Eating Disorders." *Redbook*, October 1997, vol. 189, no. 6: 120.

O'Connor, Amy. "8 Nutritional Myths: Debunking Accepted 'Truths' About Your Diet." *Vegetarian Times*, July 1997, no. 239: 78.

Parr, Jan. *The Young Vegetarian's Companion*. New York: Franklin Watts, 1996.

Pierson, Stephanie. *Vegetables Rock!* New York: Bantam Books, 1999.

Ragan, Andrews. "It's Not Easy Eating Green." Contact Kids, September 1999, 16.

Reilly, Lee. "Bites of Passage: What You Need to Know When Your Teen Goes Vegetarian." Vegetarian Times, November 1997, no. 243: 78.

Richmond, Akasha. The Art of Tofu. Torrance, Calif.: Morinaga Publications, 1997.

Robbins, John. Diet for a New America. Walpole, N.H.: Stillpoint Publishing, 1987.

Spencer, Colin. The Heretic's Feast, a History of Vegetarianism. London: The Fourth Estate, 1993.

Springer, Ilene. "Are You Ready to Go Vegetarian?" Cosmopolitan, October 1995, vol. 219, no. 4: 130.

Stepaniak, Joanne. The Vegan Sourcebook. Los Angeles: Lowell House, 1998.

VanTine, Julia. "When Kids Say 'No More Meat'!" Prevention, November 1999, vol. 51: 52.

Vegetarian Times Vegetarian Beginner's Guide. New York: Macmillan, 1996.

Visser, Margaret. Much Depends upon Dinner. New York: Macmillan, 1988.

4
FAST-FOOD TRAP

Every second in the United States about 200 people order one or more meals at a fast-food restaurant. Fast food isn't healthy eating to be sure, but just how bad is it for you? What is fast food and how is it different from junk food? Can healthy choices be made in either category? Most important, how can you eat healthy and still enjoy such favorite foods as burgers, fries, pizza, and tacos?

Fast food, foods like hamburgers, French fries, shakes, and tacos, are high in saturated fat, calories, salt, and cholesterol, but they also contain protein and some other nutrients. On the other hand, junk food includes pies, cakes, cookies, candy, and sodas. These foods are high in empty calories, which means they are mostly fat and sugar and lack any measurable nutrients, fiber, or protein. Even though they are different, fast food and junk food are used interchangeably, and both are deeply ingrained in our culture. It's hard for today's youth to imagine a world without hamburgers and fries served in bright cardboard containers, without drive-through service for quick meals, without grocery store aisles filled with different brands and flavors of chips. Yet even while people are rushing around too busy to worry about what goes into their mouths, good nutrition is more important than ever. New scientific findings constantly reinforce the need for a balanced diet for all Americans, but the grab-and-gobble eating habits of many families leave little time for meal planning, preparation, or family dinners. Instead, the typical American consumes at least three hamburgers and four orders of fries each week giving little thought to what he or she is actually eating and why.

NUTRITION MAKEOVERS

Meet Jason who sleeps as late as possible then jumps up and leaves for school. With no time for breakfast in his rushed morning, well before his lunch period he gets so hungry he eats anything he can wolf down between classes. With his serious sweet tooth, Jason usually reaches for a candy bar, or some other high-sugar vending-machine food.

Katie isn't big on breakfast either saying she's not hungry at the early hour she gets up for school. By lunch she craves greasy foods like burgers and fries leaving little room for fruits or vegetables. Since the cafeteria serves pizza and French fries every day, she has no problem finding the food she craves. When she's having a very busy day, Katie may skip lunch and just drink a diet soda to hold her over until she gets home. That's when she eats a big meal and falls into bed tired but stuffed with heavy or fried food.

Or there's Chris who has always been a picky eater and has few foods he likes. He calls himself a "meat and potatoes" lover and says he hates fruits and vegetables. A typical day's food choices would include a bagel with cream cheese for breakfast; French fries and milk for lunch; Kentucky Fried Chicken, mashed potatoes, and gravy with milk for dinner. The only way he will eat fruit is if it's in a pie, like the fried apple pies he buys from McDonald's.

Finally there's Casey, who slouches into the school with an all too obvious "I don't care" attitude, brought on by starting his day with a few beers before leaving home. Because the alcohol dulls his appetite, Casey rarely feels hungry before lunch and by the time he gets home in the afternoon his first priority is to drink another beer to stop his head from pounding. Both parents work so Casey is on his own before school and in the afternoon after school lets out. He may snack from time to time but Casey has little interest in food. When he does eat he often complains to friends that his parents don't keep food in the house, which means what his parents buy does not appeal to his adolescent tastes.

Sound familiar? Don't be surprised if you see yourself in Jason, Katie, Chris, or Casey and their eating habits. You aren't alone. In surveys conducted by the U.S. Department of Agriculture, (USDA), only 1%

of children and teens ate the daily recommended servings from all five food groups in the food guide pyramid, and the diets of all those responding showed a high consumption of fats and sugars. The Continuing Survey of Food Intakes by Individuals (CSFII) and the Diet and Health Knowledge Survey (DHKS) conducted by the USDA from 1994 to 1996 also showed that only 52 percent of teens polled were aware of the USDA's food guide pyramid. A whopping 75 percent said they are tired of hearing about foods that are supposed to be good or bad for them.

According to Anne Lehman, an instructor at First Colonial High School in Virginia Beach, Virginia, these composite students like their real counterparts are a new reality for educators. She teaches a broad cross section of grade levels in the elective classes Introduction to Food Occupations I and II. Lehman and teacher Sharlene Perry take the students through basic preparation, recipe reading, and nutrition in this 18-week course. By the end of the program, they expect the students to be able to understand a recipe, cook it, and to have the basic skills to qualify for an entry-level food service job. More important, Lehman says, "We want the students to know things that will help them in everyday life like meal planning, grocery shopping and cooking." With more family members working and schedules more rushed, the reality for these students is very different than what they are being taught in school. "The paradigm of meal planning, preparation and consumption is extinct. Teens often eat alone and getting a meal or shopping is left to the individual especially if they hold an after-school job and are away from home for all three mealtimes." When questioned on eating habits, almost all the students in Lehman's class ate dinner alone, often while doing some other activity like playing computer games or watching television. Time, convenience, and media exposure were cited as main motivators for food choices. Fast food was eaten from as infrequently as once a week up to once a day.

Lehman said this changing reality is most difficult for teens who are already seeing the results of poor eating habits. "In reality these kids may already be unhappy with the way they look or feel and know what the results (of bad nutrition) are." She added, "I need to be teaching the students how to create and maintain good habits within their lifestyle." That includes discussing what types of foods would be better choices and suggesting alternatives like smoothies, whole grain foods, and fresh vegetables. Further complicating this education process are the schools themselves. In an effort to juggle too many students and increasing academic workloads, many high schools now fail to offer students a lunch break. Lunch options at First Colonial and other high schools, according to Lehman, include giving students lunch on Monday, Wednesday, and Friday one week then rotating to Tuesday and Thursday the next. Those teens with an assigned lunch period find themselves rushing to get from classes to lockers to the cafeteria in their allotted 30 minutes. It's easy to see why students choose fries and cafeteria fast food to eat when they literally have to cram down a meal on the run between classes.

FAST FOOD IS ON THE MOVE

To further accommodate life on the run, fast food has now moved outside the restaurants and drive-throughs into public schools, airports, stadiums, Wal-Marts, shopping malls, gas stations, hospital cafeterias, and college campuses. McDonald's, synonymous with fast food, is the perfect example of that industry's success. In 1959 McDonald's had about 100 restaurants in the United States. Today, the golden arches claim some 25,000 restaurants in more than 100 countries, from Bulgaria to Germany.

In fact, the fast-food industry is the quintessential great American success story in the world of business. Those early entrepreneurs changed society, as well as our eating habits and choices, with their mass-produced burgers and fries. Fast-food dining continues to fit the flexible lifestyle that prizes speed and privacy and offers uniformity and dependability. From Tucson to Albany, from Juneau to Joliet, one burger tastes like another. Customers avoid the unknown by choosing familiar brands that offer a feeling of reassurance and predictability because the products are always the same. John F. Love wrote in McDonald's: Behind the Arches, a history of McDonald's, that the importance of these new self-service restaurants meant working-class families could finally afford to feed their children restaurant food. But the real importance of the fast-food boom went beyond families eating out. Not only has the fast-food industry affected how people eat, but that success encouraged other industries to adopt the same methods. We now have an America filled with malls, Gaps, Toys-R-Us stores, and so many franchises and chain stores that in the United States anyone can now live his or her life without ever spending a nickel at an independently owned business.

Internationally, McDonald's and other fast-food chains have carried that same message of uniformity to other countries, representing "Americana" and the excitement of modernization to their foreign customers.

Nutritionally what these restaurants really offer foreign customers are increases in such American health problems as obesity, heart disease, hypertension, and cancer. Called "diseases of affluence" they are commonplace in the United States but are growing in other parts of the world, even Asia where they once were rare. Obesity in particular continues to increase in this country and according to Healthy People 2010, "Total costs (medical cost and lost productivity) attributable to obesity alone amounted to an estimated $99 billion in 1995." The number of Americans who die annually of obesity-related diseases is over 300,000 according to former U.S. Secretary of Agriculture Dan Glickman. That figure was among statistics included in the USDA fact sheet titled *Facts about Childhood Obesity and Overweightness*, distributed at the 1998 Symposium on Childhood Obesity: Causes and Prevention. The fact sheet is reprinted in the 1999 *Family Economics and Nutrition Review*, volume 12, number 1. Glickman also said the growing problem of obesity in this country is due to several factors including eating a diet filled with fat-laden fast food.

EVERYONE IS GAINING WEIGHT

Glickman said 25 percent of children and adolescents in this country are overweight or obese, a number that has doubled since the 1960s. Although Glickman said the answer is not "to impound the Taco Bell Chihuahua or unplug the Coke machines or ban Happy Meals," is it a coincidence that those numbers began to rise following the start-up and rapid growth of fast-food restaurants in the late 1950s and early 1960s? What's the problem? The relationship between diet and disease has become painfully evident based on research and studies, and yet generations that grow up on the taste of fat, sodium, and sugar may find it hard to eat healthy foods. In fact, those surveyed believe good food does not taste good. Americans also love the convenience of letting someone else do the cooking. A two-year USDA CSFII survey ending in 1978 already showed that on any given day 43 percent of Americans ate at least one meal away from home. By 1995 the CSFII figure had climbed to 57 percent. Yet even the fast-food industry recognizes the problem of too much fat and sodium and offers lower-fat versions of popular menu items. Attempts to introduce healthy meals, such as Taco Bell border lights or the McLean deluxe burger and low-fat shake, have failed. Those choices repeatedly disappear from menus. Surely, if enough people clamored for healthier fare the fast-food restaurants would be happy to make money selling it to them. Part of the blame for our excesses in eating falls on our appetite for fat and sugar. Reasonably sized, reasonably healthful burgers are not what the American public wants.

Researchers worry that those American eating habits will continue to change for the worse even as our knowledge of what's good for us increases. Also changing for the worse are the comfort foods of yesterday, like mashed potatoes and meat loaf, which at least had some nutritional value and less fat than their new counterparts, the burger and fries. Today we reach for fast food because it is familiar, inexpensive, and convenient. Nutritionists warn that the real cost of America's love affair with fast food is still being measured and it won't be cheap.

YOU ARE WHAT YOU EAT

Unfortunately, we are what we eat, and Americans are eating fast food. Figures show that as a nation we spend $100 billion a year on fast food, a figure higher than the dollars spent on computers, higher education, or new cars. It's easier and easier to spend those dollars because fast-food outlets are now on every corner. Today it takes hard work and planning ahead to eat healthy. Smart nutrition, however, doesn't mean you have to give up all your favorite comfort foods. What you do need to learn is how to make a trade-off—to balance unhealthy choices with healthy ones. Experts agree that the best diet is one low in fat and high in fruits, vegetables, and grains. The USDA food guide pyramid contains specific recommendations for the quantities and types of foods to eat from the major food groups of grains, fruits, vegetables, dairy, and meat or protein (see Chapter 2). In fact, many groups like the American Dietetic Association and the American Heart Association are among the organizations that now recognize that a vegetarian diet may be one way to lower rates of heart disease and prevent some forms of cancer (see Chapter 3).

The first step is to keep it simple—no one food group is more important than another. Don't worry about counting every gram of this or that, but use common nutritional sense and remember how you eat over the course of a day or week is more important than what you consume at any one meal. Eat a variety of foods and emphasize fresh fruits and vegetables or a fruit juice if it's available. Choose foods low in fat, saturated fat, and cholesterol. A 1997 fast-food study made by *Consumer Reports* found that basic burgers at the major chains have about 10 to 15 grams of fat, which is relatively lean for a burger but has more fat than some of the chicken or roast beef sandwiches. The real fat traps are the signature burgers like Burger King's Double Whopper with cheese at a whopping 1,010 calories and 67 grams of fat. That's more than an entire day's fat allowance for an adult woman or man. The McDonald's Big Xtra checks in with 810 calories and 55 grams of fat. And while you are at it, hold the mayonnaise, special sauces, tartar sauce, or other salad dressings on sandwiches and salads. Without the mayo the Double Whopper with cheese drops 260 calories and 17 grams of fat. If you ask for a whole wheat or whole-grain bun at least you've added some nutrients.

POTATO: FRIEND OR FOE?

Next consider the potato, a vegetable with approximately 100 calories and no fat until you add sour cream, butter, or cheese or make it into fries. Much of the fat in French fries is a "trans-fatty" type which nutritionists fear may be as bad for your health as saturated animal fat. Trans-fatty acids are produced in oil when the liquid is processed into semisolids at room temperature such as in vegetable shortening and margarine. These trans fats increase the shelf life and improve the texture of processed foods and are commonly found in products like margarine, crackers, and cookies as well as fried foods. Gram for gram, they are believed to be twice as damaging as saturated fat. The *Nutrition Action Healthletter*, published by the Center for Science in the Public Interest (CSPI), reported in 1997 that in clinical studies trans fat raised people's blood cholesterol about as much as saturated fat did. Because trans-fatty acids are not listed on food labels, they are invisible to consumers. The CSPI found that the trans-fat content in most chains' French fries equaled or even exceeded the amount of saturated fat. That means a big order of fries has as much bad fat as a signature burger. If you "supersize" an order of McDonald's fries, it goes from 210 calories and 10 grams of fat to 610 calories and 29 grams of fat, a figure that still doesn't reflect the unlisted trans-fat grams.

If you want to eat potatoes, a better choice is mashed potatoes, even when served with gravy. According to *Consumer Reports*, the Boston Market's homestyle mashed potatoes and gravy had no more than half the fat and calories of any large serving of fries. Unfortunately other potato choices are not so light: Jack in the Box's bacon cheddar potato wedges have 800 calories and 58 grams of fat per serving.

SURPRISING FOOD CHOICES

The salad bar can be a good food choice if you are aware of the dressing trap. Wendy's blue cheese dressing has 360 calories and 38 grams of fat per package. McDonald's ranch dressing packs almost as much punch with 230 calories and 21 grams of fat per package. Customers may not realize that each dressing packet actually contains two servings. If you use the whole package, the fat in the dressing is equal to the fat content of a Quarter Pounder with cheese. Another innocent vegetable choice of a side dish is Hardee's coleslaw; a serving has as many calories, 240, and twice the fat of an order of small fries. You might think the slaw choice is a healthy one, but in fact that cabbage comes loaded with a huge amount of fat.

Pizza is another food choice that can surprise you. A popular food like pizza can actually fit into a nutritious menu with its combination of grain, cheese, and vegetables; however, mounds of greasy meat and cheese can raise the fat content too high. Good topping choices include onion and garlic, which studies suggest may ward off stomach and colon cancers, and the tomato sauce is rich in lycopene, a relative of beta-carotene that may lower the risk of several kinds of cancer. In a check of the major chains, the Pizza Hut Big New Yorker pizza proves that bigger isn't nutritionally better. Each slice in one of these big pies weighs in at 17 grams of saturated fat and 393 calories. Contrast that with Pizza Hut's Thin and Crispy Veggie Lovers pizza at only 222 calories per slice with 8 grams of fat. Remember the vegetable toppings are a better nutritional choice than the fatty sausage or pepperoni.

Chicken is a good choice, and even when it is fried, it still has less saturated fat than a burger. Roasted chicken is the best nutritional bet especially if you remove the skin since two-thirds of its fat resides in the skin. Be careful with portion sizes—what restaurants call one helping actually translates into two or more according to the Center for Science in the Public Interest. Chicken also comes now in the "wrap" sandwich stuffed in pita bread or flour tortillas. Though marketed as a healthful choice, *Consumer Reports* found in their 1997 study of fast food that the wraps vary in fat and calories. The Jack in the Box chicken fajita pita was listed at 8 grams of fat and 290 calories and the Taco Bell chicken fajita wrap had 21 grams of fat and 460 calories. A better chicken choice would be the McDonald's grilled chicken deluxe sandwich without mayonnaise at 300 calories and only 5 grams of fat.

THE THREE Bs OF BREAKFAST

Breakfast is the most important meal of the day because your body has endured a six-to-eight-hour overnight fast, and your brain is low on glucose, which it needs to perform at peak level. Though lots of breakfast choices can solve the brain's carbohydrate shortage, not all are good nutritional choices. The three Bs of fast-food breakfast menus—bagels, burritos, and biscuits—were designed with the grab-and-go mentality, but two of the three have some serious nutritional problems. Fast-food breakfast choices came on the scene to replace deep-fried doughnuts, cinnamon buns, croissants, and muffins which were all loaded with saturated fat and sugar.

Unfortunately, these fast-food replacements offer the same or more in fat and calories. Selections like the Burger King croissan'wich with sausage, egg, and cheese offers 530 calories and 41 grams of fat, enough to rival any chocolate-covered or custard-filled doughnut. Burger King's biscuit with sausage, egg, and cheese has even more calories at 620 and 43 grams of fat. Hardee's breakfast biscuits match Burger King calorie for calorie with the sausage and egg biscuit at 620 calories and 41 grams of fat. The fiesta burrito from Taco Bell offers a more reasonable choice at 280 calories and 16 grams of fat, but watch out for Taco Bell's double bacon and egg burrito at 480 calories and 27 grams of fat. The most promising newcomer to the fast-food breakfast menu is the bagel. Nutritionally speaking, bagels are the best fast-food choice available with a fat content close to zero and no sugar. In fact, the bagel, once unknown beyond New York is now one of the hottest "new" foods on the American fast-food scene. Even doughnut shops like Dunkin'Donuts have added bagels to their menus. Consumers can keep their bagel low in fat by saying no to high-fat spreads like cream cheese, butter, and margarine and using instead a "schmeer" of light cream cheese or jam.

JUNK-FOOD JUNKIES

Let's take a look at junk foods, the category of high-fat empty-calorie foods that fill you up and leave little room for nutritional snacks. Twenty-one pounds—that's how much the typical American puts away in salty snacks like potato chips, pretzels, tortilla and corn chips, popcorn, and nuts in an average year according to a 1996 report published by the CSPI in the November 1996 Nutrition Action Health letter

(p. 8). The good news is that low-fat and no-salt brands are making their way into the snack food aisles. For example the baked Lays potato chips have less than 2 grams of fat per ounce, or 12 chips, when compared to 10 grams of fat per ounce for Lays regular chips. Of course, a popular advertising slogan for many years challenged consumers "bet you can't eat just one." Snacking behavior being what it is, most people do eat more than one serving per sitting, and even though the baked Lays, like Pringles, are made from reconstituted dehydrated potatoes, too much of a low-fat food is still bad for you. The low-fat tortilla chips now on the shelves are an improved snack choice at 3 grams of fat per ounce versus 6 grams of fat for the same amount of regular tortilla chips. Choosing salsa instead of a cheese dip makes a big difference in fat and calories too.

Popcorn can be a good snack when not soaked in butter or buried in salt. Among microwave brands watch out for those with butter: labels show up to 450 calories per bag and over 30 grams of fat. The best of the microwave popcorns has just 110 calories and 3 grams of total fat— label reading can make a difference in keeping snack choices healthy. Also, when reading labels on snack packages, look at the kinds of fat as well as per serving amounts since some kinds have twice as many fat grams as others. For example, Bugles corn snacks by General Mills have 8 grams of fat per 40 bugles, a fairly high number even for a snack item, because they are made with coconut oil, an oil with more than twice the saturated fat of lard.

Vending machines may stock snacks low in fat like raisins, dry cereal, pretzels, or animal crackers, so consider those choices before buying a candy bar. If you really need to satisfy an urge for chocolate, give some thought to your candy bar choice. Almond Joy, Snickers, Milky Way, 3 Musketeers, and Butterfinger may all be beckoning. Consider that Milky Way Lite has only 170 calories and 5 grams of total fat; 3 Musketeers is not far behind at 8 grams of fat. Snickers with 6 more grams of fat has peanuts which add protein and fiber, giving you a little nutrition.

LABELS CAN HELP

In 1984 the Center for Science in the Public Interest and state attorneys general began pressuring food companies to print ingredient and nutrition information on product labels. In 1990 Congress passed the Nutrition Labeling and Education Act (NLEA) which made nutrition labeling mandatory for most foods but exempted restaurant items. It wasn't until 1996 that the FDA issued a final rule removing the restaurant menu exemption and establishing criteria under which restaurants must provide nutrition information for menu items. Nutrition and health information about fast-food selections can help people better understand what they are eating. With more and more Americans eating their meals on the run, this information is important for those people who want to limit their fat and calorie intake. Although nutrition information is not required to appear on the menu, according to the FDA it must be made available to consumers when they request it. Many fast-food restaurants have the information in a printed format, and most offer nutritional information on their web sites (Appendix G). (For more information on the NLEA, see Chapter 2.)

GOOD SNACKING TIPS

So do we stop eating fast food and junk food? That's highly unlikely with today's fast-paced lifestyle, but there are some tips that can give you a nutrition makeover. Number one on every to-do list should be to eat breakfast. Nutritious and portable foods include bagels, fruit, lowfat yogurt, or smoothies. A smoothie is made of fruit, yogurt, and ice blended into milkshake consistency. Even a peanut butter sandwich is a good breakfast choice. Peanut butter and jelly on whole wheat bread offers 27% of the daily value for protein and 13% for iron, and it is a good source for fiber, zinc, magnesium, and Vitamin E. Protein-rich foods provide lasting fuel and carbohydrates give you an energy boost. Stay away from or at least limit morning caffeine. It provides less energy than a good breakfast, it can ruin your concentration, and it increases stomach acid production.

Once you have breakfast under your belt the need to snack in the mid-morning may decrease. But if it's there try snacking on a piece of fruit instead of cookies, candy, or Twinkies. Or try munching on peanuts or sunflower seeds instead of candy. Whether snacking or eating a meal, try adding a rainbow of colors to your menu for increased vitamins and nutrients. Fuzzy green kiwi fruit is an excellent source of Vitamin C and tastes like a mixture of strawberries, bananas, melon, and lime. Sunny orange mango slices have a rich, sweet taste and are loaded with Vitamins A and C, and potassium. Peppers cut into strips create another rainbow if you use orange, purple, yellow, and red sweet peppers. Jicama is another crunchy vegetable that can be sliced into strips for a snack.

Remember to balance the foods you eat with physical activity, especially if you eat lots of fatty foods. For example, if you eat a high-fat lunch like a burger and fries, then choose lean meats, fresh vegetables, poultry, or fish for dinner. When trying to avoid trans-fat look for foods that contain no "vegetable shortening" or "partially hydrogenated" oil and avoid deep-fried foods. It stands to reason the less fat you eat the more trans-fat you'll avoid as well. Some fat is essential to a healthy diet and makes food taste good, but to be healthy eat the right fats, the mono-unsaturated kind found in olive oil, canola oil, walnut oil, or peanut oil and leave the saturated fats and the trans-fats out of your diet.

Consume calories earlier in the day; late night pig-outs don't provide the fuel you need when you need it. Don't skip meals because you are rushed or busy. When you don't eat, you often snack or overeat later when your hunger eventually gets the best of you. If you go for long periods of time without eating, your body goes into starvation mode and starts to use protein in the form of muscle mass as energy leaving fat untouched. If you skip then gorge later you take in more calories than if you just ate sensibly throughout the day. Also, take time for meals; try not to eat on the run. Instead, sit down for a family dinner including conversation. It is more satisfying and you'll be less likely to inhale your food so quickly you won't realize you have even eaten. Think twice about snacking while you study—a practice that can lead to mindless grazing. If you are concentrating it's easy to lose track of how much you have eaten. Good advice is to assemble a sensible amount of food then stop working while you eat. Nutritionists say that variety is the key to healthy eating. Try simple changes like mixing types of cereals or rotating brands. Change the type of juice you drink. There are so many different real fruit juices and blends to choose from there's no excuse to settle on just one.

A FAST-FOOD INVASION

The search for new markets has the fast-food industry setting their sights on school cafeterias and campuses across the country. They realize these locations give them access to willing customers, because today's young adults have been exposed to fast food since infancy. Also many students are away from home for the first time and making food decisions and trying to fit eating patterns into a new lifestyle. Nutrition advocates argue that school administrators need to improve, not deteriorate, food choices for their students. Motivated by financial need to make their food service programs profitable, school districts are offering Subway, McDonald's, Pizza Hut, and other fast-food choices to increasingly younger students, from college to high school to middle school all the way down to elementary school age kids. A 1996 article released by the General Accounting Office (GAO), showed that the number of school districts in the United States offering franchise fast-food items increased from 2 percent in 1990–1991 to 13 percent through 1995–1996. The October 1998, issue of *Education Digest* included the report in an article by Diane Brockett, titled "School Cafeterias Selling Brand-Name Junk Food." And there is every reason to think that figure will continue to rise.

WHAT ELSE CAN BE DONE?

It seems obvious that if America is going to do something about its weight problem, the fast-food habit must be changed. Many nutritionists parallel America's obesity problem to the antismoking crusade launched years ago to raise public consciousness about the dangers of tobacco and smoking. Like smoking, clear scientific evidence exists about the dangers of obesity, and the evidence is supported by medical authorities. The cure is no mystery: better diet and more exercise. Or the solution could be as simple as a tax on junk food, according to Dr. Kelly Brownell, the director of Yale University's Center for Eating and Weight Disorders. Brownell's proposal was published in the journal *Addictive Behaviors* in 1996 in an article titled "Confronting a Rising Tide of Eating Disorders and Obesity: Treatment vs. Prevention and Policy." Brownell has since been quoted in publications from *U.S. News and World Report* to the *New Republic* about what he calls our "toxic food environment" and his solution in the form of a "Twinkie Tax." He publicly advocates a fat tax, where foods with a high fat content are taxed at a higher rate. Although most academics and politicians consider it a far-fetched idea, the thinking behind his suggestion is based on study after study that showed when tobacco and alcohol prices increased, consumption decreased. He suggests a tax high enough to increase sharply the price of high-fat low-nutrition foods, which would in turn encourage people to buy healthy choices, especially if the government subsidized fruits and vegetables at the same time. If that happened, carrots would only cost pennies but carrot cake would be as bad for your wallet as your waistline.

ADDITIONAL READING

Ahmad, Shaheena. "Time for a Twinkie Tax?" *U.S. News & World Report*, December 29, 1997, vol. 123, no. 25: 62–63.

Crawford, Will. "Taxing for Health?" *Consumers' Research Magazine*, October 1997, vol. 80, no. 10: 34.

Critser, Greg. "Let Them Eat Fat: The Heavy Truths About American Obesity." *Harper's*, March 2000, vol. 300, no. 1798: 41–47.

"Fast, Yes, but How Good?" *Consumer Reports*, December 1997, vol. 62, no. 12: 10–15.

Hurley, Jayne, and Stephen Schmidt. "Packing the Best Snack." *Nutrition Action Healthletter*, November 1996, vol. 23, no. 9: 8–10.

Jacobson, Michael F., and Sarah Fritschner. *The Completely Revised and Updated Fast-Food Guide*. New York: Workman Publishing, 1991.

Japenga, Ann. "How America Eats: We Say Our Meals Are Healthier Than Ever, Yet Our Trash Bins Are Filled with Burger Cartons and Pizza Boxes." *Health*, July-August 1997, vol. 11, no. 5: 66–76.

Lichten, Joanne V. *Dining Lean: How to Eat Healthy in Your Favorite Restaurant*. Houston: Nutrifit Consulting, 1998.

Love, John F. *McDonald's: Behind the Arches*. New York: Bantam Books, 1986.

Maynard, Cindy. "How Does Your Diet Rate?" *Current Health 2*, March 1999, vol. 25, issue 7: 6.

McCord, Holly, and Linda Rao. "Low-fat Heaven: The Best-tasting Low-fat Brownies, Cheesecakes, Hot Dogs and Other Formerly Guilty Pleasures." *Prevention*, February 1996, vol. 48, no. 2: 65.

Natow, Annette B. *Fast Food Nutrition Counter*. New York: Pocket Books, 1994.

O'Connor, Patricia. "Smooth Moves." *Teen*, May 1998, vol. 42, no. 5: 26.

Rosin, Hanna. "The Fat Tax: Is It Really Such a Crazy Idea?" *New Republic*, May 18, 1998, vol. 218, no. 20: 18–20.

Schlosser, Eric. "Fast Food Nation: The True Cost of America's Diet." part 1: *Rolling Stone*, September 3, 1998, no. 794: 58–72.

Smyth, William. "Salty Snacks Stay Strong; Supermarkets Still Hold the Edge Because of Crisp Merchandising with a Bagful of Sizes, Savors and Specials." *Supermarket News*, June 21, 1999, 46.

Springen, Karen. "Candy and Coffee Are the New Health Foods? We Wish." *Newsweek*, May 25, 1998, vol. 131, no. 21: 14.

Stump, Bill. "When Bad Foods Happen to Good People." *Men's Health*, March 1999, vol. 14, issue 2: 118.

Tribole, Evelyn. *Eating on the Run*. Champaign, Ill.: Leisure Press, 1992.

Viegas, Jennifer. "Snack Attacks: Quick-Fix Foods for Any Time of the Day." *Vegetarian Times*, September 1997, no. 241: 56.

5
GET OFF THE COUCH

In 1998 nearly 18% of the U.S. population was obese—weighing more than 30% more than ideal weight. Young people, aged 18 to 29, were among the groups in which obesity was increasing fastest. One of the contributing reasons for obesity and weight gain is physical inactivity. This CDC research was published in the October 27, 1999, issue of the *Journal of the American Medical Association* (JAMA) in a special issue on the obesity epidemic. See additional reading for full listing of articles.

The good news is that physical activity, combined with decreasing the number of calories consumed, can result in a healthy weight loss. Plus, physical activity has benefits beyond a weigh-in. Fit people feel better. They are stronger, have greater endurance, have better coordination, have an easier time maintaining their weight, and generally can recover more quickly from illnesses or injuries. People who participate in some regular exercise also enjoy that time. They often find they can think clearly while they're exercising, or else they see it as a time of escape from nagging thoughts. The time of exercise becomes a break from daily activities, much more rewarding than a half hour spent sitting on a couch staring at a television set.

Before beginning a new exercise program, always consult your doctor. Exercise and activity have tremendous benefits, immediately and for the long term. Best of all, it's easy to begin a personal program toward greater fitness. Let logic, your own interests, and moderate increases guide you.

For example, don't sign up for aerobics classes if you hate aerobic exercises. Don't set your sights on running in a marathon three months from now if running around the block today leaves you winded. Those are recipes for failure. Instead, look for simple ways to begin to increase your physical activity.

Fitness doesn't have to cost a bundle. Walking, for example, one of the best exercises because it can be done anywhere and at almost any-time, requires only a comfortable pair of sturdy shoes and some thick socks to prevent blisters. While there's plenty of equipment available to exercise specific groups of muscles, chances are there are low- or no-cost alternatives. Why buy a stair-climbing machine if there are stairs in your school, dorm, apartment, or office? Treadmills allow you to walk or run in any weather, but many malls have walking clubs that let you do the same for free. Exercise bikes also allow you to exercise when you want, but a real bicycle provides much more variety in scenery and challenges.

Of course, if you want a stationary bike so you can "ride" while watch-ing a favorite television show, that's great, but it's not necessary to spend a lot of money to get in shape. A YMCA or gym membership can be money well spent—but only if you use the facility. The nice thing about a fitness facility is the variety of exercise options it provides. There might be a pool, weight room, basketball court, racquetball court, and team play options. Colleges generally have excellent fitness facilities and a wide range of options in a place where you'll find others who share your sports interests.

The easiest way to start is to stand up and walk out the door. Walk to and from school or classes, get off the bus a few stops before your usual stop, pack a lunch—an apple and some yogurt—and walk to the park to eat it. That's a double benefit, because the calories and fat con-tent of such a lunch are far less than those of a hamburger or heavy sandwich. Need a study break? Walk right past the candy or coffee ma-chine and take a brisk 15-minute walk instead. You'll come back feeling reenergized.

Once you begin a more active lifestyle, it becomes easier to become even more active. That's because the results can be impressive at the beginning. If you're out of shape now, find something you can do each day—take the stairs instead of the elevator or walk for 20 minutes. Then do it every day for a week. Chances are by the end of a week or two, you'll find it easier to climb those stairs. You may even find that you're walking farther in 20 minutes at the end of the week than you were on the first day. The hardest part is getting started. Once you do, though, the good cycle starts.

It will become easier to substitute other physical activities for sedentary ones. You might start riding a bike rather than taking short car trips. You might start jogging instead of walking. Once you begin to look for ways to be active, you'll be surprised at the many opportunities that present themselves rather easily.

You don't have to be a competitive athlete to be physically fit. Physical fitness has its own rewards. Fit people find they are more coordinated, stronger, more flexible, and have more endurance.

There are also numerous preventive benefits to fitness. Strong muscles are less prone to injuries and strains. Exercise helps promote a healthier weight loss. Exercise burns fat while it increases muscle strength. Although weight loss can be a little slower, the overall results are better and longer lasting. Maintaining a good weight is also important for overall heart health. Regular exercise strengthens the heart—a muscle—and also lowers blood pressure and cholesterol levels. High cholesterol and high blood pressure are major contributors to heart disease.

The other benefits of exercise are simply the way it makes you feel. Setting achievable exercise goals—and then meeting them—are wonderful morale boosters. Most people recall the effort it first took to start an exercise program and the ease with which they can do so much more now. There's a discipline to an exercise regimen which carries over to other aspects of your life. Someone who can find the half hour a day to exercise generally has good time-management skills, or has learned them. Those who start their morning with an exercise routine often report that they feel better throughout the day as a result. No matter what else happens that day, they've done their exercise. They've made that investment in themselves and their health. Plus, exercise might stimulate the release of endorphins, a chemical that acts as a natural pain killer and leaves you feeling good.

Fit people are generally sick less often, which means they can keep up with school or work demands. All of these factors combined, plus the overall feeling of good health you get from exercising, show why fit people are more confident and have a better self-image than people who are not fit.

Young people cannot rely on physical education classes alone for adequate activity. While 47 states have state mandates for physical education, only Illinois has a mandatory daily requirement for physical education for children in grades K-12. Alabama and Washington require daily physical education for students in grades K-8. The target for the Healthy People 2010 program is that 85% of adolescents in grades 9-12 get 20 minutes of vigorous physical activity three times or more per week. That's an increase of the 64% from levels in previous years.

EVERYDAY EXERCISE

So what is the appropriate amount of exercise for individuals? Experts recommend at least 30 minutes of vigorous activity five days a week. If you can't find 30 minutes, try two 15-minute intervals, or even three 10-minute intervals. Remember that what's vigorous for a sedentary person is different from a vigorous workout for an athlete. Work at your own pace.

In 1998 the American College of Sports Medicine (ASCM) created a new physical activity pyramid. Similar in design to the nutritional pyramid, the bottom, or base, shows the activities that should account for the most effort. The pyramid narrows, with less vigorous activity being required less often.

The base of the pyramid, or the bottom level, shows everyday activities, which could include walking, house or yard work, outdoor play, walking the dog. These Level 1 activities should total 30 minutes most days of the week. While that satisfies the basic requirement, there's much more people can do to become fit.

Level 2 of the pyramid is divided between active aerobics and sports and recreation. These are more vigorous activities which involve speeding up the heart rate. These activities could involve aerobic exercises, basketball, tennis, bicycling, soccer, jump roping, and hiking. Because Level 2 activities elevate the heart rate, three 20-minute intervals per week have about the same health benefits as the Level 1 activities.

Level 3 of the pyramid is divided by flexibility and muscle fitness exercises. These activities, which improve motion and flexibility, include golf, bowling, softball, and yard work. Muscle strength activities include stretching, light weight lifting, push-ups, curl-ups, and gymnastics. The ASCM recommends that people exercise each major muscle group from three to seven days a week and stretch to the point of mild discomfort, but not pain. For strength, do the muscle fitness exercises for each major muscle group two or three days a week with a day of rest in between.

The top level of the pyramid is inactivity. Remember that, in the

Figure 5.1
Participation in Regular Physical Activity, United States, 1991–1999

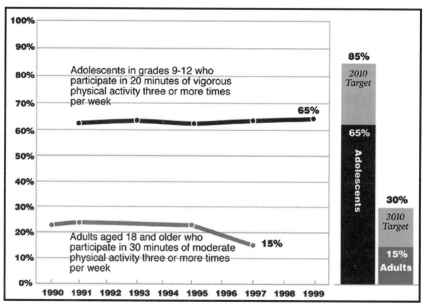

Source: Healthy People 2010.

nutritional pyramid, fats and sugars are at this level. Some are required, but they shouldn't be the mainstay of one's diet. Likewise in the activity pyramid, inactivity should be the exception, not the rule. Inactivity should be a small portion of your day—and no more than 30 minutes at a time.

START SLOWLY

The whole idea of a pyramid is to encourage people to begin to incorporate more physical activity into their days. By starting with Level 1 activities and adding more vigorous activities when you're comfortable doing so, you'll be working on an achievable schedule.

It's a logical approach—and logic and comfort should guide every exercise program. Granted, as you stretch and use muscles that haven't been used in weeks or months previously, they'll ache, but that will pass as those muscles are toned and strengthened.

From an aerobic standpoint, fitness experts refer to a target heart rate—at optimum beats per minute. There are several ways to figure

Figure 5.2
The Physical Activity Pyramid

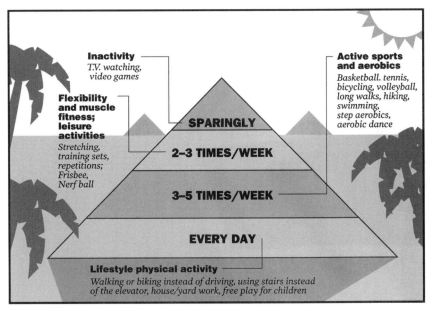

Source: U.S. Department of Agriculture, American College of Sports Medicine.

out your target heart rate—and online calculators that can help determine it—but they're based on figuring out your maximum heart rate and working at about 75% to 80% of that. The prevalent formula for figuring out your maximum heart rate is subtracting your age from 220. So a 20-year-old would have a maximum heart rate of 200 (220 − 20) and a target heart rate of 160. A 40-year-old would have a maximum heart rate of 180 (220 − 40) and a target heart rate of 146. These, of course, are ballpark figures and may not be useful if you are not "average"— either quite sedentary or extremely fit.

Use these numbers as a general guide. If you can't maintain an exercise routine at your target heart rate, slow down. You shouldn't push yourself to exhaustion—essentially your maximum heart rate. But you do need to push yourself at least hard enough to get your heart pumping. A minimum heart rate for exercise could be considered one-half of your maximum heart rate. Therefore, the 20-year-old, with the maximum heart rate of 200, should be exercising at a level to at least bring the heart rate to 100. Remember, the target is around 160.

How do you know your heart rate? The least expensive way is to measure it yourself or have a friend do it for you. Place your index and middle fingers over the pulse on the inside of your wrist. Count the number of beats in a 10-second interval and multiply by 6 to get your heart rate per minute. Take the pulse as soon as you finish exercising, or even in the middle of a workout. Your heart rate begins to slow down quickly as soon as you stop exerting yourself.

To get maximum benefit from your exercise routines, the American College of Sports Medicine recommends exercising at an intensity of from 60% to 90% of target heart rate for 20 to 60 minutes, three to five days a week. This doesn't mean taking a brisk hour-long walk every day. Exercise intervals can be as short as ten minutes to get the benefit. Just do them three times a day or more.

As some fitness experts point out, there are 336 30-minute intervals in a week. It shouldn't be too difficult to find a way to fill up 5 of those actively.

AEROBIC FITNESS

The target heart rate applies, of course, to aerobic activity—activities that make your muscles use oxygen. Aerobic exercises, which are repetitive, include bicycling, swimming, jogging, brisk walking, basketball, skating, dancing, and jumping rope.

What do aerobic exercises do for you? By strengthening your heart, aerobic exercises get fresh blood pumped more rapidly to muscle groups. That helps tone those muscle groups because they can keep moving longer. Aerobic workouts break down carbohydrates, fats, and proteins so they are the ideal workouts for losing fat.

To make the most of aerobic exercises, work out for at least 15 to 30 minutes at your target heart rate. If you can't go that long, break it down in 10-minute intervals, but aim for 30 minutes a day, three or four days a week. Have rest days in between so your body can recover and to prevent injuries. As your body gets stronger, increase the level of intensity or the time of the activity. Do it gradually, though. Don't expect to jog 30 minutes one month and an hour and a half the next. Instead, try covering more ground in that 30 minutes, or extend the slow jog to 40 minutes or so.

BUILDING MUSCLES

There are more reasons for building muscle strength than simply to look buff. Muscle-building activities are anaerobic, meaning the energy they produce comes from the burning of carbohydrates, not oxygen. Muscle strength activities let you work on specific groups of muscles by using resistance to gravity. These exercises can be performed with free weights, weight machines, or even the resistance of your own body—push-ups, chin-ups, or sprinting, for example.

Before doing a muscle-building routine, make sure you warm up with stretches to prevent painful cramping that can result from lactic acid buildup in muscle tissue. Stretching at the end of the workout is also important.

FLEXIBILITY

The more flexible you are, the less likely you are to be injured while exercising. Your muscles will stretch more easily. Flexibility exercises are essentially stretching exercises—stretching to a maximum and holding it for a few seconds. As your body becomes accustomed to these new limits, it will adjust to them. Start a flexibility workout with a warm-up. Stretch so you feel the pull, but not so much that it hurts. The point is to build up gradually. Experts suggest doing regular stretching exercises throughout the day, at least five days a week.

LOSING THE FAT

The reason many people start an exercise program is to lose weight—particularly fat. It's an excellent strategy, and combined with proper nutrition and diet, it should begin to show results fairly soon. Every human body has some fat in it. That's true, too, of lean athletes. A healthy adult male's body should have about 12 to 18 percent fat. Healthy adult females have a slightly higher body fat composition—about 15 to 22 percent fat. Fitness centers often offer body composition tests using calipers or pinchers. People can buy these in fitness and sports stores, too. It's a painless test that measures a fold of skin in several places on your body. Fat lies just below skin level. By measuring a small fold of skin, these calipers can measure how much fat is accumulated. It's a more precise measure of body composition than a simple weigh-in.

The bathroom or exercise-room scale is a good indicator, too. Remember, though, that muscle weighs more than fat. So a person beginning to exercise, turning fat into muscle, may not see as dramatic a weight loss. Don't let that deter you. What you'll see and feel is a transformation of your body that will be longer lasting and easier to maintain.

Why exercise? Exercise burns calories. That means the combination of exercise and diet does double duty. Eat less and you'll lose weight. Exercise more and you'll lose weight and tone muscles and build aerobic endurance. Do both and they'll complement each other.

The more you weigh, the more calories you'll burn. The reason is that your heart has to pump harder to get the blood to the different parts of your body. So a 130-pound person doing medium-intensity aerobic dancing for 30 minutes will burn about 174 calories in that time. A 150-pound person will burn about 201 calories in the same amount of time.

The Austin (Texas) Diagnostics Clinic put together this listing of calorie-burning levels of different activities in its fitness publication, *Classics Club Quarterly*, Spring 1998. Many such listings and online calculators exist to provide a more precise gauge on how and what you're doing.

HOW DOES EXERCISE BURN FAT?

Let's say you eat 2,000 calories worth of food, but your physical activity uses only 1,500 of these. The extra calories are stored in your body as fat. When you exercise, your body uses fuel which comes from one of two forms: stored carbohydrates called glycogen and stored body fat. Stored body fat is found in fat cells and is also stored in small droplets in the muscles.

Most activities use both carbohydrates and fat for fuel. Lower intensity workouts, such as walking, use fat as the primary fuel. As the workout intensifies, the fuel reserves come increasingly from carbohydrates. That doesn't mean, however, that walking burns more fat than running. When the carbohydrate or glycogen source runs low, the body releases fats for fuels. Also, a higher intensity workout, such as running, continues to burn fat even after the physical activity itself is over because the body continues to use fat to restore glycogen. Because higher intensity workouts burn more calories overall, even though the mix of carbohydrates and fats may be different, the body is burning more fat in the workout.

It's not necessary to create a workout regimen that burns the most fat

Table 5.1
Calorie-Burning Activities Chart

Activity	Calories Burned in 30 Minutes				
	100 lb	125 lb	150 lb	175 lb	200 lb
Basketball	192	240	288	336	284
Bicycling 10–12 mph	144	180	216	252	288
Dancing (ballroom, slow)	72	90	108	126	144
Football (flag)	192	240	288	336	384
Golf (using cart)	84	105	126	147	168
Golf (no cart)	120	150	180	210	240
Racquetball	240	300	360	420	480
Running (5 mph)	192	240	288	336	384
Step aerobics (low intensity)	144	180	216	252	288
Swimming (50 yds/min, freestyle)	192	240	288	336	384
Tennis (singles)	192	240	288	336	384
Walking (2 mph)	72	90	108	126	144
Walking (4 mph)	96	120	144	168	192

when you're starting out. Create an exercise program that you like and can follow. As long as you keep using more calories than you consume and start getting those muscle groups active, you will burn fat, strengthen your muscles and your heart, feel better, and lose weight.

STICK WITH IT

Once you've decided you're going to start exercising more, it's important to stick with it. Most people find that once they've been exercising regularly for about six weeks, it becomes a habit. Then it's much easier to find the time and motivation to do it regularly. Here are some tips to get to that point.

Work Up to It

Don't set your immediate goals too high. Start by walking, let's say. Measure how far you walk in a half hour, and over the coming days and weeks, see if you can cover more ground in the same amount of time. Or take different routes that include more hills. Even if you once were in great shape, but have let it lapse a bit, don't expect to pick up where you left off. Let's say you swam regularly in high school, but haven't been in the pool for a few years now. Don't dive in expecting to swim a mile. Work your way up. Practice different strokes, working on form. Build up your speed and endurance. This is important for two reasons: you'll minimize the chance for injuries if you build up slowly and you'll increase your chances of success.

If you set a goal you can't meet, it's easy to say, "I tried exercising and it didn't work." If you set realistic goals and meet them, you can set new goals. Seeing your own progress is a great motivator. Keeping an activity or exercise journal is a great way to assess the progress you've made. Write down the activity, the length of time you did it, and the level of intensity. Take your pulse as soon as you're through and write that down too. You'll start seeing improvements very quickly—and that will encourage you to continue.

Find a Friend

It's often more fun to exercise with someone, and two or more people will encourage each other to stick with a program. For example, if a group of two or more of you regularly walk at lunchtime, you're more likely to do it because it's fun and you don't want to disappoint the others. Friends are great motivators. Find someone who is exercising at the same level. It's not going to work if one of you walks and the other runs. Another option is to work with a personal trainer. A trainer can help provide the motivation and encouragement to stick with a program.

Exercise Smart

Make sure you stretch before and after exercising. That warms the muscles, making them easier to stretch before starting exercise and it also helps cool them down gently. A few minutes of warm-up stretching can prevent injury during the workout. Keep yourself hydrated by drinking water or a sports drink. Don't drink caffeine or alcoholic drinks before working out because both promote dehydration.

Also, don't overdo. Rest a day between strengthening exercises. If a muscle or joint hurts, stop the activity. Let injuries heal before resuming the activity.

Add Variety

Walking past the same landmarks every single day can get a little dull. If walking is your preferred activity, try some variations. Pick out a few different routes or ride a bike to a new place to walk. Add routes with hills. Also, add different kinds of workouts. Once you start walking, you'll feel more comfortable with other exercises. Try bicycling, dancing, aerobics, stretching, or bowling. The more activities you find that you like, the easier it becomes to get in your 30 minutes of daily activity.

Something Is Better Than Nothing

Simply can't find time to do 30 minutes of exercise today? Well, then do 15. Anytime you cut down on inactivity it is good for the body. Get up from the desk and do some quick stretching exercises. Run in place. Take a 10-minute walk.

Applaud Yourself

Getting started is the hardest part. Every day you complete an exercise routine, you're one day closer to having physical activity become a regular part of your day by day habit. Don't focus on any setbacks and don't slam yourself for having been "bad" by eating extra ice cream or cake that day. Enjoy the exercise and enjoy the food you eat. One day doesn't make or break a healthy body, but every day you exercise is a day you've done something good for yourself.

DO ATHLETES NEED SUPPLEMENTS?

Some studies have shown that adolescent athletes are among the greatest consumers of vitamin and mineral supplements. In a December 22, 1994, study, published in *Adolescence*, 38% of adolescent athletes surveyed responded that they took vitamin and mineral supplements. Most said they took the supplements to promote healthy growth. Boys rated muscle development and sports performance as key factors more often than girls did. Overall, 62% of the survey respondents said they believed that the supplements helped improve their performance.

The problem is that this may be a case of wishful thinking. In an April 12, 1999, story published in the *Los Angeles Times*, Gary I. Wadler, of the New York University School of Medicine, stated, "There is an absolute paucity of scientific literature on these supplements. . . . The field is built on narcissism, not on science." Much of the scientific community warns against regular use of these products, mainly because they haven't been tested in broad enough populations to support their claims.

Look through any sports-oriented magazine and you'll see lots of ads for supplements or sports bars or gels to help enhance performance. More than $1 billion of sports supplements are sold each year, and more people are using them. The idea behind sports bars is that they provide a dose of carbohydrates to help supply energy to the body during a workout. The American College of Sports Medicine recommends consuming from 30 to 60 grams of carbohydrates an hour for exercise lasting more than one hour; however, there are plenty of other sources of carbohydrates, such as bread, bagels, and pasta. And those options are less expensive—but often less convenient—than sports bars. While bars, gels, and drinks directed at athletes don't necessarily carry the hazards that performance-enhancing drugs such as steroids do, they may be unnecessary for most people. In a June 3, 1998, story printed in the *Washington Post*, Franca Alphin, the nutrition director at the Duke Diet and Fitness Center, was quoted saying, "If you're an everyday exerciser, and eat well, you don't really have a need for any of these products. . . . If you exercise less than an hour a day, all you need is water."

WHAT IF I HAVE ASTHMA?

"Fifteen million people in the United States have asthma. Of those, over five million are school-aged children," reported Nancy Sander, president and founder of the Allergy and Asthma Network • Mothers of Asthmatics, Inc., which sponsored Asthma Awareness Day Capitol Hill on May 5, 1999. Asthma and exercise are not mutually exclusive; in fact, some world-class athletes have asthma, including the Pittsburgh Steelers' running back Jerome Bettis, Olympic runner Jackie Joyner-Kersee, and Olympic swimmer Amy Van Dyken. These three athletes kicked off a 1999 public education program called Asthma All-Stars to teach others with asthma that they can control the condition, not just treat it when having difficulty breathing. Among the recommendations are avoiding the situations or things that trigger your asthma, monitor your condition, know how to use both the long-term control medicines and the quick-relief medications, and work with your doctor regularly to create and update your asthma action plan.

ADDITIONAL READING

Bailey, Covert. *Smart Exercise: Burning Fat, Getting Fit.* New York: Houghton Mifflin, 1994.

Cummings, H. J. "A Minor Problem of Size." *Minneapolis Star Tribune*, December 8, 1997.

Hainer, Cathy. "A Burst of Interest in Women's Sports and Fitness." *USA Today*, April 8, 1997, 10D.

Painter, Kim. "Weight Gain May Raise Risk of Breast Cancer." *USA Today*, November 5, 1997, ID.

Roan, Shari. "Supplements Gaining Muscle: Pills, Energy Bars, Powders and Drinks Are Increasingly Popular, but the Products are Largely Unregulated and Untested." *Los Angeles Times*, April 12, 1999, S-1.

Sobal, Jeffery, and Leonard F. Marquart. "Vitamin/Mineral Supplement Use Among High School Athletes." *Adolescence*, December 22, 1994, 29: 835–39.

VandeWater, Judith. "Kids Need Weight Training to Keep Weight Off." *St. Louis Post Dispatch*, January 6, 1997, 10.

Weinraub, Judith. "Powering Up; Sports Bars and Gels: Crunchy, Squishy and Hip?" *Washington Post*, June 3, 1998, E1.

The October 27, 1999 issue of *Journal of the American Medical Association* featured the following articles on obesity and being overweight in America.

Allison, David B., Kevin R. Fontaine, JoAnn E. Manson, June Stevens, and Theodore B. VanItallie. "Annual Deaths Attributable to Obesity in the United States," 1530–83.

Jakicic, John M., Carena Winters, Wei Lang, and Rena R. Wing. "Effects of Intermittent Exercise and Use of Home Exercise Equipment on Adherence, Weight Loss, and Fitness in Overweight Women: A Randomized Trial," 1554–60.

Ludwig, David S., Mark A. Pereira, Candyce H. Kroenke, Joan E. Hilner, Linda Van Horn, Martha L. Slattery, and David R. Jacobs, Jr. "Dietary Fiber, Weight Gain, and Cardiovascular Disease Risk Factors in Young Adults," 1539–46.

Mokdad, Ali H., Mary K. Serdula, William H. Dietz, Barbara A. Bowman, James S. Marks, Jeffrey P. Koplan. "The Spread of the Obesity Epidemic in the United States, 1991–1998," 1519–22.

Must, Aviva, Jennifer Spadano, Eugenie H. Coakley, Alison E. Field, Graham Colditz, and William H. Dietz. "The Disease Burden Associated With Overweight and Obesity," 1523–93.

Robinson, Thomas N. "Reducing Children's Television Viewing to Prevent Obesity: A Randomized Controlled Trial," 1561–76.

Wei, Ming, James B. Kampert, Carolyn E. Barlow, Milton Z. Nichaman, Larry W. Gibbons, Ralph S. Paffenbarger, Jr., and Steven N. Blair. "Relationship Between Low Cardiorespiratory Fitness and Mortality in Normal-Weight, Overweight, and Obese Men," 1547–53.

6
LOSING WEIGHT
THE HEALTHY WAY

Exercise and physical activity are important steps to overall fitness, but they make up only half of the formula. The other half is what you eat to fuel your body. Americans' eating habits are less than ideal. Generally, we're eating too few fruits and vegetables and too much fat. The result is what public health experts are calling an epidemic of obesity.

Technically, obesity means having a body mass index (BMI) of over 30. Roughly, it's being about 30 pounds overweight. The obesity rate in the United States in 1998 was nearly 18%, and fully 55% of Americans are overweight. Jeffrey P. Koplan, the director of the federal Centers for Disease Control and Prevention, has called this an alarming trend, particularly because of the increases in childhood obesity. Koplan and others believe many factors contribute to the overweight condition of Americans. In a March 24, 2000, speech, titled, "21st Century Health Challenges: Can We All Become Healthy, Wealthy, and Wise?" Dr. Koplan stated,

I believe that an increasingly rushed culture of convenience, along with flawed urban design and the proliferation of fast food and snack food marketing, have converged to create this epidemic. The technological advances that brought us automation, TV satellites, and urban sprawl have also removed many routine sources of physical activity from our daily lives and from the lives of our children. In the Steve Martin movie *L.A. Story*, there's a scene in which Steve Martin gets in his car and drives about 30 feet to his next-door neighbor's house. Sadly, this is not too far from the truth for many of us. This is particularly true for children, who watch more TV, have less P.E. in their schools, and don't play outside or walk or ride their bikes. Sixty percent of overweight children—between the ages of 5 and 10—already have at least one risk factor for heart disease; 20% of these overweight children have 2 or more risk factors such as high cholesterol. 75% of children live within 1 mile of their schools but only 25% of these students walk or bicycle to school.

Should "dieting" be a way of life for Americans? The answer is no. Dieting, if defined as a way to lose weight, is not a long-term answer. Changing your diet—your eating habits—is, and it isn't that hard to do. In fact, most people find it can be easier than following a restrictive diet because the concept of a healthy diet isn't based on deprivation.

Fad diets, or diets that are currently the rage for their weight-loss potential, are exactly that—fads. When those who have had success with a fad diet start to gain weight, the diet begins to lose its appeal. And the yo-yo weight loss and gain that results from starting and stopping restrictive dieting can be dangerous and discouraging. Again, that's why changing the way you eat, as well as the way you think about eating, can be a much more successful long-term strategy to weight loss.

DO YOU NEED TO LOSE WEIGHT?

Before starting any "diet," determine whether you really need to lose weight. Look at yourself in the mirror and get on the scale and run the BMI calculations. Don't be convinced by what your friends are doing or by making comparisons with models in magazines. If you see a healthy, active person in the right weight range, congratulate yourself.

If you see areas of your body that could use some toning up, maybe the answer is more emphasis on physical activity. What would happen if you simply began exercising more? Would you slim down or tone up enough that way?

If you're heavy, start an exercise program at the same time you begin making sensible adjustments to what you're eating. What kind of healthy food substitutions can you make easily? How about fruit salad for dessert instead of chocolate cake and ice cream? You win on two points there—

you get a more varied selection from the food pyramid and you consume many many fewer calories with the fruit choice.

Nutritionists recommend that teens generally should not drastically reduce their calorie intake because their bodies are growing and developing. Strictly limiting the variety and amount of food you eat could cause stunted development.

SENSIBLE EATING STRATEGIES

So how do you lose weight without undertaking a strict diet? The answers are so easy and logical, it almost seems too simple.

Eat Less

Continue eating the foods you like, just eat less in each serving. According to clinical studies, Americans underestimate the amount of calories they consume each day by as much as 25%. Doubt it? Measure out the food you're eating and see. Pour your usual amount of cereal into a bowl. Now take a measuring cup and see how close you are to the "serving size" listed on the nutrition box. If that microwave lasagna dinner that you ate was supposed to have 2.5 servings—and you ate it all—you'll need to multiply the calories and fat counts by 2.5 to find out what you really ate.

Nutritional information on foods is extremely useful, but if you're going to use it, make sure your starting point is the same. The best way to do this is to measure out portions for a week or so. By measuring the specific amount considered to be one serving of a variety of foods, you'll begin to understand and visualize on your own what a "serving" is.

What if one of these designated servings isn't enough for you? It's possible that you can eat a serving of cereal or other food and not feel satisfied. The point isn't necessarily to limit the food you eat to one serving, but to recognize what it is you are eating. If you're routinely eating 1.5 servings of cereal, realize that the calories and fat you've consumed are 1.5 times what's listed on the box.

Eat Slowly While Sitting Down at the Table

Have you ever been so ravenous that you gobbled down an entire plate of food and about 20 minutes later felt like your stomach would burst? Plain and simple, you overate. When you eat too quickly, your brain doesn't have a chance to send the signal that you were full. So you ate past the point of satiation and, as a result, ate too much.

Almost everybody overeats at some time. Thanksgiving dinner is a good example of a meal where most people push away from the table as stuffed as the turkey itself. An occasional belt-loosening meal isn't going to cause great weight gain. However, it is a problem if most meals are eaten like that because your body will begin to accommodate these greater amounts of food, and the weight piles on.

Eating while standing up, or grazing through the refrigerator, can result in the same overstuffed feeling. By portioning out your food, sitting down to eat it, and enjoying some conversation at dinner, you regulate the amount of food you eat. What you'll find is that you'll be satisfied with smaller amounts.

Cut the Fat

Fatty foods are a definite culprit in weight gain. Keep fats at about 30% or less of daily calories. Someone eating a 1,200-calorie-a-day diet shouldn't eat more than 40 grams of fat. If you're eating an 1,800-calorie-a-day diet, keep fat intake below 60 grams of fat, and if your daily calorie intake is 2,200 calories, keep the fat intake below 83 grams of fat.

Avoid fried foods. Foods cooked in fats from oil or butter absorb some of that fat. Baking or broiling food doesn't add fat. If you must fry, use polyunsaturated oils.

Lowering fat intake is relatively easy to do, thanks to nutrition labels. Look for lower fat substitutions—drink 1% or skim milk instead of whole milk. There are no- and low-fat yogurts and ice creams, too. You don't necessarily have to give up your favorite snack foods.

Recognize, too, that if you reduce your overall fat during the day, having a thin slice of chocolate cake isn't going to undo the rest of the day's healthy eating.

Eat Less Meat, More Fiber

Red meats and processed meats are typically more fattening than fish and poultry. Limit meat to one serving a day. Fiber, found in fruit, beans, bran, green leafy vegetables, whole grains, and root vegetables, is an important part of a healthy diet.

Cut the Sugars

Take a look at how many additional "empty" calories you're eating. For example, a one-half cup serving of sweetened or regular applesauce contains at least 90 calories. Substitute unsweetened applesauce and the calorie content drops to around 50. You don't have to sacrifice taste. If unsweetened applesauce tastes too bland, add a little cinnamon or nutmeg.

Make It Fresh

Fresh fruits are great dessert options. Be creative and get away from the more fattening cakes and cookies and ice creams.

Use a Smaller Plate

If you don't feel happy unless you've got a heaping plate of food in front of you, fill up a smaller plate. You'll see the same abundance at the same time you cut portion sizes.

Get Moving

Diet alone isn't the best weight-loss option. A healthy balanced diet provides a variety of tastes, textures, and nutritional complements. To lose weight and create better overall health and fitness, you're going to have to get out of the kitchen and start moving around (see Chapter 4).

FADS AND PILLS: AN EASIER WAY?

There is no short cut to good health. It's a process that continues for your whole life. But the sooner you develop the eating and activity habits that will help you achieve and maintain a healthy weight and level of fitness, the easier it becomes.

Unfortunately, many young people think of dieting as a quick way to lose a few pounds, or they feel they need to diet continually to achieve some kind of unachievable body shape. These approaches can lead to an altered body image, which can in turn lead to anorexia nervosa or bulimia or other eating disorders (see Chapter 10), and they can lead to yo-yo weight gains and losses. Go on a diet, lose weight, rebound, find another diet, lose weight. Some people joke that over the course of their lives, they've lost hundreds of pounds. To their hearts and vital organs, which constantly have to adjust to these extremes, that's no joke.

Eat the foods you like in moderation. Add variety and substitute healthier choices for current high-fat high-sugar favorites. That's a better approach than skipping meals, which only makes you hungrier and more likely to overeat at the next meal. Don't deprive yourself of good meals by going on a grapefruit and black coffee diet. You'll begin to crave the foods you're missing, again increasing the likelihood of binging when you can eat them again. These very-low-calorie diets can be damaging because the body is probably not getting enough minerals and vitamins. The results can be weakness, diarrhea, and hair loss, for example.

"GUARANTEED WEIGHT LOSS"—SAVE YOUR MONEY

So you're still not happy with your weight, but like so many people you wish you could eat what you want, as much as you want, and never gain an ounce. What you need is a magic solution, a pill or a plan without a brutal exercise program or the endless counting of calories and fat. The promise of quick, easy weight loss is hard to resist, so much so that, according to a 1998 report published by industry analyst Marketdata Enterprises, cited by Jane Bennett Clark in her article "Worth the Weight," 45 million dieters yearly drop $30 billion, an average of $667 each, on strategies that include commercial programs, meal replacements, and diet drugs. From Sugar Busters! to Dr. Atkins' new diet revolution to fen-phen, if it offers a quick, easy, get-it-off now solution, Americans will buy it. Unfortunately, although the pills and programs promise a lot, the majority of people regain what they lost when they get tired and return to their old eating habits.

The simple solution doesn't cost a cent; it's as easy as exercising more and eating fewer calories. There are no shortcuts or magic pills, yet that is exactly what some diets offer. Known as magic-food diets, these are plans that suggest that a single food group will make weight magically disappear. Examples include the grapefruit diet, the cabbage soup diet, the whipped cream and martini diet, the rice diet, and Dr. Cooper's fabulous fructose diet. The most obvious problem with magic-food diets is the lack of variety, which means you don't get the nutrients you need to stay healthy. Plus, people get tired of eating the same thing all the time, and once they stop the weight comes right back.

NEW DIETS FROM OLD IDEAS

High-protein diets like Dr. Atkins' diet advocate eating protein but tell participants to exclude most carbohydrates. When Dr. Atkins first published his diet book in 1977 it joined the high-protein regime led by the very popular Scarsdale diet. Now, with his new effort, *Dr. Atkins' New Diet Revolution*, published in 1997, the high-protein plan is back and bigger than ever. It can be found on the best-seller lists with a large crop of other low-carbohydrate diets, including sugar busters! protein power, the carbohydrate addict's diet, and the eat right 4 your type diet. According to nutritionists, you do lose weight at first on a low-carbohydrate diet because, when you restrict carbohydrates, you cut calories and lose fluid. Since your body stores carbohydrates with water, fewer carbohydrates results in your shedding water weight. Cutting carbohydrates puts your body into a state of ketosis, an abnormal metabolic state caused by carbohydrate depletion. In this state you can dramatically lose pounds while eating all the beef, bacon, and cheese you want. Ketosis causes nausea, which unfortunately works as an appetite suppressant. Other side effects of carbohydrate depletion include bad breath, dizziness, dehydration, diarrhea, and, later, constipation.

Sugar busters! promises that if you eliminate refined sugar and high-glycemic carbohydrates that spike blood sugar, you can lose weight while eating meat, eggs, cheese, and wine. The theory behind this diet is a variation on the low-carbohydrate diet. Sugar busters! maintains that cutting down on carbohydrates decreases blood-sugar levels causing the pancreas to produce less of the energy catalyst insulin. With less insulin to draw on, the body is forced to burn fat reserves for energy. Opponents maintain that excess insulin is caused not by too many carbohydrates but by being too fat. They argue that, like the Atkins diet, when dieters stop eating huge numbers of foods, especially carbohydrates, they immediately experience water-weight loss. Nutritionists caution that this diet is low in essential vitamins and minerals including calcium and zinc. In addition, many foods that raise blood sugar are also high in calories so you lose weight by cutting them out. A simpler solution is to eat foods that are higher in fiber and lower in calories. Another popular low-carbohydrate diet book bases its theory on eating tailored to your specific blood type. Peter J. D'Adamo's book *Eat Right 4 Your Type* sets up specific eating plans with Type A's relegated to mostly vegetables and fruits but Type O's restricted to lots of red meat but little in the way of fruits or vegetables. Nutritionists worry that since most Ameri-

cans don't eat enough produce as it is, diets like these will push more
people away from the USDA's food guide pyramid and the government
supported "5 a-day" plan. Information on the national 5 A-Day for
Better Health Program is available at the Produce for Better Health
Foundation web site, www.5aday.com. The foundation is a nonprofit
organization working in cooperation with the National Cancer Institute
to encourage Americans to eat five servings of fruits and vegetables each
day.

For traditional dieters, calorie-reduction programs still exist, including
Weight Watchers and Jenny Craig. According to a 1997 national survey
of high school students, by the National Centers for Disease Control
and Prevention published in the May 1997 FDA article "On the Teen
Scene: Should You Go on a Diet," more than 43 percent of the girls
reported being on a diet, and the most common dieting methods were
skipping meals, inducing vomiting after eating, and taking diet pills.
Fasting or skipping meals for weight loss means mostly water and muscle
loss. Inducing vomiting can lead to an eating disorder called bulimia,
which can result in serious health problems (see Chapter 10). The FDA's
Office of Over the Counter (OTC) Drug Evaluation noted a surprising
fact about weight loss and diet pills in a May 1999 report titled "Ways
to Win at Weight Loss." They found that dieters taking pills with phen-
ylpropanolamine, PPA, such as Dexatrim and Acutrim, lost only one-
half pound more per week than dieters not taking any OTC pills. They
also reported possible side effects of OTC pills—elevated blood pressure
and heart palpitations—and they reported that long-term use of OTC
diet pills, which contain amphetamines, could become addictive. Many
dieters don't realize amphetamine-based pills should not be used in combination with other drugs; even some over-the-counter cold medicines
can interact badly with them. Besides OTC pills, the FDA has approved
several prescription drugs for the treatment of obesity. Those pills, however, can have even more serious side effects, and in some cases, the
pills can kill you.

COMPLICATIONS FROM FEN-PHEN AND REDUX

The prescription diet drugs fen-phen and Redux are a perfect example
of how pills can turn deadly. The once popular prescription combination
fenfluramine and phentermine, otherwise known as fen-phen, was vol-
untarily withdrawn from the market in 1997 when some users died or
developed serious side effects. The FDA had approved these drugs for

individual use in short-term obesity management: phentermine had been on the market since 1959, and fenfluramine was approved in 1973. Independently, neither the fenfluramine nor the phentermine had been that successful, largely due to such side effects as jitteriness, constipation, extreme drowsiness, and diarrhea. In 1992, when they were combined, they seemed to improve each other's side effects, and the pair doubled the weight loss of study participants. Until the first reports of heart-valve disease surfaced, the only serious side effect of fenfluramine or dexfenfluramine, sold under the brand name Redux, noted in human trials was a rare, but often fatal, type of pulmonary hypertension. With pulmonary hypertension, the arteries carrying blood from the heart to the lungs thicken, and this in turn creates a life-threatening high blood pressure in the lungs.

Josie Freeman, a 36-year-old wife and mother of three children, died in 1996 from this rare lung disease after taking the fen-phen combination to lose weight she gained during pregnancy. Her problem began as a nagging cough, diagnosed as bronchitis. Her symptoms worsened, and she died while waiting for a double lung transplant. Josie was one of the 18 to 46 of every million fenfluramine users who died from pulmonary hypertension, a number considered "statistically insignificant," so doctors continued to prescribe the drug combination convinced that the untreated obesity posed greater risks for patients than this rare disease. That attitude changed when researchers found fen-phen users were developing a fatal form of heart-valve disease. Fenfluramine was clearly the problem because no cases of similar disease were found in patients taking phentermine alone. At the same time, the FDA received reports of the same heart-valve disease in some patients taking Redux. With the cooperation of the manufacturers, the two weight-loss drugs were pulled off the market. The bad news is that as many as 30 percent of dieters who took these drugs may have developed heart-valve abnormalities according to a February 1998 report published by the Medical Education and Research Foundation. The report was in Medical Update titled, "The Fen-phen Furor: Advice for Users," by Edwin W. Brown. Was the weight loss worth the price dieters paid? In dollars and cents, those using fen-phen paid over $1,000 for a six-month supply of pills. Unfortunately, many dieters are still paying with damaged health.

Coincidentally, when fen-phen was pulled off the market, the FDA approved a new diet drug called sibutramine, sold under the brand name Meridia. Meridia affects brain chemistry like fen-phen: both cause the brain to release serotonin, which makes you feel full. Meridia keeps the serotonin in circulation rather than increasing its production as fen-phen did. Early studies of Meridia do not show the same risks for heart-valve problems or lung disease. Nevertheless, its side effects include elevated pulse and blood pressure, dry mouth, headache, constipation, and insomnia. It costs roughly $100 for a one-month supply of pills. A second prescription obesity drug, orlistat, sold under the brand name Xenical, differs from Meridia in that it is not an appetite suppressant. Instead it works as a lipase inhibitor and acts by blocking the enzyme that breaks down dietary fat in the intestine, preventing the body from absorbing about one-third of the fat eaten. The undigested fat is ex-creted. If the dieter eats too much fat, the side effects include flatulence, greasy stools, and incontinence. On the plus side, those problems create a powerful incentive to eat less fatty foods, which is what most dieters need to do no matter how they approach weight loss. However, doctors caution that Xenical can also flush Vitamins A, D, E, and K out of the system, and they suggest users take a multivitamin at least two hours before taking the drug. Although many patients using this and other diet drugs do lose weight with pills, those who eat for reasons other than hunger may not. Plus, both drugs offer only limited help and are not intended for people who only want to lose a few pounds.

HERBAL SUPPLEMENTS ARE NOT "NATURAL" CHOICES

Even more worrisome to doctors and nutritionists are herbal supple-ments that contain ephedra or ma huang, a powerful stimulant that can cause high blood pressure, heart attacks, and even death. The herbal weight-loss remedy Metabolife 356 is one of several supplements, in-cluding Therma Pro, Diet Pep, and Diet Fuel, which combine caffeine with ephedra and a laxative. Derived from the Chinese herb ma huang, ephedra constricts the blood vessels while speeding the heart and ner-vous system. It also suppresses appetite. The FDA has received reports of seizures, strokes, heart attacks, and deaths from users, but because ephedra is a naturally occurring substance it can legally be sold as a dietary supplement without the regulations and testing undergone by prescription medicines. One Metabolife caplet contains 12 milligrams of ephedra and 40 milligrams of caffeine, which is roughly the amount of caffeine in an espresso or cappuccino. Metabolife developer Michael J. Ellis said his packages carry voluntary warnings which advise users to reduce their consumption if nervousness, tremor, or nausea occurs. The company warns users against taking more than eight tablets per day. In an October 4, 1999 *Newsweek* interview, Ellis admitted that ephedra can be dangerous, but he insisted that his product is safe when used as directed. However he also said in the article titled "Mad About Metabolife," he would welcome laws barring sales to kids under 18 as long as his competitors have to follow his lead on doses and warnings. The other ingredients in Metabolife contain no magic. They simply include unspecified amounts of Vitamin E, magnesium, chromium, ginseng, ginger, lecithin, zinc, bee pollen, bovine complex, sarsaparilla, goldenseal, nettles, gotu kola, royal jelly, and spirulina algae.

No matter what you want to believe, no successful weight-loss plan involves magic. What you need is a balanced diet based on the food guide pyramid, an exercise program, and changes in eating behavior. Forget the fantasy of a magic pill. The reality is that with thought and planning you can improve your health. If you answer yes to these questions, you are ready to do just that.

• Are you ready to lose weight and keep it off for better health?
• Does your diet include all the food groups every day?
• Will the plan help you make positive behavior changes?
• Does your plan encourage a safe, regular program of physical activity?

SHOULD I JOIN A WEIGHT-LOSS PROGRAM?

Numerous weight-loss programs are in existence. Generally, the good ones espouse a change in attitude and approach toward diet and exercise. What they can also provide is contact with people who are in the same boat, trying to lose weight, and counselors, who support and encourage people in the program.

With adequate motivation to lose weight and become more active, many young people find they can muster the willpower to lose weight on their own, or they can make it a family affair. If you're living with your family or roommates, do some menu planning. Agree to bring healthier snack foods into the house or apartment. If you're in college, or working, find a friend who will take daily walks with you. Keep a journal of what you're eating and see how it changes over time as you move away from high-fat high-sugar foods and into a variety of healthier options. Periodically review your weight, BMI, and body fat composition to see how you're doing. Progress is one of the strongest motivators.

ADDITIONAL READING

Antonella, Jean. *How to Become Naturally Thin by Eating More: The Anti-Diet Book*. St. Paul, Minn.: Heartland Book, 1989.

Barasch, Douglas S. "Killer Diets: The New Fat-pill Junkies." *Cosmopolitan*, April 1997, vol. 222, no. 4: 178–82.

Clark, Jane Bennett. "Worth the Weight." *Kiplinger's Personal Finance Magazine*, April 1999, vol. 53, issue 4: 102.

Cowley, Geoffrey, and Karen Springen. "After Fen-Phen." *Newsweek*, September 29, 1997, vol. 130, no. 13: 46–49.

Czarnecki, Joanne, and Shelley Drozd. "Rating the Fat-Fighters." *Men's Health*, January 1999, vol. 14, issue 1: 60.

Denny, Sharon. "Nutrient Robbers: Food Habits and Teenagers." *Current Health 2*, March 1997, vol. 23, no. 7: 6–13.

Gleick, Elizabeth. "Available from a Doctor near You." *Time International*, October 25, 1999, issue 43: 65.

Krowchuk, Daniel P. "Problem Dieting Behaviors Among Young Adolescents." *Journal of the American Medical Association* 280, no. 20 (November 25, 1998): 1728.

Levine, Hallie. "Fen-phen Killed My Wife." *Cosmopolitan*, December 1997, vol. 223, no. 6: 196–200.

"Mad About Metabolife: Some Call It a Dieter's Dream; Others Say It's a Health Hazard. But Americans Can't Get Enough of This Herbal Weight-Loss Remedy." *Newsweek*, October 4, 1999, vol. 134, no. 14: 52–53.

Pipher, Mary Bray. *Hunger Pains: From Fad Diets to Eating Disorders—What Every Woman Needs to Know About Food*. Holbrook, Mass.: Adams, 1995.

Rhodes, Maura. "America's Top 6 Fad Diets." *Good Housekeeping*, July 1996, vol. 223, no. 1: 100–103.

Rover, Elena. "Rethinking Diet Pills." *Ladies Home Journal*, March 1997, vol. 114, no. 3: 60.

Shute, Nancy. "FDA Approves a New Diet Drug." *U.S. News & World Report*, December 8, 1997, vol. 123, no. 22: 38.

Stapleton, Stephanie. "Diet Drugs: Problems and Prospects." *American Medical News*, November 9, 1998, 31.

Stoppard, Miriam. *Healthy Weight Loss*. New York: DK Publishers, 1999.

Underwood, Anne. "The Battle of Pork Rind Hill: When the Nation's Best-selling Diet Gurus Squared Off in a Raucous Food Fight, One Thing Was Clear: There's No Easy Way to Shed That Ugly Flab. So Get Out the Jogging Shoes." *Newsweek*, March 6, 2000, vol. 135, no. 10: 50–52.

Welch, Christine B. "The Miracle That Wasn't: Fen-phen and Redux." *Diabetes Forecast*, April 1998, vol. 51, no. 4: 40–46.

7

RISKY BUSINESS: TOBACCO, ALCOHOL, AND DRUGS

We've all heard the stories about the promising young athlete who blows his professional career chances, or worse, overdoses or drinks too much and gets behind the wheel of a car. We wonder when we hear these stories about what it was that caused this person to take the risk. Why risk a lucrative professional career in sports by taking drugs or drinking alcohol? Why spend all that time and effort working to get in the best shape of your life if you're going to take such risks? Because alcohol and drugs, and even cigarettes, are addictive substances. Not only do they leave the user craving more, they also damage the brain and other organs. If you want to live a healthy life, there's no room for these addictive substances.

Why talk about tobacco, alcohol, and drugs in a book on nutrition and fitness? Actually, it's precisely the place to the talk about them. Health is an overall state of well-being. It relies on a good and varied diet, physical activity, and treating your body well. Each of the substances talked about in this chapter are in direct contrast to these goals. Let's see what researchers have learned about the ill effects of these substances on your health. Just as good nutrition can be a good habit for life, addictive substances can easily become bad habits for life.

CIGARETTES

In 1997, an estimated 64 million Americans smoked—including one in five teenagers, according to an August 21, 1998 press release from the U.S. Department of Health and Human Services, "Annual National Drug Survey Results Released: Overall Drug Use Is Level, But Youth Drug Increase Persists." Cigarette smoking is clearly linked to cancers and other diseases; as a result, nearly 450,000 deaths in America each year are related to cigarette smoking. Smoking is particularly dangerous for teens because their bodies are still developing and changing, and the 4,000 chemicals (including 200 known poisons) in cigarette smoke can adversely affect this process.

In its 1994 report to the Surgeon General, "Preventing Tobacco Use Among Young People," the CDC reports, people who smoke are less healthy than those who don't. Smoking hurts young people's physical fitness in terms of both performance and endurance, even young people trained in competitive running. Smokers are more susceptible to colds, a smoker's cough, gastric ulcers, chronic bronchitis, an increase in heart rate and blood pressure, premature and more abundant face wrinkles, emphysema, heart disease, stroke, and cancer of the mouth, larynx, pharynx, esophagus, lungs, pancreas, cervix, uterus, and bladder. Smokers tend to have a diminished sense of smell and taste. High school seniors who are regular smokers and began smoking by grade nine are 2.4 times more likely than their nonsmoking peers to report poorer overall health; 2.4 to 2.7 times more likely to report cough with phlegm or blood, shortness of breath when not exercising, and wheezing or gasping; and 3 times more likely to have seen a doctor or other health professional for an emotional or psychological complaint.

What nonsmoking friends of smokers see is someone with bad breath who is forcing them to breathe their second-hand smoke. Many smokers resent the fact that they are forced into smoking sections of restaurants or that more smoke-free zones are put in place. But nonsmokers resent that someone else's personal choices can directly affect their health. Second-hand smoke is responsible for approximately 3,000 lung cancer deaths annually of nonsmokers in the United States.

Cigarettes are highly addictive, both mentally and physically. Adolescent cigarette smokers are 100 times more likely to smoke marijuana and are more likely to use other illicit drugs such as cocaine and heroin in the future. One-third of young people who are just "experimenting" end up being addicted by the time they are 20.

Cigarettes contain nicotine. Most smokers develop a tolerance for nicotine and need greater amounts to produce the desire effect—so they smoke more. Smokers become physically and psychologically dependent and will suffer withdrawal symptoms when they stop smoking. Physical withdrawal symptoms include changes in body temperature, heart rate, digestion, muscle tone, and appetite. Psychological symptoms include irritability, anxiety, sleep disturbances, nervousness, headaches, fatigue, nausea, and cravings for tobacco that can last days, weeks, months, years, or an entire lifetime.

Cigarette smoking also puts young people at risk for a host of behaviors that on the surface seem unrelated. Teens who smoke are 3 times more likely than nonsmokers to use alcohol, 8 times more likely to use marijuana, and 22 times more likely to use cocaine. Smoking is associated with a host of other risky behaviors, such as fighting and engaging in unprotected sex according to the Centers for Disease Control and Prevention (CDC) in its publication, *Preventing Tobacco Use Among Young People*. Smoking may also be a market for underlying mental health problems, such as depression, among adolescents.

Although the emphasis is often on cigarettes, other tobacco products—smokeless (chewing), pipes, bidis, and kreteks (clove cigarettes)—carry the same risk. Bidis (also known as beedis or beedies) are small, brown cigarettes, often flavored, consisting of tobacco hand rolled in tendu or temburni leaves and secured with a string at one end. They are produced primarily in India and in some Southeast Asian countries and are imported into the United States. Some young people are under the impression that bidis are a safe alternative to cigarettes, but they contain just as much, if not more, nicotine, more carbon monoxide, and more tar than a cigarette. Bidi smokers have an increased risk of coronary heart disease and cancers of the mouth, pharynx and larynx, lung, esophagus, stomach, and liver. Bidi use during pregnancy can cause perinatal mortality.

STARTING YOUNG

Studies have indicated that about 90% of adult smokers began smoking when they were teens. A January 2000 press release, "Tobacco Use Among Middle and High School Students—United States, 1999," detailed the findings of an October 1999 National Youth Tobacco Survey conducted by the American Legacy Foundation and the CDC and the CDC Foundation. The survey found that 12.8% of middle school students and 34.8% of high school students currently use some form of tobacco—cigarettes, smokeless, cigars, pipes, bidis (herbal cigarettes), or kreteks (clove cigarettes). African American high school students smoked at much lower rates than other students; however, the survey found that African American middle school students were smoking at about the same rate (9.0 percent) as white (8.8 percent) and Hispanic (11.0 percent) middle school students.

About one in 10 (9.2 percent) middle school students and more than a quarter (28.4 percent) of high school students were current cigarette smokers. Cigar use was the second most preferred tobacco product used by middle and high school students. Among middle school students, 6.1 percent reported smoking cigars in the past month. African American middle school students (8.8 percent) were significantly more likely to smoke cigars than white students (4.9 percent). Cigar use among high school students was 15.3 percent. An estimated 1 in 5 male students (20.3 percent) had used cigars compared to about 1 in 10 female students (10.2 percent).

Current use of novel tobacco products, such as bidi and kretek cigarettes, is an emerging public health problem among young people in the United States. The use of bidis (5.0 percent) and kreteks (5.8 percent) among high school students nearly equaled the use of smokeless tobacco (6.6 percent).

Researchers Jessica Hochberg and Andrew Siber from the University of Massachusetts Medical School were under the impression that many young people begin smoking only when they get to college. They developed a survey for college students and in October 1999 posted their results on the Stop Teenage Addiction to Tobacco (STAT) web site (http://stat.org). Almost all, 92% of smokers, had started smoking before college, and 72% responded they had smoked regularly in high school. More than 50% of the respondents said they began to smoke more when they arrived at college; only 6% reduced their smoking. "When asked why they thought they smoked more in college the four most common reasons were stress, their friends smoke, there is less supervision, and there is much more free time. Many students stated that smoking was something to do and now they were able to do it almost anytime or in any place they wanted," reported the researchers.

These young smokers saw themselves as part of a large crowd. The researchers found that the majority of smokers greatly overestimated the percentage of smokers on their campus. "The average for most campuses across the country is around 30% (close to the numbers for noncollege smokers). Only 16% of our survey guessed even close to this number. Over one third (38%) thought that greater than 60% of the campus was smoking."

Other findings from this survey included the fact that 61% of the student smokers surveyed had a family member who smoked—often one or both parents. Men appeared to smoke more than women, and nearly one-quarter of the respondents also used other tobacco products, such as cigars, chewing tobacco, pipes, and bidis. The researchers said they were most surprised by the fact that 64% of the respondents said they wanted to stop smoking. Nearly 70% said they didn't expect to continue smoking once they finished college. "There is a general feeling that they will be able to stop by then. Most studies done show that the percentage of adults smoking after college does not decrease by much, indicating that many of these student smokers will not be able to quit so easily. Perhaps one of the problems is that students do not realize how addicted they may become to nicotine."

For these reasons, smoking is one of the leading public health concerns. The Healthy People 2010 initiative has set as a goal a reduction in adolescent smoking rates.

HOW DO I QUIT?

Quitting isn't easy. If you have developed an addiction to nicotine, you'll have to make a commitment and work hard at quitting. The rewards are huge: you'll reduce your risk of cancers and other diseases, and you'll eventually start to feel better. Former smokers often report they're able to participate in sports and activities longer because they don't feel as out of breath.

The Anne Arundel County Department of Health in Annapolis, Maryland, developed a booklet titled, "I Quit," which is distributed by the CDC. It is also available online at http://www.cdc.gov/tobacco/iquit.html. The booklet offers the following tips:

The Day You Quit

1. Throw away all your cigarettes, lighters and ashtrays.
2. You will feel the urge to smoke, but it usually passes in 2–3 minutes. When you feel the urge, do something else. Take deep breaths and let them out slowly. Drink a glass of water.
3. Carry things to put in your mouth, like gum, hard candy or toothpicks.

Figure 7.1
Cigarette Smoking, United States, 1990–1999

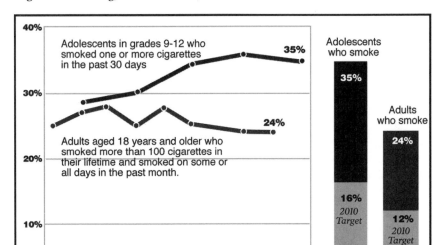

Source: Healthy People 2010.

4. Keep busy: Go to the movies, ride your bike, walk the dog, play video games, call a friend.

5. Go to places where you're not allowed to smoke, like the movies or the mall.

The First Few Days

1. The first few days after you quit, don't hang around people and places where you used to smoke. If your family or friends smoke, ask them not to:

• smoke around you

• offer you cigarettes

• leave cigarettes where you can find them

• tease you about not smoking.

2. Turn your room into a "no smoking zone," especially if your family smokes.

3. Spend a lot of time in places where you're not allowed to smoke.

4. Drink lots of water and fruit juice, but don't drink anything with caffeine in it, like soda, coffee or tea.

When you quit smoking, you may have to put up with some stuff like bad nerves and crabbiness for awhile. That's because tobacco contains nicotine—a drug—and smokers get hooked on nicotine. When you quit, your body craves nicotine and you feel withdrawal symptoms: the Crazies.

How Bad Will It Be?

The Crazies usually last for 1–2 weeks after you quit. After that, your body begins to forget about nicotine and you start feeling better. For some people— like heavy smokers—the Crazies may be tougher and last longer.

Even after the Crazies are gone, there will be times you'll still want to smoke. That's because nicotine is a powerful addiction. Even after you quit, you can get hooked again with just a few cigarettes. The only way to be safe is to become a nonsmoker—for good.

How Do I Handle It?

Here's what to do when the Crazies hit.

Grouchy, nervous: Exercise. Walk the dog. Keep busy.

Headaches, dizziness: Take deep breaths. Exercise.

Tired: Take naps and get plenty of rest.

Dry mouth, sore throat: Drink cold water or juice. Chew gum.

The blues: You may get really depressed and feel like crying. These feelings will pass. Until they do, call a friend or someone else who understands.

Pigging out: When people quit smoking, they need something else to do, so they eat. If you don't want to gain weight, try these things:

• Eat regular meals. Don't just eat whatever or whenever you feel like it.

• Don't eat lots of candy and sweet stuff. Try sugarless gum, fresh fruit, popcorn and vegetable sticks.

• Drink extra water, especially at meals.

• Keep active—take walks, shoot baskets, ride your bike.

The Crazies are a pain, but they only last a little while. And they're better than dying from something like lung cancer or a heart attack. Even if smoking doesn't kill you, it'll probably make you sick with emphysema or other diseases.

Lots of people quit smoking for a few days, but it's harder to stay off cigarettes for good. Remember, lots of other people have quit, and you can too. Here's what you need to do to really beat smoking.

1. Don't pull the triggers. All smokers have "triggers," certain times and places that make them want to smoke. For you, it may be leaving school or hanging out with friends. Learn what your smoking triggers are and try to avoid them. Or figure out how to get through them without smoking.

2. Plan ways to handle stress. When you get stressed, you may want to reach for a cigarette. Think of things you can do instead of smoking when stress hits— like chewing gum or taking deep breaths.

3. If you blow it, try again. All smokers have trouble quitting, and most of

them will blow it and smoke once in a while. Some people have to quit several times before they stop for good. If you blow it, you're not a failure. Quit again!

4. Pat yourself on the back. When you quit, you're doing something great and you deserve a reward! Treat yourself to a movie or a new tape or something else—and pay for it with the money you used to spend on cigarettes.

If you try all the tips listed here and are still having trouble quitting, talk to your doctor about whether using nicotine gum or the patch would be right for you.

ALCOHOL

The legal drinking age is 21 in every state, but many young people know someone who has bought or consumed alcohol before their 21st birthday—or have done so themselves. If it's okay for adults to drink, why shouldn't you? That's a fair question. While it is legal for adults to drink, the penalties can be severe for those adults who drink too much or put themselves or other people in danger because of their drinking. Plus, there are particular dangers for the developing bodies of young people. Long-term effects of heavy alcohol use include loss of appetite, vitamin deficiencies, stomach ailments, sexual impotence, liver damage, heart and central nervous system damage, and memory loss.

Because alcohol goes directly into the bloodstream, it affects every system of the body. Alcohol blocks the messages going to your brain and alters your perceptions and emotions, vision, hearing, and coordination. It slows reaction time, dulls senses, and blocks memory functions. That's why alcohol is a factor in so many serious and fatal injuries. In 1993, for example, 40% of the 5,905 traffic fatalities of 15- to 20-year-olds were alcohol related and more than 38% of drownings are alcohol related according to a fact sheet "Tips for Teens about Alcohol," by the U.S. Department of Health and Human Services, Substance Abuse and Mental Health Services Administration.

It doesn't take much alcohol to impair your ability. Studies have shown that certain driving skills—such as steering a car while responding to changes in traffic—can be impaired by blood alcohol concentrations (BACs) as low as 0.02 percent. A 160-pound man will have a BAC of about 0.04 percent one hour after consuming two 12-ounce beers. The more alcohol you consume, the more impaired you will be. Although most states set the BAC limit for adults who drive after drinking at from 0.08 to 0.10 percent, impairment of driving skills begins at much lower levels.

Telling yourself, "It's just a beer," is no excuse. One 12-ounce beer has as much alcohol as a 1.5-ounce shot of whiskey or a 5-ounce glass of wine. The same is true of a wine cooler. Other excuses young people sometimes offer for themselves is that they have a designated driver. Certainly, that's far better than driving drunk, but it doesn't undo the other damage that can be caused.

On July 12, 1999, Mothers Against Drunk Driving (MADD) and the U.S. Justice Department's Office of Juvenile Justice and Delinquency Prevention (OJJDP) announced a partnership to fight underage drinking in 14 communities. The two groups also released a study showing that the costs of underage drinking in America totals more than $58 billion annually. Earlier research had shown that underage drinking is the nation's largest youth drug problem, killing 6.5 times more young people than all other illicit drugs combined.

"Alcohol is the number one drug of choice among our nation's youth, and it is costing our society an average of $577.91 per year for every household in the United States," asserted MADD National President Karolyn Nunnallee in the press release announcing the study and partnership. "It's time for our nation's youth to join forces with our law enforcement community to change the social environment that condones illegal alcohol consumption as an accepted rite of passage."

According to the study, "Underage Drinking: Immediate Consequences and their Costs," the costs of alcohol use by youth breaks down this way:

Traffic crashes: $18,200,000,000

This figure is only for those crashes with a driver under age 21 that are attributable to alcohol. Another $289 million is attributable to accidents involving pedestrians and cyclists under age 21.

Violent crime: $36,400,000,000

Incidents of interpersonal violence committed by individuals under age 21 account for approximately:

32 percent of murders

45 percent of rapes

44 percent of robberies

37 percent of assaults

16 percent of child abuse.

Both perpetrators and victims of this violence are often under the influence of alcohol. Numerous studies reveal that both perpetrators and victims of violence are often under the influence of alcohol at the time of the offense. Nearly 3,000 of the approximately 31,000 completed suicides that occurred in 1994 involved individuals under age 21. An additional 60,000 people under age 21 attempted suicide but weren't successful. Experts estimate that 12% of male suicides and 8% of female suicides are attributable to alcohol.

Burns: $459,000,000
Drownings: $771,000,000
Suicide attempts: $1,510,000,000
Fetal Alcohol Syndrome: $493,000,000
Fetal Alcohol Syndrome (FAS) is one of the leading causes of mental retardation. It results when a developing fetus is exposed to alcohol. However, the amount of alcohol exposure that triggers FAS has not been determined, so experts advise that pregnant women, or those trying to conceive, avoid alcohol entirely.

Alcohol poisonings: $948,000,000
Treatment: $1,008,000,000
TOTAL = $58,379,000,000
Many of the conditions described above are the immediate results of alcohol use, but alcohol use over a long period of time can result in long-term health problems, including liver disease; heart disease; cancer of the esophagus, mouth, throat, and voice box; and pancreatitis—inflammation of the pancreas which helps regulate the body's blood sugar level by producing insulin. Women who drink heavily are at a slightly increased risk of developing breast cancer, and there may be a correlation between drinking and the risk for developing cancer of the colon and rectum.

Alcohol-related liver disease affects more than 2 million Americans. Long-term heavy drinkers can develop alcoholic hepatitis, or inflammation of the liver. The symptoms of this disease include jaundice, or a yellowing of the skin, eyeballs, and urine; abdominal pain; and fever. It is reversible if the person stops drinking. However, cirrhosis or scarring of the liver is permanent. Liver function may improve when these people stop drinking, but once done, the damage cannot be undone. Long-term heavy drinking increases the risk for high blood pressure, heart disease, and some kinds of stroke.

The federal Healthy People 2010 initiative sets as a goal decreased use of alcohol and drugs among young people.

Figure 7.2
Use of Alcohol and/or Illicit Drugs, United States, 1994–1998

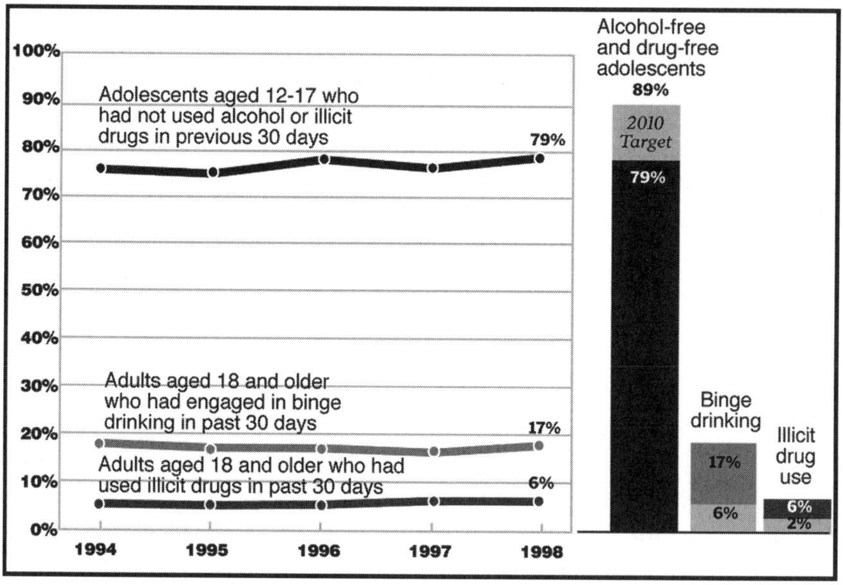

Source: U.S. Department of Health and Human Services.

DRUGS

Marijuana

Marijuana, the most widely used illicit drug in the United States, tends to be the first illegal drug used by teens. In a 1994 survey conducted of high school seniors, 30.7% had used marijuana sometime within the past year, but 69.3% did not use marijuana. Furthermore, most marijuana users do not go on to use other illegal drugs, according to "Tips for Teens About Marijuana," a fact sheet published by the U.S. Department of Health and Human Services Substance Abuse and Mental Health Services Administration.

The negative physical and mental effects of marijuana use include impairment or reduction of short-term memory and comprehension, an altered sense of time, and a reduced ability to perform tasks requiring concentration or coordination.

Short-term effects also include sleepiness and hunger. When the munchies hit, most users don't turn to vegetable snacks either. Favored foods are sweet and high-fat foods, which contribute to overall poorer eating habits and possible weight gain. Marijuana can increase the risk of paranoia or intense anxiety and decrease social inhibitions, which can contribute to a foolishness factor some users regret.

The drug also has long-term effects, including the increased risk of chronic pulmonary disorders and cancer, a decrease in testosterone levels for men, an increase in testosterone levels for women, lower sperm counts and difficulty having children in men, an increased risk of infertility in women, diminished sexual pleasure, and a psychological dependence—meaning that the user needs more of the drug to achieve the same effect.

Hallucinogens

Hallucinogenic drugs, PCP (phencyclidine), LSD (lysergic acid diethylamide), mescaline, peyote, and psilocybin mushrooms, are substances that distort the physical senses as well as the senses of direction, distance, and time. They alter the perception of objective reality. Users can feel disoriented and display bizarre behavior. Used regularly, hallucinogenic drugs can lead to permanent changes in cognitive thinking, memory, and fine motor function. Babies who have been exposed to PCP while in the womb often have visual, auditory, and motor problems.

While hallucinogens are not technically "addictive" in that they produce compulsive drug-seeking behavior—as do cocaine, alcohol, and nicotine—use of drugs such as LSD can produce a tolerance. In other words, the user must use higher doses to achieve the same sensation.

Heroin

Heroin is a highly addictive opiate. Attempts to withdraw from the drug can be physically painful, and addicts who want to kick the habit often undergo years of methadone treatment, a synthetic substitute that keeps the withdrawal symptoms at bay but doesn't provide the "rush" of heroin. Some of the effects of heroin are shallow breathing, nausea, panic, insomnia, and an increasing addiction to the drug.

Heroin is generally consumed by intravenous injection, shooting the drug from a needle into a vein. Drug users who share needles are putting themselves at risk for contamination with the AIDS virus, which is carried in contaminated blood left in the needles or syringe. Because the purity of the heroin is different depending on what it's combined with and where it comes from, users can't be too sure of the dosage they're injecting. An overdose of heroin could lead to a coma or death. Heroin use during pregnancy can lead to miscarriages or a stillborn baby. Babies can also be born addicted to heroin. Those babies who have to experience withdrawal from the drug are often left with a number of developmental problems.

Analogs

Analogs are drugs that have been chemically altered to create a drug that's just different enough that it isn't listed on the Drug Enforcement Administration's list of controlled substances. That loophole has since been changed as these so-called designer drugs have been added to the list. One analog of methamphetamine is known as "ecstasy." One problem with these drugs is that they are underground drugs so stronger potency than the original drug and contamination of the analog are risks.

Stimulants

Stimulants provide the user with a temporary feeling of power and energy; however, when the drug wears off, the user often feels depressed, edgy, and craving more. That cycle contributes to stimulants' addictiveness.

One of the most common stimulants is cocaine—also called coke, C, snow, blow, toot, nose candy, flake, and The Lady. Cocaine is a white powder that comes from the leaves of the coca plant and is typically snorted—rapidly inhaled through the nasal passages—or injected intravenously. Crack is cocaine chemically altered so it can be smoked.

Methamphetamine is another powerful stimulant. It's often manufactured illegally in underground labs, and the street version is known as "speed" or "crystal" when it is swallowed or sniffed, "crank" when it is injected, and "ice" when it is smoked.

The physical effects of stimulants include increases in blood pressure, heart rate, breathing rate, and body temperature. Heart attacks, strokes, respiratory failure, hepatitis or AIDS through shared needles, and brain seizures are also physical risks. Psychological risks include violent or erratic behavior, hallucinations, confusion, loss of interest in food or sex, and loss of interest in friends, family, sports, and hobbies. In addition, cocaine habits can be extremely costly, and some users will do almost anything to support the habit—including selling drugs, prostitution, and other crimes.

Inhalants

Inhalants include any substance that is sniffed or huffed to give the user a high. Use of these substances are increasing, especially among younger teens. According to a survey conducted by the Substance Abuse and Mental Health Services Administration, of the U.S. Department of Health and Human Services, and published in "Tips for Teens About Inhalants," "Inhalant use among all grades has risen steadily since 1991. Nearly 20 percent of all adolescents report using inhalants at least once in their lives. Current use is highest among eighth graders."

Inhalants are not safe. Possible effects are sudden death, suffocation, visual hallucinations and severe mood swings, numbness, and tingling of the hands and feet. Long-term use has been associated with brain damage. The use of inhalants can also lead to damage or decreased function of senses such as smell, the body's nervous system, and kidneys, and can cause nausea, nosebleeds, violent behavior, irregular heartbeat, and the involuntary passing of urine and feces.

Researchers point out that inhalant use can become a habit. As users develop a tolerance to inhalants, they'll need more of the substance to get the same head rush. Also, when users try to give up the habit, they can suffer withdrawal symptoms, such as hallucinations, headaches, chills, tremors, and stomach cramps.

Steroids

Anabolic steroids have some medical uses. They are used for treating specific types of anemia, some breast cancers, and testosterone deficiency, but they are more commonly known to young people for their body-building and performance-enhancing characteristics. Steroids include the male hormone testosterone and its artificial derivatives. Nonmedical use by athletes to improve their athletic ability, as well as nonathletes who use them to look better, is illegal.

Steroids have some unpleasant side effects. Users can suffer from paranoid jealousy, extreme irritability, and impaired judgment which might be caused by the feeling of invincibility evoked by steroids. Researchers are also concerned that there might be lasting psychiatric effects from long-term steroid use. Some of the known major side effects include liver tumors, jaundice, fluid retention, high blood pressure, and severe acne.

Because steroids are derived from a natural or synthetic male hormone, they can mix up the signals to the body. Males using steroids can experience testicular shrinkage, reduced sperm count, infertility, baldness, and the development of breasts. Female users report these side effects: facial hair, irregular menstrual cycles, and a deepened voice. Of particular concern to adolescents is the side effect of stunted growth.

Steroids can be taken orally or injected. If young people are injecting steroids with shared needles, they are also risking exposure to hepatitis and AIDS.

AIDS AND HIV

The Human Immunodeficiency Virus (HIV) is transmitted through unprotected sexual intercourse and through sharing needles or syringes with someone infected with the virus. HIV can be in the body for 10 years before symptoms of Acquired Immunodeficiency Syndrome (AIDS) begin to show up.

While many people know how the virus is transmitted, many continue to engage in high-risk activities. According to an August 1999 fact sheet from the CDC, titled "Young People at Risk: HIV/AIDS Among America's Youth":

In the United States, HIV-related death has the greatest impact on young and middle-aged adults, particularly racial and ethnic minorities. HIV is the fifth leading cause of death for Americans between the ages of 25 and 44. Among African American men and women in this age group, however, it is the *leading* cause of death. Many of these young adults likely were infected as teenagers. It is estimated that at least half of all new HIV infections in the United States are among people under 25, and the majority of young people are infected sexually.

In 1998, 1,798 young people (ages 13 to 24) were reported with AIDS, bringing the cumulative total to 27,860 cases of AIDS in this age group. Among 13- to 24-year-olds, 51% of all AIDS cases reported among males in 1998 were among young men who have sex with men (MSM); 10% were among injection drug users (IDUs); and 9% were among young men infected heterosexually. In 1998, among young women the same age, 47% were infected heterosexually and 14% were IDUs. . . .

A CDC study that analyzed data from 25 states with integrated HIV and AIDS reporting systems for the period between January 1994 and June 1997 found that young people (aged 13 to 24) accounted for a much greater proportion of HIV than AIDS cases. The study also showed that even though AIDS incidence (the number of new cases diagnosed during a given time period, usually a year) is declining, *there has not been a comparable decline in the number of newly diagnosed HIV cases among youth*.

One of the first-line protections against HIV is to avoid alcohol or drugs of any kind. Young people might wonder why drinking beer could be considered a risk factor for HIV, but studies have shown that people who drink or use other drugs increase the likelihood of following up with additional risky behavior. Under the influence of alcohol or other drugs, someone might not have the good judgment to say no to unprotected sex, for example.

Don't share needles. That's not just limited to drug use, but to any needles—whether they've been used for tattooing, piercing, or injecting steroids or other substances. Contaminated blood remaining in the needle or syringe can be spread to the next user.

Another first-line avoidance strategy is sexual abstinence. If you are having sex, avoid contact with a partner's semen, blood, or vaginal fluid. Use a latex condom.

ADDITIONAL RESOURCES

The first place to look for information on treatment and support is in your local Yellow Pages. Try "Alcoholism Information" or "Drug Abuse and Addiction Information." Alcoholics Anonymous (AA) or Narcotics Anonymous (NA) may also be listed. For AIDS or HIV information and support, look in the Yellow Pages under AIDS Counseling or Social Service Organizations. Or use the following list for referrals to local groups or information.

AIDS/HIV

AIDS Action Council
1875 Connecticut Avenue, NW
Suite 700
Washington, DC 20009
202-986-1300

AIDS & Adolescents Network of New York
666 Broadway, Suite 520
New York, NY 10012
212-505-9115

AIDS Prevention League
136 West Wood Avenue
Akron, OH 44302
216-376-4384

Gay Men's Health Crisis
129 W. 20th Street
New York, NY 10011
212-807-6664

Health Education Resource Center
101 W. Read Street, Suite 825
Baltimore, MD 21201
410-685-1180

Names Project Foundation
2362 Market Street
San Francisco, CA 94114
415-863-5511

National AIDS Clearinghouse
P.O. Box 6003
Rockville, MD 20849
301-217-0023
1-800-458-5231

National AIDS Hotline
1-800-342-AIDS
1-800-344-SIDA (Spanish)
1-800-AIDS-TTY (TTD/TTY for deaf and hard of hearing)

National Minority AIDS Council
300 I Street, NW, Suite 400
Washington, DC 20002
202-544-1076

Teens Teaching AIDS Prevention
3030 Walnut
Kansas City, MO 64108
816-561-8784 or

AIDS Hotline for Teens
1-800-234-Teens

Alcohol/Drug Use

Al-Anon/Alateen Family Group Headquarters, Inc.
P.O. Box 862
Midtown Station
New York, NY 10018-0862
212-302-7240
1-800-334-2666 (U.S.)
1-800-443-4525 (Canada)

Alcoholics Anonymous (AA) World Services, Inc.
475 Riverside Drive
New York, NY 10115
212-870-3400

American Council for Drug Education
164 West 74th Street
New York, NY 10023
212-758-8060
1-800-488-DRUG

Center for Substance Abuse Treatment
Information and Treatment Referral Hotline
11426–28 Rockville Pike, Suite 410
Rockville, MD 20852
1-800-622-HELP

Children of Alcoholics Foundation, Inc.
Box 4185, Grand Central Station
New York, NY 10115
1-800-359-COAF
212-754-0656

Cocaine Anonymous
3740 Overland Avenue, Suite G
Los Angeles, CA 90034

213-559-5833
1-800-347-8998

CoAnon Family Groups
P.O. Box 64742-66
Los Angeles, CA 90064
310-859-2206

Cocaine Helpline
Monday through Friday, 9:00A.M.–3:00A.M.
Saturday and Sunday, 12:00 P.M.–3:00 A.M.
1-800-COCAINE

Families Anonymous, Inc.
P.O. Box 3475
Culver City, CA 90231-3475
310-313-5800
1-800-736-9805

MADD
www.madd.org
214-744-6233

Nar-Anon Family Groups
P.O. Box 2562
Palos Verdes Peninsula, CA 90274
310-547-5800

Narcotics Anonymous (NA)
P.O. Box 9999
Van Nuys, CA 91409
818-773-9999

National Clearinghouse for Alcohol and Drug Information
P.O. Box 2345
Rockville, MD 20847-2345
301-468-2600
1-800-729-6686

National Council on Alcoholism and Drug Dependence
12 West 21st Street, 7th Floor
New York, NY 10010
1-800-622-2255

National Families in Action
2296 Henderson Mill Road
Suite 300
Atlanta, GA 30345
404-934-6364

National Federation of Parents for Drug-Free Youth
Monday through Friday, 9:00 A.M.–5:00 P.M.
1-800-554-KIDS

National Institute on Drug Abuse Information and Referral Line
Monday through Friday, 9:00 A.M.–3:00 A.M.
1-800-622-HELP

Parent's Resource Institute for Drug Education (PRIDE)
Monday through Friday, 8:30 A.M.–5:00 P.M. (recorded service other times)
1-800-241-9746

Students Against Driving Drunk (SADD)
Box 800
Marlboro, MA 01752
1-800-787-5777
1-508-481-5759 (FAX)
www.saddonline.com

Smoking

American Cancer Society (AMC)
1-800-ACS-2345 (1-800-227-2345)
www.cancer.org

American Lung Association (ALA)
1740 Broadway
New York, NY 10019
212-315-8700
www.lungusa.org

Office on Smoking and Health
Centers for Disease Control and Prevention
Mail Stop K-50
4770 Buford Highway, NE

Atlanta, GA 30341-3724
404-488-5708

Steroids

American Academy of Sports Physicians
17113 Gledhill Street
Northridge, CA 91325
818-886-7891

American College of Sports Medicine
P.O. Box 1440
Indianapolis, IN 46206
317-637-9200

American Orthopedic Society for Sports Medicine
2250 E. Devon Avenue
Suite 115
Des Plaines, IL 60018
708-803-8700

American Osteopathic Academy of Sports Medicine
7611 Elmwood Avenue
Suite 201
Middleton, WI 53562
608-831-4400

Joint Commission on Sports Medicine and Science
Oklahoma State University
Student Health Center
Stillwater, OK 74078
405-744-7031

ADDITIONAL READING

Blue, J. G., and J. A. Lombardo. "Steroids and Steroid-like Compounds." *Clinics in Sports Medicine* 18, no. 3 (1999): 667-89.
Goldberg, L., et al. "The ATLAS Program: Preventing Drug Use and Promoting Health Behaviors." *Archives of Pediatrics and Adolescent Medicine* 154 (April 2000): 332-38.
Legwold, Gary. "More Teenage Girls Using Steroids." *Better Homes and Gardens* 76, no. 8 (August 1998): 76.

Pierce, Charles P. "Ten Years Later, He Can Laugh About It." (Ben Johnson profile) *Esquire* 131, no. 2 (February 1999): 50.

Stephenson, Joan. "Curbing Teen Steroid Use." *JAMA, The Journal of the American Medical Association* 283, no. 19 (May 17, 2000): 2514.

Yesalis, C. E. *Anabolic Steroids in Sports and Exercise.* 2d ed. Champaign, Ill.: Human Kinetics, in press.

Yesalis, Charles and Virginia Cowart. *The Steroids Game.* Champaign, Ill.: Human Kinetics, 1998.

8

BE A SMART
FOOD SHOPPER

Teenagers today face a cornucopia of some 30,000 products each time they step into a grocery store thanks to the twentieth century and its related food technology. After entering these behemoth buildings, many inexperienced shoppers are overwhelmed by the variety of choices in frozen, canned, dehydrated, fresh, and processed foods. What should you buy? What's really healthy? What's safe? These are important questions because what you eat is one of the major influences on how healthy you are now and how healthy you will be as you age.

Some of the factors that shape what you buy are family preferences, convenience, and advertising. Just how much of what we eat is influenced by advertising? Advertisements are everywhere: in expected places like television and radio, but also in unexpected places like shopping carts, food products, and even inside grocery packaging. Plus, advertisers recognize the growing wealth in the youth market. U.S. teenagers spent $153 billion on everything from clothing to food in 1999, a figure 8% higher than the 1998 figure of $141 billion. Those numbers were reported in the *Spring 2000/Wave 35 Teenage Marketing and Lifestyle Study* conducted and released by the Illinois-based Teenage Research Unlimited (TRU). TRU is a marketing-research firm that specializes in surveying teen attitudes. Another interesting finding from this study shows

47% of teens grocery shop for their family in a given week and 62% cook and/or prepare meals weekly. TRUs' Spring 2000 Study surveyed over 2,034 teens nationwide between the ages of 12 and 19. Today's teens represent approximately 11% of the total U.S. population.

Many companies like Procter & Gamble or Coca-Cola recognize the buying power of young consumers and are investing tremendous thought and energy into satisfying these young consumers knowing they are brand-loyal shoppers, according to researchers like Lawrence Lepisto, professor of business administration at Central Michigan University in Mount Pleasant, Michigan. Lepisto is the director of a long-term study that measures the ways in which consumers change as they age. The study, which began in the late 1980s, also looks at how life changes affect people as consumers. According to Lepisto, most consumers are surprisingly consistent and stable in their purchasing behavior, but he adds, "Older shoppers are more quality conscious while young buyers are novelty prone." This stands to reason since those teenage years are all about figuring out who you are and wrestling with the question of iden-tity which makes image very important to young consumers. "Self-image isn't solidified for a while and teens don't want to be linked with something that isn't cool or that they associate with their parent's gen-eration." Lepisto encourages his students to slow down and think about purchases before they buy as part of the course he teaches on consumer behavior. For his class, and others like it, raising awareness among stu-dents of what they are buying and why is part of the class objective. The main objective, however, is to help marketers better understand consumers. Advertisers target everything from toothpaste to snack food toward the youth market. Commercial jingles and slogans are aimed at the young and the hip. The good news, according to Lepisto, is that basic consumer behavior courses can teach people to recognize their own power as consumers and help them recognize advertisements designed to push their buttons.

CONVENIENCE MATTERS

In supermarkets and grocery stores everything is designed to be quick, easy, and convenient, creating a generation that may not realize soup can be made without opening a can or bread can be baked instead of bought. Analysts say convenience is the most important factor driving the food industry today. To give us that convenience, our food must travel great distances from fields around the world to packinghouses and processing plants, finally making its way to those conveniently located stores. Once the food reaches the grocery shelves U.S. consumers of all ages are ready to shop. U.S. Department of Agriculture (USDA) statistics on food spending are charted in the *Statistical Abstract of the United States* (1998). According to the USDA Americans spent over $423 billion in retail food stores in 1996—between 10% and 15% of most people's budgets. Food is the largest expense after housing for a majority of people (p. 770).

When one adds in the expense of foods eaten outside the home, it's even higher. According to the Consumer Expenditure Survey released by the Bureau of Labor Statistics of the U.S. Department of Labor, on November 16, 1999, Americans spent 3.5% less on food purchased for home preparation and 5.7% more for food away from home. The average expenditures on food away from home per consumer increased from $1,921 in 1997 to $2,030 in 1998. In contrast, spending on food at home fell from $2,880 in 1997 to $2,780 in 1998.

You may be thinking, "Why should I care?" Here's a reason: you can save dollars, time, and energy and improve your overall nutrition and health if you follow a budget, plan meals, and make a grocery list instead of impulse shopping for your food. If you want an example of how it's done, the Department of Agriculture provides a list of average amounts spent by Americans on thrifty, low-cost, moderate, or liberal grocery spending plans. Using USDA June 1999 examples, a family of four with moderate grocery purchases spend between $579 and $684 per month, depending on the ages of the children. A single man between the ages of 15 and 19 spends close to $200 a month or $2,400 per year for foods and snacks prepared at home. But watch out, impulse purchases can mean spending two or three times that amount of money on your groceries. Remember, those USDA figures do not include dollars spent at fast-food or other restaurants, only money spent in grocery stores, supermarkets, convenience stores, superstores, or warehouse shopping clubs.

PLANNING STARTS AT HOME

The best way to organize your trip to the supermarket is to read your daily newspaper or the sale inserts that list weekly food specials. Put together a weekly menu, check recipes, and add needed ingredients to your list. If you wait to choose dinner ideas in the store it's very easy to overspend. A "quick trip" to pick up one item is a sure way to waste

Table 8.1
Cost of Food at Home at Four Levels, U.S. Average, June 2000

Age-Gender Groups	Weekly Cost				Monthly Cost			
	Thrifty	Low	Moderate	Liberal	Thrifty	Low	Moderate	Liberal
Individuals								
CHILD:								
1–2 years	$ 15.70	$ 19.20	$ 22.60	$ 27.40	$ 68.00	$ 83.20	$ 97.90	$118.70
3–5 years	17.00	21.10	26.10	31.30	73.70	91.40	113.10	135.60
6–8 years	21.00	28.10	35.00	40.70	91.00	121.80	151.70	176.40
9–11 years	25.00	31.80	40.80	47.20	108.30	137.80	176.80	204.50
MALE:								
12–14 years	25.80	36.00	44.70	52.60	111.80	156.00	193.70	227.90
15–19 years	26.50	37.20	46.30	53.30	114.80	161.20	200.60	231.80
20–50 years	28.40	36.90	46.10	55.90	123.10	159.90	199.80	242.20
51 years +	25.70	35.20	43.30	52.00	111.40	152.50	187.60	225.30
FEMALE:								
12–19 years	25.90	31.00	37.80	45.60	112.20	134.30	163.80	197.60
20–50 years	25.80	32.30	39.40	50.50	111.80	140.00	170.70	218.80
51 years +	25.30	31.40	39.00	46.60	109.60	136.10	169.00	201.90
Families								
FAMILY OF 2								
20–50 years	59.60	76.10	94.10	117.00	258.40	329.90	407.60	507.10
51 years +	56.10	73.30	90.50	108.50	243.10	317.50	392.30	469.90
FAMILY OF 4:								
Couple, 20–50 years and children—								
1–2 and 3–5	86.90	109.50	134.20	165.10	376.60	474.50	581.50	715.30
6–8 and 9–11	100.20	129.10	161.30	194.30	434.20	559.50	699.00	841.90

Source: USDA. *Family Economics and Nutrition Review*, p 70.

money. If you like to shop "creatively," it may seem rigid and calculating to preplan meals and buy only what is on a shopping list; however, over time, that planning will save you many dollars and help you eat more nutritiously, a huge benefit for giving up a little spontaneity in the store. While you are at it, keep a list going during the week of goods you run out of, writing them down at the time so you won't forget when you get to the market to shop.

Still not convinced that planning is important? Let's see just how easy it is to spend a lot of money on very few groceries. Andrew has his own apartment, attends community college during the day, and works by shelving books at the college library at night. In between classes and work he usually eats fast food although his parents tell him he could save money if he bought groceries. His cupboards are often bare because he doesn't like to shop. Today he has some extra time and decides to "pick up a few things" at the supermarket since it is just across the street from his apartment. Because he gets to the store around noon, he is already hungry, and the smells from the bakery grab his attention. He selects a loaf of sandwich bread for $1.89 and sees fresh-baked cinnamon rolls on special for $4.00 for two rolls. Because they smell so good he gets a package for breakfast. He steps over to the deli and buys a pound of sliced turkey in the deli for $4.99 and picks up a package of sliced Swiss cheese displayed next to the deli case. This imported cheese costs $5.25, double the regular price, but Andrew doesn't notice. Next he grabs two bags of name-brand chips at $3.99 each. He needs laundry detergent and heads for the middle of the store and puts a jug of $4.99 laundry soap in his cart. Since Andrew is on the other side of the store, he selects a meat-lovers frozen pizza for dinner for $6.95. He needs milk and picks up a gallon for $2.89. He sees a carton of orange juice for $3.50 and adds it to his groceries. While waiting in line he is so hungry he spends an extra $2.00 on a candy bar and soda he takes from the drink case in the checkout line. His bill with tax totals about $50, but it doesn't include any fruits or vegetables and only a few foods that will last beyond one day.

UNDERSTANDING LABELS

Are you spending a lot for food but feeling like you get little for your money? Successful grocery shopping doesn't require you to be a mathematician or an accountant. All you need is some knowledge. The food guide pyramid, developed by the USDA, can guide you in choosing a variety of foods to get the nutrients you need and, at the same time, the right amount of calories to maintain a healthy weight. Labels on packaged foods can help you identify good sources of fiber, vitamins, and minerals while helping you balance your intake of fat, saturated fat, cholesterol, and sodium. In fact, the information on food labels is one of the most important sources of data you have about any food item you intend to purchase. It is also one of the most important shopping habits you can develop. Prior to 1994, however, food labels only listed ingredients and lacked any specifics. Serving sizes were any size the manufacturer wanted them to be; there was no uniformity to the information. The government developed those labels in 1990 with the passage of the National Labeling and Education Act (NLEA), which requires that manufacturers of food products put a uniform nutrition fact label on each package (see Chapter 2 for more information on food labels).

Serving size is important because it is the calculation upon which all other numbers on the food label are based. Other food label categories include servings per container, calories, calories from fat, total fat, cholesterol, sodium, total carbohydrate, protein, and other nutrients. Food label information follows a standard format. First is the size of one serving or portion, then the number of portions in the container. After that comes the number of calories per portion and the amount of protein, carbohydrate, and fat, all expressed in grams. Following that basic information, the label gives the product's percentages of the U.S. recommended daily allowance (RDA) of vitamins and minerals (see Chapter 2 for more information on RDAs).

Another direct source of information is the list of ingredients on the label. This list is put in order of the largest ingredient to the smallest. A good example is sugar. If it is the very first ingredient listed on the label, that food contains more sugar than any other ingredient. Clear labeling information helps consumers deal with specific health concerns and conditions. For example, not all additives are safe for everyone. By carefully reading ingredients, someone with asthma could avoid sulfites, which have been known to cause strong reactions in people with asthma. Or someone who is allergic to MSG, nuts, dairy products, eggs, or wheat could avoid those allergens.

Food labels can also help someone who has high blood pressure or hypertension. Because labels list the amount of salt or sodium per serving, anyone trying to control high blood pressure could easily limit their salt intake. Labeling information is especially important to people with diabetes since diet is very important in controlling and treating this condition. Diabetics need to monitor their fat intake as well as sweets and refined starches so they can better evaluate and stabilize their blood sugar (see Chapter 11 for more information on Diabetes).

Since the enactment of the NLEA, the Food and Drug Administration (FDA) has strictly enforced the NLEA's provisions concerning health claims in food labels. Health claims are another aspect of food labeling used to show a relationship between a nutrient or substance in a food and a disease or health-related condition. An example of a health claim would be the statement found on some sugarless candy and gum: "Does not promote tooth decay." The FDA has approved 10 health claims that link the following foods and diseases: calcium-rich foods and reduced risk of osteoporosis; low-sodium foods and reduced risk of high blood pressure; a low-fat diet and reduced risk of cancer; a diet low in saturated fat and cholesterol and reduced risk of heart disease; high-fiber foods and reduced risk of cancer; soluble fiber in fruits, vegetables, and grains and reduced risk of heart disease; soluble fiber in oats and psyllium seed husk and reduced risk of heart disease; a fruit-and-vegetable-rich diet and reduced risk of cancer; folate-rich foods and reduced risk of neural tube defects; less sugar and reduced risk of dental cavities. It's also the job of the FDA to test new food additives. In 1958 Congress approved the FDA's Generally Recognized as Safe, or GRAS, list when it enacted the Delaney Clause. The Delaney Clause prohibits the human use of chemicals shown by research to cause cancer in animals. After the law was passed, scientists reviewed several thousand additives already in use and those considered safe made it onto the GRAS list. The list was reviewed again in 1977.

COMPARING PRICES

Another important tool for shoppers who want to compare the jumble of odd package sizes, weights, and prices is the establishment of unit pricing or per-unit cost. To understand unit pricing, look at any item on the grocery shelf. Paper towels are a good example. Years ago one brand might cost 38 cents and contain 165 square feet. A different brand might cost 45 cents but contains 180 square feet. The problem would be repeated over and over again, aisle after aisle, as you looked at packages and tried to determine what you were getting and how to compare different sizes and costs. On the shelf underneath the products shoppers can now find the unit-price label. It states the price for each item per a standard quantity. All paper towel brands are priced per the same 100 square feet. Comparing is easy when you can see one brand costs 50 cents per 100 square feet and another brand costs 55 cents per 100 square feet. This same technique applies to products from mouthwash to meat. The unit pricing makes comparison shopping simple and practical because the information is right in front of you on the product label or shelf label.

MONEY-SAVING TIPS

Now that you know where to find helpful information, with a few more shopping strategies you can save money and think of your grocery shopping as an exercise rather than an ordeal. Your first stop inside the store should be the produce department since fruits and vegetables make great meals or snacks and are rich sources of vitamins, minerals, and fiber. With all the varieties available it is easy to choose lots of colors as well as a mix of leaves, stems, fruits, and roots. Based on data released in a March 3, 1999 report by the Produce for Better Health Foundation, 90% of Americans snack an average of twice a day, but fruits and vegetables are their snack choice only 10% of the time. The report, "Health Officials Urge Dietary Change for Year 2000 Guidelines," can be found on the Foundation's web site, www.5aday.com. Grocery stores know that soda, chips, and crackers are irresistible snack choices, as well as impulse purchases, and they position them throughout the store to tempt you repeatedly. Try to avoid those items and choose fruit juices for beverages and fruits and vegetables for snacks. Also keep in mind that you will probably pay more for snack items the closer you get to the checkout station. For example, a 20-ounce bottle of Coca-Cola from a small refrigerator case at the checkout stand may sell for 75 cents; two aisles away, a large, warm, two-liter bottle of Coke may cost only 99 cents.

Another important rule of smarter shopping is to not shop when hungry. Supermarkets are devoting more and more space to deli and bakery items hoping to catch a hungry shopper with delicious fresh baked breads and appealing cases of entrées. For every fat-laden cake or doughnut, for every oil-drenched salad, there are better choices. The in-store bakery and deli are actually double trouble for shoppers because many of their items have no nutrition labeling. Don't worry, even without labels the ingredient listing can provide useful information. Since the ingredients are listed in order of predominance, you can estimate the basic nutritional merit of something by finding out what it is made of. For example, a glazed doughnut lists sugar, enriched bleached flour, water, partially hydrogenated soybean oil, and high-fructose corn syrup. A cinnamon-raisin bagel lists high-gluten flour, water, raisins, malted barley flour, sugar, salt, and yeast. By finding in what order ingredients are listed, you can determine that the bagel has a much lower sugar content and less oil than the doughnut. On the plus side, the raisins in the bagel provide fiber and iron making it a more nutritious breakfast choice.

The deli section can be equally treacherous because there are no food labels on premade dishes. Start with the salad bar with its fresh seasonal fruit pieces or the greens and fresh vegetables like carrots, beet slices, green peppers, and tomatoes. Stay away from the prepared macaroni, potato, and pasta salads, which are usually high in fat due to their dress-ings. Without being able to see ingredient lists or recipes, you will not know how much fat has been added. It pays to ask store personnel to show you recipes or other ingredient information they may have for their prepared foods. Then at least you can make an educated choice. The store may also stock those same salads in individual take-out containers in the deli case and the containers may have ingredient labels. Whether they do or not, don't be afraid to ask—if more people ask, more healthful options might be made available.

Another interesting move made by consumers has been the switch away from expensive brand name foods to the less costly store brands. Supermarkets are working hard to match the quality of brand-name products and to offer these products priced as much as 30 percent below their national-brand competitors. Store brands are profitable for stores since they do not require huge advertising budgets or costly television advertisements. Surprisingly, name-brand manufacturers often make the same items for the supermarkets; in other words, consumers are buying the same products and paying more for the brand-name recognition. Buying store-brand items is a great way to cut your food bills.

WHAT ABOUT ORGANIC FOOD?

Many people are committed to the idea of purchasing organic pro-duce, and stores are responding by carrying at least a few offerings of organic fruits and vegetables. Unfortunately, you can expect to pay more for them. According to a January 1998 survey made by *Consumer Reports*, organic foods cost 57 percent more on average than conventional foods. Just what does the term organic mean? Organic produce is a fruit or vegetable grown without chemical fertilizers or pesticides on land that has been chemical free for a number of years. Pesticides are poisonous compounds made to kill the insects, weeds, and fungal pests that damage crops. Although organic farms make up less than 2% of U.S. crop acreage, sales are growing. The Produce Marketing Association stated, in an April 19, 1999 release of data in an issue of *Discount Store News*, that sales of organic produce reached $1.33 billion in 1998, a gain of 20 percent over the previous year. With organic food production increasing, the organic-food industry has been pushing for national standards to help consumers understand what the "organic" label signifies. In 1990 the federal government passed a law allowing for a federal organic standard. The act established the National Organic Program and a fifteen-member National Organic Standards Board (NOSB) to advise the USDA in developing regulations to certify organic foods. In December 1997 the USDA issued the first National Organic Program Proposed Rule, and since that time it has taken public comments on the proposed rule. Criticism over the first draft of the rule brought about a second public comment period and a revision of the rule. The NOSB and USDA hope to have a final rule in place in the near future.

Because of the public's growing interest in organic food, farmers market vendors also offer organic produce. In its biannual National Directory of Farmers Markets the USDA counted 1,755 in 1994 and 2,411 in 1996, a 37 percent increase. Farmers markets appeal to people looking for old-fashioned face-to-face shopping as well as to those with an interest in organic food. The markets are good for small farmers, who save dollars normally spent in packaging and labeling and save having to pay middlemen to distribute their products. Another plus for small farmers is that they can sell ripe fruit long considered too fragile to ship. Produce at a farmers market may have been picked the day before or even as late as that morning. Consumers who want organic food often want food that was harvested locally, not three weeks ago and 1,500 miles away.

NEW FOOD FRONTIERS: IRRADIATION AND BIOENGINEERING

At the same time demand for fresh and healthful food is on the rise, consumers have shown increased interest in irradiated foods. Food irradiation, zapping food with gamma rays from radioactive material in the name of food safety, over the years had little consumer support. In a 1988 study of Consumer Attitudes Toward Irradiation, commissioned by the Food Marketing Institute (FMI), the Grocery Manufacturers of

America (GMA), the National Restaurant Association (NRA), and the American Meat Institute (AMI), figures showed 80 percent of consumers say they would be likely to buy food products if they were labeled "irradiated to kill harmful bacteria." With several recent outbreaks of deadly food poisonings in this country, irradiation has received a more positive reception.

How does irradiation work? Food is packed in containers and moved by conveyer belts into a shielded room. There it is passed through a chamber containing rods of radioactive cobalt or cesium. Powerful gamma rays kill most of the bacteria, insects, and molds. The food is left virtually unchanged, but the number of bacteria, parasites, and fungi is reduced or eliminated. Despite its rather limited use, irradiation is more intertwined in food production than most Americans realize. The FDA first approved wheat flour and white potatoes for irradiation in 1960. But it was the U.S. Army that used irradiated foods on a large scale in the 1960s to improve shelf life and prevent microbial and insect contamination in troop rations. Subsequent approvals included dried spices and vegetable seasonings in 1983, pork in 1986, fruits and vegetables in 1986, poultry in 1992, and red meat in 1997. One of the most important uses of food irradiation in the United States is providing astronauts with uncontaminated food. In fact, the largest U.S. food-irradiation facility is located in Florida and counts NASA among its regular customers.

Irradiation has some proven benefits, including retarding spoilage so potatoes won't sprout tubers and lettuce can last weeks when refrigerated. It also kills bacteria and parasites including *Salmonella, Trichinella spiralis*, and *E. coli*, all of which can cause death. Food-irradiation opponents argue that it may produce byproducts that are carcinogenic and it may affect the nutritional content of the foods treated. The Food Safety and Inspection Service of the USDA developed rules outlining the requirements for the manufacture and sale of irradiated products, especially meat. Those rules went into effect in February 2000. The guidelines mandate that packages include a green international radura symbol accompanied by a simple declarative statement, such as "Treated by irradiation." Optional labeling statements about the purposes of irradiation are also allowed. For example, "Treated by irradiation to kill harmful bacteria," or ". . . for your protection."

Opponents worry that setting up irradiators for even a small percentage of the food purchased in this country could be a daunting task. For example, with 13 billion pounds of hamburger eaten each year in the

United States, irradiation would mean producing, transporting, working with, and eventually disposing of a huge amount of radioactive cobalt and cesium rods. Because of these concerns, another type of irradiation called electron-beam irradiation is being considered. This technology is already used to sterilize medical equipment. It works with an electron generator that produces electrons with ionizing energy that kills bacteria. There are no radioactive materials involved, and supporters say it can be used right on the production line like an x-ray machine.

BIOENGINEERED OR GENE-ALTERED FOODS

As biotechnology improves, food producers will continue to use new findings to improve yields and the disease resistance of plants. Proponents say it's an enormous benefit. For example, about half of the American soybean crop planted in 1999 has a gene that makes it resistant to an herbicide used to control weeds, and about a quarter of U.S. corn planted in 1999 has been bioengineered to produce a protein toxic to certain caterpillars to avoid use of conventional pesticides.

However, genetic modifications aren't unanimously applauded. In Europe, manufacturers are finding it a public relations bonus to assure buyers their products are not genetically modified, and there are some indications that the perception of dangers of bioengineering are hitting home. On April 28, 2000, the *Wall Street Journal* reported that McDonald's told its French fry suppliers to stop using genetically modified potatoes, and Frito-Lay asked its farmers not to grow genetically modified potatoes. It had already told its corn growers to stop growing genetically modified crops.

On May 3, 2000, the Food and Drug Administration announced its plans to refine the regulatory approach to these bioengineered or gene-altered foods. "FDA's scientific review continues to show that all bioengineered foods sold here in the United States today are as safe as their non-bioengineered counterparts," stated Jane E. Henney, the commissioner of food and drugs. "We believe our initiatives will provide the public with continued confidence in the safety of these foods." Henney's comments were included in a May 3, 2000 press release titled "FDA to Strengthen Pre-Market Review of Bioengineered Foods."

The proposed rule mandates that developers of bioengineered foods and animal feeds notify the FDA when they intend to market such products, but the rule falls short of requiring that foods be labeled as being bioengineered or requiring mandatory premarket safety testing.

Instead, the FDA will rely on mandatory consultations with producers. Opponents of the plan immediately seized on that point, saying consumers have a right to know whether the foods they buy have been genetically modified or whether the livestock has been fed genetically modified feed.

The independent Center for Food Safety, in its May 3, 2000 press release decrying the policy, quoted Andrew Kimbrell, the group's executive director, as saying, "Under the new FDA policy, tens of millions of American consumers will still be the guinea pigs testing the safety of these foods. Voluntary labeling means consumers won't see any labels out of this, and won't have a right to choose."

However, consumers can expect to see "GE Free" labels to begin appearing on foods. While the FDA created the labeling plan to allow producers of foods to show their products aren't genetically modified, it doesn't require that genetically engineered foods be labeled that way. The Center for Food Safety opposed this as well, saying the labeling policy

reverses the labeling burden from those using GE to those who are not using this technology. Clearly, those who are introducing GE food into the market should be required to label their foods as "genetically engineered." FDA's new voluntary labeling idea will punish those not using the technology by putting the burden on them to certify, test, and label their foods as "GE Free." Many companies will not want to undergo the considerable time, expense, and liability of testing, certifying, and labeling their foods as "GE Free." As a result, consumers will not be informed which foods have been genetically engineered and which have not. The only sure way to ensure consumers' right to know about GE foods is to require labeling of foods which have been genetically engineered.

The group also created a partial list of processed foods that tested positive in September 1999 for genetically engineered ingredients. The list, again from September 1999, included Frito-Lay Fritos Corn Chips, Bravos Tortilla Chips, Kelloggs's Corn Flakes, General Mills Total Corn Flakes Cereal, Post Blueberry Morning Cereal, Heinz 2 Baby Cereal, Enfamil ProSobee Soy Formula, Similac Isomil Soy Formula, Nestle Carnation Alsoy Infant Formula, Quaker Chewy Granola Bars, Nabisco Snackwell's Granola Bars, Ball Park Franks, Duncan Hines Cake Mix, Quick Loaf Bread Mix, Ultra Slim Fast, Quaker Yellow Corn Meal, Light Life Gimme Lean, Aunt Jemima Pancake Mix, Alpo Dry Pet Food,

Gardenburger, Boca Burger Chef Max's Favorite, Morning Star Farms Better'n Burgers, Green Giant Harvest Burgers (now called Morningstar Farms), McDonald's McVeggie Burgers, Ovaltine Malt Powdered Beverage Mix, Betty Crocker Bac-Os Bacon Flavor Bits, Old El Paso Taco Shells, and Jiffy Corn Muffin Mix.

The FDA states that concerns about the safety of bioengineered foods is unwarranted. The January/February 2000 issue of *FDA Consumer* magazine featured a Q&A with FDA Commissioner Henney. One of the questions posed was whether genetically engineered food is safe. She answered,

All of the proteins that have been placed into foods through the tools of biotechnology that are on the market are nontoxic, rapidly digestible, and do not have the characteristics of proteins known to cause allergies.

As for the genes, the chemical that encodes genetic information is called DNA. DNA is present in all foods and its ingestion is not associated with human illness. Some have noted that sticking a new piece of DNA into the plant's chromosome can disrupt the function of other genes, crippling the plant's growth or altering the level of nutrients or toxins. These kinds of effects can happen with any type of plant breeding—traditional or biotech. That's why breeders do extensive field-testing. If the plant looks normal and grows normally, if the food tastes right and has the expected levels of nutrients and toxins, and if the new protein put into food has been shown to be safe, then there are no safety issues.

SHOPPING HISTORY

There is little doubt that supermarkets will continue to invest tremendous thought and energy into new technology as well as tried-and-true marketing strategies: appealing displays, placement of items, and specials to encourage shoppers. In fact, years ago, grocers learned to increase profits by positioning the staples milk, and bread at the back of the store. With this standard store design, shoppers must walk down the aisles or around the perimeter of the store to get to the basics. Everything else is arranged to entice you. The luscious strawberries beckon even though they are imported and expensive. The shortcake is thoughtfully placed near the strawberries so you can put the two together for dessert. Notice the special displays and how attractive they are. Is the item on sale, or is it just on display? According to Vince Staten, in his book *Can You Trust a Tomato in January?*, supermarkets in America owe their design to a 1964 USDA experiment. The study tested 1,300 shoppers by putting them in redesigned markets with staples in the middle aisles and nonperishables, like canned goods, on the perimeter. With a fixed amount of time to shop, the results showed that the average shopper's purchases went down 33 percent with drastically less items from the perimeter and more produce from the middle aisle. The study concluded that the distance a shopper walks, not the time spent shopping, is what determines how much money is spent. Today's stores are clearly designed with staples strategically placed around the store so shoppers spend the maximum time finding what they need.

The modern grocery store actually dates back to the specialty shops of colonial America—shops like the Great American Tea Company. Formed in 1861 in Manhattan, this tea shop later took the name the Great Atlantic & Pacific Tea Company. After several years, owners George Gilman and George Hartford started adding staples to their inventory and the store, nicknamed the A&P began to grow, and eventually it became a major chain grocery store. According to Staten, by 1912, the A&P had over 400 stores and $24 million in sales. Other early supermarkets included the Piggly Wiggly Store in Memphis, Tennessee; Ward's Grocereteria in Ocean Park, California; King Kullen the Price Wrecker in Queens, New York; and Big Bear in Elizabeth, New Jersey.

OTHER PLACES TO SHOP

Supermarkets also face increasing competition from nontraditional retailers, "supercenters," warehouse club operators, convenience stores, and restaurants, all vying to attract customers with take-out options and family-friendly atmospheres. According to the USDA, although supermarkets were the primary source of retail food sales with over 57% of the total dollars spent in 1996, that percentage has been in decline since 1992. It isn't a new idea to combine a grocery store, drugstore, and mass merchandiser under one roof. The only difference in the new supercenters is the tremendous size of these giants. Retailers like Kmart, Wal-Mart, and Meijer offer one-stop shopping, but they do it in buildings that can measure up to 200,000 square feet, twice the size of a regular Wal-Mart and as big as six or seven typical supermarkets put together. Their massive size provides a great price advantage, but it can also mean tiring hours spent shopping. Warehouse or shopper clubs are overgrown stores dating back to the 1970s, but they deal with volume in a slightly different way. Shopping clubs like Sam's Club, Costco Wholesale or the Price Club, and BJs Wholesale Club stock merchandise on huge shelves in large warehouses and offer minimal service all for an annual membership fee. They combine groceries with a host of other products and use aggressive pricing on the food to draw shoppers in to the store where they can sell more profitable soft goods. Unlike supercenters, the variety of grocery products is small, just a few brands and sizes for each product. For those who need a 100-ounce jar of peanut butter, the warehouse is a great option, but for one person living alone, the volume and lack of choice are significant problems.

Convenience stores are also in strong competition for grocery dollars. Not only can you purchase gasoline, a big drink, and a hot dog, but today's convenience stores offer fresh foods, cappuccinos, smoothies, and a host of nonfood products. The *National Petroleum News* recorded $164 billion in motor fuel and in-store merchandise sales in 1998. In the October 1999 issue, in an article titled "Steady Growth in a Changing Retail Landscape," they report the total number of convenience stores has grown almost 3 percent since 1996, registering some 96,700 stores across the United States (p. 24). Convenience stores have continued to update by allying with fast-food chains. Companies from Subway, to Taco Bell, Burger King, McDonald's, and Baskin Robbins are combining with over 12 percent of the convenience-store owners according to the NPN 1998 report.

VIRTUAL SHOPPING

Some entrepreneurs now offer at-home convenience for grocery shopping through online businesses by way of virtual carts instead of physical carts. While some online grocery services work in partnership with supermarket chains by offering their complete assortment, others use resource centers to process online orders. Some online grocery companies work from a central warehouse but offer only nonperishable items and ship nationally. Other variations include providers where customers place orders in the morning and go to a drive-through center to pick up their food later that same day. In the next decade, these businesses may become formidable alternatives to or partners with conventional supermarkets and grocery stores. These and other major changes in technology could revolutionize the way people grocery shop. It's not science fiction that someday you may be able to scan the bar code on an empty item at home, thereby putting it on a computer list. When the list is finished, the order will be sent over the Internet to the grocery store for later delivery. Or consider prototype refrigerators by Frigidaire, Microsoft, and ICL built with a touch-screen, PC monitor attached to allow users to check e-mail, bank online, pay bills, or place a grocery order. No matter whether you order your groceries from home or select them in the store, it still pays to be a smart shopper.

ADDITIONAL READING

Barfield, Rhonda. *Eat Healthy for $50 a Week: Feed Your Family Nutritious, Delicious Meals for Less.* New York: Kensington Publishing, 1996.

Bingham, Joan, and Dolores Riccio. *The Smart Shopper's Guide to Food Buying and Preparation.* New York: Simon & Schuster, 1982.

Cony, Sue. *At the Market.* New York: Viking Penguin, 1998.

Ebenkamp, Becky. "Tipping the Balance." *Brandweek*, May 10, 1999, vol. 40, no. 19: 4–5.

Farrington, Jan. "Are Ads Making You Sick?" *Current Health 2*, April 1999, vol. 25, no. 8: 6–7.

Haas, Elson M. *The Staying Healthy Shopper's Guide.* Berkeley, Calif.: Celestial Arts, 1999.

Havala, Suzanne. *Shopping for Health.* New York: HarperCollins, 1996.

Henkel, John. "Irradiation: A Safe Measure for Safer Food." *FDA Consumer*, May-June 1998, vol. 32, no. 3: 12–18.

Hunter, Beatrice Trum. "More Precise RDAs?" *Consumer Research Magazine*, May 1998, vol. 81, no. 5: 8–10.

Jacobson, George T. *50 Secrets Your Grocer Doesn't Want You to Know: An Insider's Guide to Stretching Your Grocery Shopping Dollars.* Redmond, Wash.: Andante Publishing, 1995.

Jacobson, Michael F., Lisa Lefferts, and Anne Witte Garland. *Safe Food: Eating Wisely in a Risky World.* Los Angeles: Living Planet Press, 1991.

Janoff, Barry. "Foods for Thought." *Progressive Grocer*, January 2000, vol. 79, no. 1: 59–62.

Klein, Jennifer. "Debate Continues over Federal Standard for Organic Produce." *Knight-Ridder/Tribune Business News*, August 6, 1999.

Maradino, Cristin. "Is Zapping Food the Answer?" *Vegetarian Times*, December 1997, no. 244: 12–14.

Marietta, Anne B., Kathleen J. Welshimer, and Sara Long Anderson. "Knowledge, Attitudes and Behaviors of College Students Regarding the 1990 Nutrition Labeling Education Act Food Labels." *Journal of the American Dietetic Association* 99, no. 4 (April 1999): 445.

Mogelonsky, Marcia. *Everybody Eats: Supermarket Consumers in the 1990s.* Ithaca, N.Y.: American Demographics, 1995.

"Organic Food: Green Greens?" *Consumer Reports*, January 1998, vol. 63, no. 1: 12–17.

Renders, Eileen. *Food Additives, Nutrients & Supplements, A to Z: A Shopper's Guide*. Santa Fe, N.M.: Clear Light Publishers, 1999.

Stanton, John L. "The Teen Scene: Why Teens Can Be a Great Market for Food Products." *Food Processing*, April 1999, vol. 60, no. 4: 32–34.

Staten, Vince. *Can You Trust a Tomato in January?* New York: Simon and Schuster, 1993.

Surowiecki, James. "The New Teen Spirit." *Rolling Stone*, May 27, 1999, no. 813: 49–52.

Tanner, Lisa. "7-Eleven Hoping to Bring More In." *Denver Business Journal*, November 26, 1999, vol. 51, no. 14: 60A.

Vosburg, Robert. "Final Irradiation Rules for Meat Are Published." *Supermarket News*, January 24, 2000: 62.

Yu, Winifred. "Blue-Chip Foods: A Baker's Dozen of Healthful Picks from the Supermarket." *Vegetarian Times*, June 1996, no. 226: 76–79.

9

SETTING UP
YOUR FIRST KITCHEN

More than any other room in your home or apartment, the kitchen is the energy center of your living space. Cooking and eating are at the heart of all the activity and yet so much more happens there: homework gets done, bills get paid, schedules are arranged, important conversations happen, or a romantic candlelight dinner takes place. How can you create a kitchen that meets all your cooking needs but also provides for the pleasure of eating with your family and friends?

For "unseasoned" beginners, a well-tooled kitchen can ease the transition from "take-out" king or queen to good cook, and your kitchen equipment doesn't have to include the latest gadgets. Start with the most essential tools and build a collection based on your personal preferences and cooking expertise. Many chefs and cooking enthusiasts agree the most essential kitchen tool is a decent knife. Prices for good to excellent knives go from a low of $25 to $80, and sets can cost from $60 to over $140. Knives come with different types of blades, from fine edged types that require sharpening, to no-maintenance and serrated types. The most expensive knives are forged from stain- and rust-resistant high-carbon steel. Carbon steel is softer than stainless steel, making it easier to keep the knives sharpened. Sharp knives are better and safer than dull ones because a dull knife forces you to push harder, which means more opportunities to cut yourself. A sharp knife allows you to cut easily and smoothly and reduces the risk of injury.

The two most important knives for a well-equipped kitchen are the paring knife, great for peeling and making finer cuts, and an 8-inch blade known as the chef's knife for all other cutting. A chef's knife's primary purpose is chopping, but its heavy weight helps it cut easily through meats and tough vegetables, and the curved blade makes it easy to handle for light chopping and mincing. Beyond those two essential knives, other knives in a set might include the serrated or bread knife, a knife for carving and one for boning, a cake knife, and a cheese knife. The serrated knife is best for foods whose inside is softer than the outside like bread, tomatoes, or citrus. If you make an investment in good knives, a sharpening steel is worth the dollars spent. By keeping your own knives sharpened you save the cost of repeated professional sharpening.

Of course a knife is only as good as the cutting board underneath it. The two basic choices are synthetic boards and wooden boards. Many people prefer synthetics like polyethylene and polypropylene because they are soft and forgiving to the blade and are easy to clean and sanitize. Wooden boards are less wearing than countertop surfaces like marble, granite, and porcelain, which will quickly dull a knife. However, any and all cutting boards should be sanitized after they are used, either by running them through the dishwasher or, in the case of wood, cleaning them with the USDA-suggested sanitizing solution: 1 teaspoon of household bleach mixed with 1 quart of water. Sanitizing a cutting board prevents cross contamination when boards and knives used to prepare raw meat, poultry, and fish come into contact with vegetables or other ready-to-eat foods. Always sanitize a cutting board after cutting meat; better still, keep two boards, one for meats and one for fruits, vegetables, and other foods that need no cooking.

RIGHT TOOLS FOR THE RIGHT JOB

In terms of electric equipment, basic necessities for a new kitchen include a toaster, a can opener, a blender, and a mixer either handheld or standing. A coffeemaker, a pasta machine, a coffee grinder, a food processor, and a juicer are also great tools for a new cook. Don't forget these essential handheld tools: a vegetable peeler, a vegetable brush, a corkscrew, a meat thermometer, a colander, and a cheese grater. Reduce preparation time by using an electric rice cooker, a steamer basket and wok, a pressure cooker, and a teakettle. Finally, every kitchen needs utensils like a ladle, cook's fork, measuring spoons and cups, and cooking spoons.

Spoons, spatulas, and tongs extend the reach of any cook. The most basic spoons are solid and are designed for mixing; perforated or slotted spoons are used to lift and drain foods from broth. Tongs, usually made of stainless steel, can pick up foods on the grill or stovetop; wooden tongs are helpful for pulling pieces of toast from the toaster. Tongs come in a number of sizes from the very long barbecue tongs to tiny serving tongs. Whisks, available in a variety of sizes and materials, are used to whip anything from potatoes to egg whites and custards. The balloon whisks have a round shape that helps aerate foods such as egg whites; sauce whisks are more pear-shaped and are designed to emulsify sauces; and flat whisks are curved out on the bottom for scraping along the pan bottom when making sauces or custards. Spatulas also come in a variety of lengths and sizes with long handles and flat rubber ends. They are essential for scraping out pans and bowls and should be replaced when the rubber end becomes cracked or badly scored.

A set of 2 or 3 mixing bowls is as necessary as a basic set of pots and pans. Glass bowls work well because glass holds hot or cold and does not react like aluminum does with acidic ingredients. Glass bowls are better than stainless steel if you plan to put them in the microwave and will last longer than plastic ones. For baking you'll need a bread pan, two layer-cake pans, and a cookie sheet. New cooks will also want to invest in an oven-proof casserole dish, two different sized sauce pans with lids, and a stock pot or pasta pot that holds up to 8 quarts. A roasting pan and rack, an 8-inch skillet, and a 12-inch sauté pan are also very useful. A sauté pan is a straight-sided heavy-bottomed pan about 3 inches deep.

With cookware manufacturers constantly making improvements in nonstick technology, many types or brands of frying pans, also known as skillets and sauté pans are available, and these offer a great way to cut down on added fat when cooking or frying. Avoid pans with a light or flimsy nonstick coating that may chip or peel. Although nonstick is great for skillets, it is not necessary to buy saucepans or pots to match. In fact, pots and pans with heavy bottoms and tight-fitting lids are a better choice because they distribute heat more evenly than their thinner nonstick counterparts. Heaviest of all, of course, are the cast-iron pans, but if you invest in cast-iron cookware be aware that it takes more care and upkeep. Cast-iron ware must be seasoned and cleaned carefully to prevent rust. Stainless steel pans with copper bottoms also evenly conduct heat while cooking, making them another fine choice.

BASIC EQUIPMENT

Having the right kitchen equipment means producing the best results from a recipe. Start with the basics, then add equipment as your experience, style, and taste develop. This list includes the bare essentials for setting up your first kitchen.

Knives

Boning knife

Carving or slicing knife—10-inch blade

Chef's knife—8- or 10-inch blade

Cleaver

Paring knife—3- or 4-inch blade

Serrated or bread knife—8-inch blade

Sharpening steel

Pots and pans

Pots and pans are not the same thing. A pot has two small side handles, and a pan has one long handle.

1-quart covered saucepan

2- or 2 ½-quart covered saucepan

4- or 6-quart casserole dish

5- or 6-quart Dutch oven or heavy kettle

8- or 9-inch covered skillet or frying pan

8-quart soup/pasta pot

10- or 12-inch covered skillet

14- by 11-inch roasting pan

Double boiler, a two-pot set used for melting chocolate or cooking delicate foods.

Tools

2-tined fork

Can opener

Cheese grater

Colander

Corkscrew

Cutting boards, synthetic or wood

Ladle

Measuring spoons

Measuring cups, liquid and dry

Meat thermometer

Spatulas

Tongs, metal or wood

Vegetable peeler

Vegetable brush

Whisk

Wooden spoons

Basic appliances

Blender

Can opener, electric

Coffeemaker

Crock-Pot or slow cooker

Food processor

Mixer, handheld or stand

Toaster or toaster oven

Baking equipment

Bread pan

Cake pans—8- or 9-inch, round or rectangular

Cookie sheets

Cooling wire rack

Rolling pin

Flour sifter

Mixing bowls

Muffin pan

Pie pans—8- or 9-inch, glass or aluminum

Springform pan

Other kitchen essentials

Ceramic dinnerware—porcelain, stoneware, bone china, or earthenware

Flatware—sterling, silver plate, or
stainless-steel

Glassware—short or tall tumblers,
wineglasses, tall fluted glasses

Pot holders and oven mitt

Tablecloths and napkins

Trivets or small pads to protect the table
from a hot platter or dish

STOCKING THE LARDER

Experienced cooks know that using good-quality ingredients is as important to the final product as having well-made equipment. Call it a pantry, cupboard, or larder—any name will do—but keep your pantry stocked with staples that will give you the makings for healthy meals. Pantry essentials:

canned tomatoes, sauce and paste

herbs

spices

mustard

ketchup

mayonnaise

olive oil

Balsamic vinegar

white vinegar

oatmeal

rice

barley

bulger

dried pasta

bullion or powdered broth

canned beans

dried beans and lentils

canned fruit

vegetable cooking spray

flour

baking soda

baking powder

brown and white sugar

cornstarch

honey

eggs or pasteurized egg products

dairy or soy milk

cheese

lemon juice

butter or margarine

frozen vegetables

Some versatile items that store well include prepared pasta sauces, tuna fish, fresh salsa, bottled minced garlic, pickled vegetables, canned and dried fruits; instant coffee and corn or flour tortillas. (See Appendix E for a list of staples.)

SETTING UP A SAFE KITCHEN

No matter how up to the minute your kitchen technology and equipment are, the safety of the foods you cook still depends on old-fashioned rules of cleanliness. The kitchen has often been called the most germ-infested spot in the house, but if you follow these commonsense rules you can prevent the spread of disease or food-borne illness. Let's start with the basics everyone should know. Wash your hands always, but especially before preparing or eating a meal; after using the bathroom; and after handling raw meat, poultry, fish, or produce. Special antimicrobial soaps are nice but regular soap and water will do. When washing rub your hands together vigorously for a minimum of 20 seconds, and dry your hands with a paper towel rather than a reused cloth towel which can harbor germs.

Wash everything. Even prewashed produce should be washed before it is eaten according to experts who point to recent outbreaks of illness linked to lettuce, raspberries, and other plant foods. After produce is washed don't store it in the same package it came home in. While washing, remember regularly to sanitize all kitchen surfaces, including cutting boards, countertops, and other high-traffic surfaces like the refrigerator door or faucet handles. Throw sponges into the dishwasher once a day, boil them on the stovetop or microwave them for two minutes on high while moist, or soak them in a diluted bleach solution of 1 teaspoon bleach in one quart of water. Sponges soaked in bleach should be allowed to air dry. Better yet, food safety experts suggest using paper towel for cleanups, especially juices from raw meat. Sponges and dishtowels will harbor the bacteria from the juice; a paper towel can and should be thrown away immediately. Before you think there is too much to remember, it all boils down to three simple rules.

HOT, COLD, AND CLEAN: THE THREE RULES OF FOOD SAFETY

Americans are lucky. We have one of the safest food supplies in the world. Even so, it is not 100% free of bacteria, and food can be contaminated with viruses that cause illness. Sue Snider, extension specialist at the University of Delaware, says that three simple rules go a long way to making sure that the food you are eating is safe: keep hot foods hot, keep cold foods cold, and keep foods clean. "They sound like three very easy things to do but people unknowingly violate these three principles all the time."

Keep hot foods hot. Foods that are served hot should not be allowed to sit out at room temperature for long—certainly no longer than two hours. "Anytime you've got food at room temperature, there's the potential that bacteria will be growing. It's important to keep foods out of the danger zone—from 40 to 140 degrees Fahrenheit." In her conversations with young people, Snider often finds there's a mistaken belief that if the food doesn't contain meat, it's safe to leave it out. She cringes when she hears students say they keep their cheese pizza in an unheated oven overnight and eat it the next day. Any food—not just meat products—are susceptible to bacteria.

There's a lower likelihood with certain foods that bacteria will grow, but bacteria are capable of growing on most every food. There have even been outbreaks on acidy foods, such as tomatoes, orange juice, and apple juice, which were thought to be safe. "Now I even caution people that they need to think about keeping those products in the refrigerator." The temperature danger zone, in which bacteria will grow, also applies to cold foods. That's why frozen food shouldn't be thawed on the counter at room temperature. They should either be thawed slowly in a refrigerator, placed in a waterproof container and surrounded by cold water, or thawed in a microwave. Then it should either be prepared immediately or put back in the refrigerator.

The final rule is to keep foods and food-preparation areas clean. Some of the concern is for cross contamination. Using a cutting board as a surface to mix meatloaf, wiping it off with a paper towel, and then chopping vegetables for a salad on it is a recipe for cross contamination. One option is to have two cutting boards—one for meats and the other for vegetables and fruit. Even so, all cutting boards should be washed thoroughly with hot soapy water or run through the dishwasher. Replace cutting boards when the surface has lots of cuts in it because they're harder to clean. That cleaning should be sufficient for most people; however, if there's someone in the household with an immune-compromised condition, the cutting board should be cleaned with a chlorine solution (1 teaspoon bleach in 1 quart of cold water) and left to air dry. Bacteria aren't the only food safety concern. "Viruses don't multiply like bacteria. They are transferred and food-borne viruses are transferred primarily because of human fecal contamination." In other words, the person preparing the food didn't wash his or her hands well. What's most frightening is that some viruses, such as hepatitis, can be spread even though the person passing it along is completely free of symptoms. "It doesn't take many viral particles to cause people to get sick," Snider said. There have been examples of viral contamination in foods ranging from cake frosting to salad. In Delaware, there was a hepatitis outbreak when a pizza server, who didn't know she was sick, was transferring the virus to customers.

Tracking down the cause of food-borne illnesses can be quite a challenge, according to Snider. Many times, the flu-like symptoms of a food-borne illness are simply not recognized for what they are. Even when people suspect it's food-related, they tend to think back only to the meals they had the day before. "Very few of the organisms you're looking at have that short of an incubation period. Two to five days is more typical, and with Hepatitis A, the incubation period is up to 30 days. So it becomes complicated to figure out what the culprit is." You can't tell by looking at it. Since you can't see bacteria growing on food, it's even more important to stick to the three rules. People generally throw away food that has spoiled—when it looks old and slimy or doesn't smell good. "That's spoilage and it is not necessarily going to make you sick. But with food-borne organisms and viruses, it may look great and taste delicious. That's the reason handling it appropriately becomes so critical." You may not want to throw away the big pan of chili you left out for three hours during a dinner party, but the risk of eating food that potentially harbors bacteria that can make you very ill simply isn't a good one. If you didn't follow the three rules of keeping it hot, keeping it cold, and keeping it clean, don't take the chance.

Think you know everything there is to know to have a safe and sanitary kitchen? Try this food quiz from the FDA and test your knowledge.

CAN YOUR KITCHEN PASS THE FOOD SAFETY TEST?

A clean kitchen is more than shiny floors and neat, clutter-free countertops. More than how it looks, a "clean" kitchen is a safe kitchen, and safety is measured in three main areas: proper food handling, cooking, and storage. To see how well you're doing in each, take this quiz, and then read on to learn how you can make the meals and snacks from your kitchen the safest possible.

QUIZ

Choose the answer that best describes the practice in your household, whether or not you are the primary food handler.

1. The temperature of the refrigerator in my home is:

a. 50 degrees Fahrenheit (10 degrees Celsius)

b. 41° F (5° C)

c. I don't know; I've never measured it.

2. The last time we had leftover cooked stew or other food with meat, chicken, or fish, the food was:

a. cooled to room temperature, then put in the refrigerator

b. put in the refrigerator immediately after the food was served

c. left at room temperature overnight or longer

3. The last time the kitchen sink drain, disposal, and connecting pipe in my home were sanitized was:

a. last night

b. several weeks ago

c. can't remember

4. If a cutting board is used in my home to cut raw meat, poultry, or fish and it is going to be used to chop another food, the board is:

a. reused as is

b. wiped with a damp cloth

c. washed with soap and hot water

d. washed with soap and hot water and then sanitized

5. The last time we had hamburgers in my home, I ate mine:

a. rare

b. medium

c. well done

6. The last time there was cookie dough in my home, the dough was:

a. made with raw eggs, and I sampled some of it

b. store-bought, and I sampled some of it

c. not sampled until baked

7. I clean my kitchen counters and other surfaces that come in con-tact with food with:

a. water

b. hot water and soap

c. hot water and soap, then bleach solution

d. hot water and soap, then commercial sanitizing agent

8. When dishes are washed in my home, they are:

a. cleaned by an automatic dishwasher and then air-dried

b. left to soak in the sink for several hours and then washed with soap in the same water

c. washed right away with hot water and soap in the sink and then air-dried

d. washed right away with hot water and soap in the sink and immediately towel-dried

9. The last time I handled raw meat, poultry, or fish, I cleaned my hands afterwards by:

a. wiping them on a towel

b. rinsing them under hot, cold, or warm tap water

c. washing with soap and warm water

10. Meat, poultry, and fish products are defrosted in my home by:

a. setting them on the counter

b. placing them in the refrigerator

c. microwaving

11. When I buy fresh seafood, I:

a. buy only fish that's refrigerated or well iced

b. take it home immediately and put it in the refrigerator

c. sometimes buy it straight out of a local fisher's creel

12. I realize people, including myself, should be especially careful about not eating raw seafood, if they have:

a. diabetes

b. HIV infection

c. cancer

d. liver disease

Answers

1. Refrigerators should stay at 41° F (5° C) or less, so if you chose answer B, give yourself two points. If you didn't, you're not alone. According to Robert Buchanan, Ph.D., food safety initiative lead scientist in the Food and Drug Administration's Center for Food Safety and Applied Nutrition, many people overlook the importance of maintaining an appropriate refrigerator temperature.

"According to surveys, in many households, the refrigerator temperature is above 50 degrees (10° C)," he said. His advice: Measure the temperature with a thermometer and, if needed, adjust the refrigerator's temperature control dial. A temperature of 41° F (5° C) or less is important because it slows the growth of most bacteria. The temperature won't kill the bacteria, but it will keep them from multiplying, and the fewer there are, the less likely you are to get sick from them. Freezing at zero F (minus 18° C) or less stops bacterial growth (although it won't kill all bacteria already present).

2. Answer B is the best practice; give yourself two points if you picked it.

Hot foods should be refrigerated as soon as possible within two hours after cooking. But don't keep the food if it's been standing out for more than two hours. Don't taste test it, either. Even a small amount of contaminated food can cause illness.

Date leftovers so they can be used within a safe time. Generally, they remain safe when refrigerated for three to five days. If in doubt, throw it out, said FDA microbiologist Kelly Bunning, Ph.D., also with FDA's food safety initiative. "It's not worth a food-borne illness for the small amount of food usually involved."

3. If answer A best describes your household's practice, give yourself two points. Give yourself one point if you chose B.

According to FDA's John Guzewich, epidemiologist on FDA's food safety initiative team, the kitchen sink drain, disposal and connecting pipe are often overlooked, but they should be sanitized periodically by pouring down the sink a solution of 1 teaspoon (5 milliliters) of chlorine bleach in 1 quart (about 1 liter) of water or a solution of commercial kitchen cleaning agent made according to product directions. Food particles get trapped in the drain and disposal and, along with the moistness, create an ideal environment for bacterial growth.

4. If answer D best describes your household's practice, give yourself two points.

If you picked A, you're violating an important food safety rule: Never allow raw meat, poultry and fish to come in contact with other foods. Answer B isn't good, either. Improper washing, such as with a damp cloth, will not remove bacteria. And washing only with soap and water may not do the job, either.

5. Give yourself two points if you picked answer C.

If you don't have a meat thermometer, there are other ways to determine whether seafood is done:

- For fish, slip the point of a sharp knife into the flesh and pull aside. The edges should be opaque and the center slightly translucent with flakes beginning to separate. Let the fish stand three to four minutes to finish cooking.
- For shrimp, lobster and scallops, check color. Shrimp and lobster and scallops, red and the flesh becomes pearly opaque. Scallops turn milky white or opaque and firm.
- For clams, mussels and oysters, watch for the point at which their shells open. Boil three to five minutes longer. Throw out those that stay closed.

When using the microwave, rotate the dish several times to ensure even cooking. Follow recommended standing times. After the standing time is completed, check the seafood in several spots with a meat thermometer to be sure the product has reached the proper temperature.

6. If you answered A, you may be putting yourself at risk for infection with *Salmonella enteritidis*, a bacterium that can be in shell eggs. Cooking the egg or egg-containing food product to an internal temperature of at least 145° F (63° C) kills the bacteria. So answer C—eating the baked product—will earn you two points.

You'll get two points for answer B, also. Foods containing raw eggs, such as homemade ice cream, cake batter, mayonnaise, and eggnog, carry a *Salmonella* risk, but their commercial counterparts don't. Commercial products are made with pasteurized eggs; that is, eggs that have been heated sufficiently to kill bacteria, and also may contain an acidifying agent that kills the bacteria. Commercial preparations of cookie dough are not a food hazard.

If you want to sample homemade dough or batter or eat other foods with raw-egg-containing products, consider substituting pasteurized eggs for raw eggs. Pasteurized eggs are usually sold in the grocer's refrigerated dairy case.

Some other tips to ensure egg safety:

• Buy only refrigerated eggs, and keep them refrigerated until you are ready to cook and serve them.
• Cook eggs thoroughly until both the yolk and white are firm, not runny, and scramble until there is no visible liquid egg.
• Cook pasta dishes and stuffings that contain eggs thoroughly.

7. Answers C or D will earn you two points each; answer B, one point. According to FDA's Guzewich, bleach and commercial kitchen cleaning agents are the best sanitizers—provided they're diluted according to product directions. They're the most effective at getting rid of bacteria. Hot water and soap does a good job, too, but may not kill all strains of bacteria. Water may get rid of visible dirt, but not bacteria.

Also, be sure to keep dishcloths and sponges clean because, when wet, these materials harbor bacteria and may promote their growth.

8. Answers A and C are worth two points each. There are potential problems with B and D. When you let dishes sit in water for a long time, it "creates a soup," FDA's Buchanan said. "The food left on the dish contributes nutrients for bacteria, so the bacteria will multiply." When washing dishes by hand, he said, it's best to wash them all within two hours. Also, it's best to air-dry them so you don't handle them while they're wet.

9. The only correct practice is answer C. Give yourself two points if you picked it.

Wash hands with warm water and soap for at least 20 seconds before and after handling food, especially raw meat, poultry and fish. If you have an infection or cut on your hands, wear rubber or plastic gloves. Wash gloved hands just as often as bare hands because the gloves can pick up bacteria. (However, when washing gloved hands, you don't need to take off your gloves and wash your bare hands, too.)

10. Give yourself two points if you picked B or C. Food safety experts recommend thawing foods in the refrigerator or the microwave oven or putting the package in a watertight plastic bag submerged in cold water and changing the water every 30 minutes. Gradual defrosting overnight is best because it helps maintain quality.

When microwaving, follow package directions. Leave about 2 inches (about 5 centimeters) between the food and the inside surface of the microwave to allow heat to circulate. Smaller items will defrost more evenly than larger pieces of food. Foods defrosted in the microwave oven should be cooked immediately after thawing.

Do not thaw meat, poultry and fish products on the counter or in the sink without cold water; bacteria can multiply rapidly at room temperature.

Marinate food in the refrigerator, not on the counter. Discard the marinade after use because it contains raw juices, which may harbor bacteria. If you want to use the marinade as a dip or sauce, reserve a portion before adding raw food.

11. A and B are correct. Give yourself two points for either.

When buying fresh seafood, buy only from reputable dealers who keep their products refrigerated or properly iced. Be wary, for example, of vendors selling fish out of their creel (canvas bag) or out of the back of their truck.

Once you buy the seafood, immediately put it on ice, in the refrigerator or in the freezer. Some other tips for choosing safe seafood:

- Don't buy cooked seafood, such as shrimp, crabs or smoked fish, if displayed in the same case as raw fish. Cross-contamination can occur. Or, at least, make sure the raw fish is on a level lower than the cooked fish so that the raw fish juices don't flow onto the cooked items and contaminate them.

- Don't buy frozen seafood if the packages are open, torn or crushed on the edges. Avoid packages that are above the frost line in the store's freezer. If the package cover is transparent, look for signs of frost or ice crystals. This could mean that the fish has either been stored for a long time or thawed and refrozen.

- Recreational fishers who plan to eat their catch should follow state and local government advisories about fishing areas and eating fish from certain areas.

- As with meat and poultry, if seafood will be used within two days after purchase, store it in the coldest part of the refrigerator, usually under the freezer compartment or in a special "meat keeper." Avoid packing it in tightly with other items; allow air to circulate freely around the package. Otherwise, wrap the food tightly in moisture-proof freezer paper or foil to protect it from air leaks and store in the freezer.

- Discard shellfish, such as lobsters, crabs, oysters, clams and mussels, if they die during storage or if their shells crack or break. Live shellfish close up when the shell is tapped.

12. If you are under treatment for any of these diseases, as well as several others, you should avoid raw seafood. Give yourself two points for knowing one or more of the risky conditions. People with certain diseases and conditions need to be especially careful because their diseases or the medicine they take may put them at risk for serious illness or death from contaminated seafood. These conditions include:

- liver disease, either from excessive alcohol use, viral hepatitis, or other causes
- hemochromatosis, an iron disorder
- diabetes
- stomach problems, including previous stomach surgery and low stomach acid (for example, from antacid use)
- cancer
- immune disorders, including HIV infection
- long-term steroid use, as for asthma and arthritis

Older adults also may be at increased risk because they more often have these conditions. People with these diseases or conditions should never eat raw seafood—only seafood that has been thoroughly cooked.

Rating Your Home's Food Practices

24 points: Feel confident about the safety of foods served in your home.

12 to 23 points: Reexamine food safety practices in your home. Some key rules are being violated.

11 points or below: Take steps immediately to correct food handling, storage and cooking techniques used in your home. Current practices are putting you and other members of your household in danger of food-borne illness. (*Written by Paula Kurtzweil, a member of FDA's public affairs staff.*)

ADDITIONAL READING

Ambrose, Jeanne. "Kitchen Cleanup Checklist." *Better Homes & Gardens*, June 1999, vol. 77, no. 6: 132.

Clark, Melissa. "Essential Cookware." *Vegetarian Times*, May 1998, no. 249: 26.

Cunningham, Marion. *Learning to Cook with Marion Cunningham*. New York: Alfred A. Knopf, 1999.

Gallo, Nick. "Are You Safe at the Plate?" *Better Homes & Gardens*, January 1998, vol. 76, no. 1: 66.

Gerber, Suzanne. "Soulful Kitchens." *Vegetarian Times*, May 1998, no. 249: 74.

Johnson, Sharlene K. "Danger in the Kitchen." *Ladies Home Journal*, November 1997, vol. 114, no. 11: 282.

Morganthau, Tom. "E. coli Alert." *Newsweek*, September 1, 1997, vol. 130, no. 9: 26.

Sass, Lorna J. *Recipes from an Ecological Kitchen.* New York: William Morrow, 1992.

Schindler, Martha. "How Safe Is Your Kitchen?" *Prevention,* May 1999, vol. 51, no. 5: 126.

Schofield, Deniece. *Kitchen Organization Tips and Secrets.* Cincinnati, Ohio: Betterway Books, 1996.

Schrambling, Regina. "New World Order." *House Beautiful,* April 1999, vol. 141, no. 4: 66.

Taft, Mimi Shanley. "Last-Minute Meals." *Working Mother,* April 1999, 77.

Zweigenthal, Gail. "Tools of the Trade." *Gourmet,* June 1993, vol. 53, no. 6: 20.

10

EATING DISORDERS

There are healthy ways to lose weight, and there are ways that are dangerous. Eating disorders, such as anorexia and bulimia, fall into the second category. The vast majority of people affected by these eating disorders are adolescent and young adult women. Males and older women can also develop eating disorders, but young women are often the most influenced by idealistic—and generally unachievable—standards of beauty. In a survey conducted by the Centers for Disease Control and Prevention, more than one-third of the high school girls surveyed thought they were overweight. That compares to 15% of the boys who answered the same way.

According to the National Institutes of Health, approximately 1% of adolescent girls develop anorexia nervosa, and another 2% to 3% develop bulimia nervosa. As girls approach adulthood, the numbers increase. Studies indicate that by the time they reach college, somewhere between 4.5 to 18 percent of women have a history of bulimia. The National Center for Health Statistics estimates that about 9,000 people admitted to hospitals were diagnosed with bulimia in 1994 and about 8,000 were diagnosed with anorexia. Males account for from 5% to 10% of bulimia and anorexia cases. While people of all races develop the disorders, the vast majority of those diagnosed are white.

Both eating disorders are destructive conditions and can lead to serious damage, even death. One in ten cases of anorexia nervosa leads to death from starvation, cardiac arrest, other medical complications, or suicide. About 1,000 women die of anorexia each year, according to the American Anorexia/Bulimia Association. The National Center for Health Statistics show that anorexia nervosa was the underlying cause of death noted on 101 death certificates in 1994, and it was mentioned as one of the multiple causes of death on another 2,657 death certificates. In the same year, bulimia was the underlying cause of death on two death certificates and mentioned as one of several causes on 64 others. These statistics were reported in the article, "On the Teen Scene: Eating Disorders Require Medical Attention," by Dixie Farley, printed in FDA Consumer, September 1997.

The two conditions are similar in as much as both reflect a lessening self-esteem, an unrealistic view of body image, and skewed views of food and diet. The paths they take are quite different.

ANOREXIA NERVOSA

Anorexia nervosa is an intentional starving. It often begins around the time of puberty and involves extreme weight loss—defined as at least 15% below one's normal body weight. For regularly menstruating adolescent girls and women, skipping three menstrual cycles (except during pregnancy) is another medical indicator of a serious problem. Even though someone with anorexia may look emaciated, she may still be convinced she's too heavy.

Researchers estimate that half of those with anorexia will develop bulimia.

BULIMIA NERVOSA

Bulimia nervosa is characterized by a binge-and-purge eating pattern. This person will eat large amounts of food and then force herself to vomit, or she will take laxatives, diuretics, or enemas, or she will exercise compulsively to "purge" herself of the food. People with bulimia often maintain their body weight, and if the purging is done in secret, they can keep the condition hidden for quite a while. There is also "non-purging" bulimia, characterized by some other method of keeping the weight off, such as compulsive exercising or fasting.

Binges and purges can range from once or twice a week to several times a day. What is visible to family and friends, however, may only be strident dieting. Symptomatic of the disorder is the excessive amount of food being eaten. Someone with bulimia will eat more food and more frequently than most people. Often, while eating, the person seems to lack control or feels as if he or she can't stop eating. For example, normal food intake for women and teens is between 2,000 and 3,000 calories per day, but bulimic binges often account for more than that in a span of less than two hours. Some people with the disorder have reported consuming up to 20,000 calories in binges lasting up to eight hours.

Rapidly purging food, through abuse of laxatives, enemas, diuretics, or induced vomiting, upsets the body's balance of chemicals, including sodium and potassium. The results are often fatigue, an irregular heartbeat, thinner bones, and seizures. Repeated vomiting can also damage the stomach and esophagus and can erode tooth enamel. It can also result in skin rashes and broken blood vessels in the face.

Bulimia typically begins during adolescence and can continue for years undetected by others. The longer someone waits to seek help with an eating disorder, the more ingrained their eating habits become and the more difficult the recovery will be.

An eating disorder is not just about food. It's about self-esteem, stress, fear of becoming overweight, and a feeling of helplessness. However, food becomes the focus, and the farther the condition progresses, the larger food issues loom. What someone eats—or doesn't eat—becomes a tool of control—self-control or even control over others.

Researchers are not precisely sure what causes eating disorders. They suspect it can be a combination of factors—behavioral, genetic, and biochemical. People who develop anorexia often have some similar characteristics: they are obedient, perfectionists, good students, and often excellent athletes. People who develop bulimia and binge eating often eat large amounts of junk food and then feel guilty about it. They eat to relieve stress, but the subsequent guilt increases stress. And the cycle continues.

Genetics also seems to play a factor. People who develop an eating disorder sometimes find other women in the family have struggled with a similar challenge. One of two studies published in the March 2000 *American Psychiatric Association Journal* concluded that "anorexia nervosa commonly occurred in female relatives of those suffering an eating disorder, but rarely among family members of persons with similar characteristics who have never suffered an eating disorder. Although bulimia nervosa occurred more frequently than anorexia among the relatives of never-ill subjects, it too occurred at a higher rate among families of those with the illnesses." The study seems to indicate a familial predisposition to the disorders.

In another study published that month, titled "Controlled Family Study of Anorexia Nervosa and Bulimia Nervosa: Evidence of Shared Liability and Transmission of Partial Syndromes," researchers studied twins and found that anorexia nervosa was estimated to have an inherited risk factor of 58%. Because the pool of subjects was small, the study did suggest genetic factors play a role in risk for developing anorexia nervosa.

There is also ongoing research into the role played by excessive or lacking brain neurotransmitters and medications that can counteract either condition.

FAMILY GET-TOGETHERS AND EATING DISORDERS

The end-of-the-year holidays present some special challenges to people with eating disorders. In a November 10, 1999, press release titled, "Anorexia Nervosa and Major Depression: Shared Genetic and Environmental Risk Facts," from the Center for Change, Randy K. Hardman, a national expert in the treatment of eating disorders, stated,

In American society, the celebration of Thanksgiving and Christmas center primarily around food and family. It's oversimplifying to say that these are the two things that people with anorexia and bulimia fear most, but for many this is basically a true statement. Food, to them, causes weight gain and with the distorted view that eating disorder sufferers have of their bodies, any weight gain is bad. Holiday activities can amplify these feelings leading to increased social isolation or withdrawal, secrecy and deceit, an escalation of the negative eating disorder behaviors, and an increase in personal feelings of failure, inadequacy and contempt. Those with anorexia respond by starving themselves and bulimics respond with binge eating and purging.

The direct approach offered by friends or family may be more harmful than helpful. According to Hardman, offering advice about eating often "compounds the intense sense of guilt that most young women with eating disorders already feel and can alienate them even further from those who can support them best."

Instead, he suggested speaking openly about the eating disorder and helping plan those activities that might be most supportive. Focus less on food and meal preparation and more on the celebration. Break activities down into smaller family groups. According to Hardman, family members need to understand that eating disorders have less to do with food than they have to do with pain. Eating disorder behavior is one method that anorexics and bulimics use to communicate their intense need for unconditional acceptance and love. "Families should be prepared over the holidays and beyond to provide that kind of acceptance and love," he added.

Although Hardman offered these tips specifically for the holiday seasons, they apply as general guidelines for any get-together with friends or family that has food as a main part of its focus.

Eating disorders cannot always be overcome by supportive hugs from friends and family—although those could always help; counseling can help someone with anorexia or bulimia find different, less destructive, coping mechanisms; and medical intervention is needed if the person with eating disorders has reached dangerously low weights or developed other complications.

FOOD AS AN OBSESSION

Christi R. Carver, a Fredericksburg, Virginia, psychiatric nurse practitioner, says it often begins this way. A young girl is having trouble with self-esteem, or the eating disorder signals an underlying problem— family substance abuse, sexual abuse, or significant problems with her peer group. Even if she is doing well in school or other areas, she may feel she's not doing well enough. She begins to eat less. The result is that she loses weight—and, initially, that seems promising. People notice and comment, and she begins to feel that she's found something she can do really well. So it continues and after a while, what she's eating or not eating becomes an obsession. It pushes other interests out of the way. Family, friends, sports, or hobbies can all fall by the wayside.

Someone with anorexia seems to convince herself that she'll be able to stop losing weight as soon as she loses another 10 pounds, or some other weight-related goal. "But when she achieves that goal, nothing inside her has changed. Losing the weight doesn't make her feel any better emotionally," Carver said.

Most alarming is that someone with anorexia doesn't see herself as thin, even as she becomes dangerously skinny. Nor does she think of other people of a healthy weight as being overweight. Carver is astounded by these rail-thin women who look at her and ask her how she stays thin. "Yet when they look at themselves, they think they are overweight. Their own body image is distorted."

Not only is their view of themselves distorted, their view of the fundamentals of nutrition can be completely out of whack. That's why counseling is often a multipronged effort. Carver, for example, typically refers people with eating conditions to a nutritionist. Most people with eating disorders need to learn or relearn the basics of nutrition. She'll touch on nutritional concepts but likes to leave the instruction to someone else. One reason is that she wants to minimize the amount of time actually spent talking about food.

For most people with eating disorders, food is the primary topic of conversation. Young people living at home may hear little else from their families other than what they've eaten or not eaten. Food truly becomes a form of control for them. That's why Carver wants to spend the time talking about other things, such as what triggers the need to eat compulsively or not to eat.

By searching for the emotional roots of the problem, and by avoiding key triggers—or at least recognizing them—people with eating disorders can begin to recover. For example, Carver often recommends to the mother of an anorexic that she stop making disparaging remarks about her own weight or her daughter's weight. She'll recommend that the person with the eating disorder talk to her friends about how they can help. "She can say, 'Let's stop buying the fashion magazines and comparing ourselves to the models. Let's not talk about food.' Her friends could be extremely helpful if they asked her how she was feeling, and took the time to listen. Or if they did something active together."

Family therapy and group therapy sessions are often part of the recovery process for people with eating conditions. Getting started on the road to recovery brings on its own positive cycle, Carver said. Women with anorexia who begin to eat and gain a little weight begin to feel better. As they regain some of the body fat, little things, like sitting on a wood chair, don't hurt as much. They feel warmer, they have more energy, they feel less depressed, and those relationships and interests that they had driven out of their lives to focus on dieting can come back. The hair gets shinier, and the skin becomes more resilient and less dry looking. Part of the process is an acceptance of the body. "She might say to herself, 'I'll never have thighs as thin as my friend's, but that's OK. My thighs don't define who I am.' "

What people with—and those who haven't been affected by—eating disorders need to figure out is what their ideal body weight is. Carver defines that as the weight range in which you feel comfortable and energetic and one which you can maintain without great difficulty. Constant dieting to try to attain a body weight that is lower than your ideal weight leads to problems. Deny yourself ice cream, or another favorite, for a long period of time and you start to crave it. Give in to the craving and you feel guilty. This cycle could evolve into a binge-and-purge behavior. It's better to judge your ideal weight, not based on comparisons with models in fashion magazines, but on your health. If you're winded after walking up a flight of stairs, you're probably either out of shape or overweight or both. There are healthy ways to eat less and exercise more, both of which contribute to a slow, steady weight loss. Resorting to fasting or purging isn't a healthy alternative. Above all, said Carver, don't envy the anorexic. "I've heard people say, 'Oh, I wish I could have anorexia, at least until I lose 15 pounds.' They mean it as a joke, but they have no idea of the emotional difficulty of eating disorders. People with eating disorders aren't living. The eating disorder itself has taken the place of living."

DO YOU HAVE AN EATING DISORDER?

Let's say you just polished off an entire bag of chocolate chip cookies. Does that mean you have a binge-eating problem? Not based on one incident, it doesn't. The American Psychiatric Association has listed these specific symptoms as characteristic of eating disorders.

Bulimia Nervosa

- Recurrent episodes of binge eating (minimum average of two binge-eating episodes a week for at least three months)
- A feeling of lack of control over eating during the binges
- Regular use of one or more of the following to prevent weight gain: self-induced vomiting, use of laxatives or diuretics, strict dieting or fasting, or vigorous exercise
- Persistent overconcern with body shape and weight.

Anorexia Nervosa

- Refusal to maintain weight that's over the lowest weight considered normal for age and height
- Intense fear of gaining weight or becoming fat, even though underweight

• Distorted body image
• In women, three consecutive missed menstrual periods without pregnancy.

ADDITIONAL RESOURCES

American Anorexia/Bulimia Association, Inc.
165 West 46th Street
Suite 1108
New York, NY 10036
212-575-6200

National Association of Anorexia Nervosa and Associated Disorders
P.O. Box 7
Highland Park, IL 60035
847-831-3438

ADDITIONAL READING

Bennett, Bev. "Teen Dieting Backfires. Study Says Girls Who Diet Face Greater Risk of Obesity Than Nondieters." *Newsday*, April 3, 2000, B15.
Bordo, Susan, *Unbearable Weight: Feminism, Western Culture and the Body*. Los Angeles: University of California Press, 1993.
Brumberg, Joan Jacobs. *Fasting Girls: The History of Anorexia Nervosa*. New York: Plume, 1989.
Chernin, Kim. *The Hungry Self: Women, Eating, and Identity*. New York: Harperperennial Library, 1994.
———. *The Obsession: Reflections on the Tyranny of Slenderness*. New York: Harperperennial Library, 1994.
Cooke, Kaz. *Real Gorgeous: The Truth About Body and Beauty*. New York: W. W. Norton, 1996.
Fairburn, Christopher. *Overcoming Binge Eating*. New York: Guilford Press, 1995.
Fraser, Laura. *Losing It: America's Obsession with Weight and the Industry That Feeds on It*. New York: Dutton Books, 1997.
Freedman, Rita. *Bodylove: Learning to Like Our Looks and Ourselves*. New York: Harper & Row, 1988.
Hall, Lindsey, and Leigh Cohen. *Bulimia: A Guide to Recovery*. Carlsbad, Calif.: Gurze Books, 1993.
Hutchinson, Marcia Germaine. *200 Ways to Love the Body You Have*. Freedom, Calif.: Crossing Press, 1999.
Kano, Susan. *Making Peace with Food*. New York: HarperCollins, 1989.
Lemberg, Peter. *Controlling Eating Disorders with Facts, Advice and Resources*. Phoenix, Ariz.: Oryx Press, 1992.

Normandi, Carol Emergy, and Laurelee Roark. *It's Not About Food: Change Your Mind; Change Your Life; End Your Obsession with Food and Weight.* New York: Penguin USA, 1999.

Orbach, Susie. *Fat Is a Feminist Issue.* New York: Budget Book Service, March 1997.

Roth, Geneen. *Breaking Free from Compulsive Eating.* New York: Plume, 1993.

————. *Feeding the Hungry Heart: The Experience of Compulsive Eating.* New York: Plume, 1993.

Siegal, Michelle, Judith Brisman, and Margot Weinshel. *Surviving an Eating Disorder: Strategies for Families and Friends.* New York: HarperPerennial, 1997.

Strober, Michael, et al. "Controlled Family Study of Anorexia Nervosa and Bulimia Nervosa: Evidence of Shared Liability and Transmission of Partial Syndromes." *American Journal of Psychiatry* 157 (March 2000): 393–401.

Thompson, Becky W. *A Hunger So Wide and So Deep.* Minneapolis: University of Minnesota Press, 1996.

Vreeland, Leslie. "Dying to Be Thin—After 30." *Good Housekeeping*, March 1, 1998, pp. 137–39.

Wade, Tracey D. "Anorexia Nervosa and Major Depression: Shared Genetic and Environmental Risk Facts." *American Journal of Psychiatry* 157 (March 2000): 469–71.

Zerbe, Kathryn J. *The Body Betrayed: A Deeper Understanding of Women, Eating Disorders, and Treatment.* Carlsbad, Calif.: Gurze Books, 1993.

11
SPECIAL DIETS

Something in your digestive tract is causing a problem. It may be temporary, or it may be permanent, but either way it means restricting what you eat. The best thing to do is to accept the fact that you need to follow a special diet. Special diets are designed for people who discover that what they are eating is undermining their health. You may find out that you suffer from allergies to food, or have diabetes or high cholesterol. Proper nutrition is an important part of health; it's also an important part of managing illness, and it's a tool to use in the fight against disease. When faced with a diagnosis that involves a carefully controlled diet, it's important to remember that proper nutrition, calorie intake, and appealing and appetizing foods do go together. Because of nutrition's recognized role in health care, many people now consult a registered dietitian to create an eating plan that provides the energy and nutrients needed to maintain or improve health. This chapter addresses some of the most common special dietary needs. Many such conditions require oversight or a diagnosis from a health care provider. The information in this chapter is not intended to be a substitute for that; it is intended only to supplement information from a doctor or a qualified nutrition professional.

DIABETES

Diabetes is a disease in which the body can no longer produce or properly use insulin, a hormone required to convert sugars and starches from the food we eat into the energy we need. One of the most common chronic illnesses today, it affects an estimated 16 million people in the United States and an estimated 120 to 140 million people worldwide, and the number is increasing. The World Health Organization in their November 1999 Fact Sheet predicts that the total number of people with diabetes worldwide may rise to 280 million by 2025.

There are two major types of diabetes. In Type 1, once known as juvenile diabetes or insulin-dependent diabetes, the pancreas no longer produces insulin. Between 500,000 and 1 million people in the United States have Type 1 diabetes. It usually strikes children or young adults, though it can develop at any age. It occurs when the body's immune system mistakenly attacks the insulin-producing cells in the pancreas. People with Type 1 diabetes must take daily insulin injections to stay alive. While the cause of Type 1 diabetes is unknown, it is likely that heredity plays a role. However, in susceptible individuals, a virus can trigger the disease.

In Type 2 diabetes, the body does produce insulin, but either makes too little or has become resistant to it. More than 90% of people with diabetes have Type 2. It most often strikes older people and those with a history of obesity and inactivity, though increasingly it is appearing in younger people—even children—who are overweight and inactive. Type 2 diabetics can often control their blood sugar levels through weight loss, exercise, and better nutrition, but many also need oral medications and insulin.

A third type of diabetes, gestational diabetes, is a temporary condition that occurs during pregnancy when the mother's body fails to produce the extra insulin needed during some pregnancies. Gestational diabetes requires that the pregnant woman monitor her food and blood sugar levels carefully. It usually goes away after the pregnancy, but women who have had it are at an increased risk of developing Type 2 diabetes later.

Risk Factors and Complications

Heredity plays a role in development of Type 1 diabetes. Siblings of people with Type 1, as well as children of parents with Type 1, are at a higher risk of developing the disease. Type 1 most often strikes in puberty, according to researchers, though it can occur at any age. Type 2 diabetes has a hereditary factor as well—people with a family history of Type 2 are more likely to develop the disease themselves. Type 2 is commonly a disease of middle or old age, though it is increasingly striking young people who are overweight and physically inactive. Some racial and ethnic groups have higher rates of diabetes; African Americans and Latinos are nearly twice as likely to develop Type 2 diabetes as the general population.

The warning signs for Type 1 diabetes include frequent urination, excessive thirst, unusual hunger, extreme fatigue, and unexplained weight loss. Victims of Type 2 diabetes can experience the same symptoms, as well as blurred vision, tingling or numbness in hands or feet, and cuts, bruises, and infections that are slow to heal. Often, though, people with Type 2 diabetes will have no symptoms at all, and the disease won't be discovered until complications develop.

According to the American Diabetes Association's "Facts and Figures," diabetes is the seventh leading cause of death in the United States and the sixth leading cause of death by disease. Each year, nearly 200,000 people die as a result of diabetes and its long-term complications, which include kidney disease, heart disease and stroke. It is often described as a "silent killer" because, in its Type 2 form, it can go undetected for years. It is only when serious and sometimes life-threatening complications develop that many people learn they have the disease. Complications of diabetes—which often take years to develop—stem in many instances from the damage that high blood sugar levels do to the tiny blood vessels in the body. In instances of kidney failure, for example, damage has been done to the blood vessels inside the kidney that act as filters to remove wastes, chemicals, and excess water from the blood. Poorly controlled diabetes can cause blindness by damaging the tiny blood vessels in the retina.

The most serious short-term complication of Type 1 diabetes is called ketoacidosis. When the body doesn't have enough insulin, it begins to burn fat for energy. Burning fat produces ketones, an acid that can poison the body, leading to coma and even death. Ketoacidosis usually develops slowly—early warning signs include thirst, a dry mouth, and frequent urination and high levels of ketones in the urine. Later, the person may feel nausea, have a fruity odor on the breath, and have difficulty breathing. Ketoacidosis is a serious condition that requires immediate medical attention.

Treating Diabetes

People with diabetes have a lot of responsibility to make sure their treatment plan works. People with diabetes must balance a variety of factors every day—deciding what to eat and when, or determining how much medication to take and when to take it. Physical activity or illness can also mean adjusting the treatment regimen. The best way to learn that responsibility is to seek advice from health care professionals.

A primary care physician is a good place to start, but treating diabetes almost always involves specialists in other areas as well. A diabetes care team usually involves an eye doctor, a dietitian, and a certified diabetes educator. If complications arise, a patient might be sent to other specialists.

For people with Type 1 diabetes, insulin is the only option, but there is a wide variety of approaches to insulin therapy. More than 20 kinds of insulin are available—some act very quickly or peak at different times, and some last all day long. There are also different ways to deliver insulin—syringes, insulin pens, and insulin pumps.

Most people with Type 1 begin by taking two injections of two types of insulin per day. Later they take multiple injections, usually three or four a day, depending on what they're eating or their level of activity. A person with Type 1 diabetes often calculates the amount of carbohydrates he or she will consume and then inject himself or herself with a number of units of insulin. This formula depends on the individual's reaction to insulin as well as expected activity level.

Injecting insulin before every meal or snack is the most targeted approach to diabetes treatment and allows the greatest flexibility, but some diabetics find it cumbersome. Another approach is to inject a specific amount of insulin in the morning and then eat only those foods that will be covered by that amount of insulin. This approach is more regimented and doesn't allow for spontaneous snacking.

Another recent introduction to insulin delivery is the insulin pump, a device that looks like a beeper and provides a steady, incremental dose of fast-acting insulin through a tiny tube inserted in the person's abdomen. Insulin pumps are the most expensive approach to diabetes care, but the device is the closest thing to the normal delivery of insulin that a person with diabetes can achieve. Pumps can be programmed to deliver different amounts of insulin at different times of the day or night, giving a person the ability to fine-tune the treatment regimen.

If you have an insulin-dependent diabetic friend, or if you are insulin-dependent, discuss this openly with friends. An insulin-dependent diabetic may need help at some point. He or she may experience an episode of hypoglycemia and need help getting a snack or sugared drink. It's much less intimidating to help a diabetic prepare an insulin injection or provide a sweet snack after discussing the symptoms and learning what to do.

People with Type 2 diabetes have a different set of treatment options. Sometimes, Type 2 diabetes can be controlled through diet and exercise alone, but, in many cases, the body needs help because the body doesn't make enough insulin and doesn't use the insulin it does make very well.

Oral medications can help the body reduce blood sugar levels. There are three classes of drugs for Type 2. The first kind stimulates the body to produce more insulin. The second makes the body more sensitive to the insulin it does have. The third blocks the breakdown of starches and certain sugars, which slows the rise of blood sugar levels. People with Type 2 may take a combination of oral medications, or take pills in combination with insulin. For every person with Type 2, medication combined with improved nutrition and regular exercise is the best treatment.

A key part of self-treatment of diabetes is frequent blood sugar testing. Pharmacies sell a variety of small blood glucose monitors and test strips that diabetics can (and should) carry with them. The diabetic places a drop of blood on the test strip and within a minute or so has a reading of the blood sugar levels. The general goal is to achieve blood sugar levels as close to normal as possible. People without diabetes generally maintain blood sugar levels between 70 and 120 milligrams per deciliter before eating, and less than 180 milligrams per deciliter after eating.

People with diabetes can also gauge how well they're controlling their blood sugar by taking a glycated hemoglobin test every three months. The test, done at a doctor's office, measures the presence of excess glucose in the blood over a three- or four-month period and gives a better picture of the effectiveness of the person's diabetes care than a single test on a glucose monitor.

Tight Control

Research has shown that the best way to avoid complications is to keep blood sugar levels as close to normal as possible. A 10-year study sponsored by the National Institute of Diabetes and Digestive and Kidney Diseases that was completed in 1993 showed the benefits of tight control. The Diabetes Control and Complications Trial (DCCT) followed 1,441 people with Type 1 diabetes for several years. Half of the participants followed a standard diabetes treatment, while the other half followed an intensive-control regimen of multiple injections and frequent blood sugar testing.

Those who followed the intensive-control regimen had significantly fewer complications. Only half as many developed signs of kidney disease, nerve disease was reduced by two-thirds, and only one-quarter as many developed diabetic eye disease.

Achieving tight control means taking several injections of insulin every day, or using an insulin pump to mimic the release of insulin that occurs in people without diabetes. It also means doing several blood tests a day to gauge how much insulin is needed.

Though the DCCT followed only people with Type 1, researchers believe tight control can have the same effect on people with Type 2. Since most people with Type 2 diabetes do not take insulin, they must take a different approach to tight control. Losing weight is one of the best ways to bring down glucose levels. Regular exercise helps, too, not only to bring down weight but also to reduce glucose levels. A recent study of 1,263 men with Type 2 diabetes showed that over 12 years, the men who did not exercise and stay active were more than twice as likely to die as those who did exercise.

Tight control has obvious benefits, but it's not necessarily the right choice for everyone. The DCCT found that people who followed tight control had three times the number of low blood glucose episodes as those using conventional treatment. Plus, people using the tight control approach gained more weight than those on conventional treatment— an average of 10 pounds, according to the DCCT.

Those who should avoid tight control include people who already have complications, young children whose developing brains need glucose, and the elderly who can suffer strokes or heart attacks from episodes of hypoglycemia.

Waiting for a Cure

The wait for a cure might be difficult for people with diabetes, but the progress in treating this disease has been remarkable. It wasn't until 1920 that a Canadian doctor, Frederick Banting, first conceived the idea of insulin. The first patient treated with insulin was a 14-year-old Canadian boy. Oral medications weren't available until the 1950s.

Today, researchers are making progress in solving the riddle of diabetes. More is known today about the genetic causes of diabetes, and
scientists are closing in on a way to prevent Type 1 diabetes by preventing the body's immune system from attacking the cells in the pancreas that produce insulin. Other researchers are working on ways to
transplant insulin-producing cells into the bodies of Type 1 diabetics.

Other researchers, meanwhile, are finding new ways to help people
who have the condition to control it. There are new oral medications
for Type 2 diabetes, new fast-acting insulins for people with Type 1, and
new devices that make it easier to test blood sugar levels.

Diabetes is the most well-known diet-related condition, but it is by
no means the only one.

ALLERGIES AND FOOD INTOLERANCE

A food allergy differs from a food intolerance, and each affects different mechanisms in the body. Normally the immune system works to
keep the body healthy, and when all is well it also fights off colds or
infections. If you have a food allergy your immune system reacts to foods
as it would toward unwanted bacteria or virus by developing antibodies.
When people form antibodies against a food, that food becomes the
allergen and this creates a genuine food allergy. With each exposure to
the offending food, your body reacts more strongly, producing more antibodies. When enough antibodies build up, the food causes the release
of chemicals such as histamine, which leads to symptoms like wheezing
or a runny nose. There is a huge difference in the degree of sensitivity
to various allergens. Some people experience only mild symptoms; others
can have an anaphylactic reaction, in which blood vessels leak, causing
blood pressure to drop which, in turn, inhibits blood and oxygen from
reaching the brain. Within minutes or even seconds, the airways tighten
and the tongue and throat may swell. Anyone suffering an anaphylactic
reaction must be treated immediately. Adults are most often allergic to
shellfish, such as shrimp, crab, and lobster, and peanuts, nuts, fish, and
eggs. Children are often allergic to eggs, milk, and peanuts. Because
antibodies can be detected in the blood, a test called the radioallergo-
sorbent test or RAST can be ordered by your doctor find out if you do
suffer from allergies. Doctors may also use skin tests that inject an extract
of the suspected allergen into the skin. This test is especially helpful in
diagnosing a food allergy.

Celiac Disease

Celiac disease, also known as nontropical sprue and gluten-sensitive enteropathy, is a classic food allergy. It was first identified in 1888 but wasn't specifically linked with wheat until World War II. The disease develops when someone's immune system attacks certain glutens or proteins found in wheat and rye. The attack mimics how the body would respond to an invading virus, and the more gluten that person consumes, the more the body defenses attack. Eventually, the lining of the small intestine becomes damaged and unable to absorb nutrients. Symptoms range from a feeling of heaviness after a meal to persistent diarrhea, weight loss, abdominal swelling, and pain. Because the symptoms are so variable and similar to other diseases, the diagnosis of Celiac disease should always be made by a doctor. The only treatment is to eliminate gluten from the diet. This means saying no to all foods that contain wheat, rye, barley, and oats. Eliminating gluten is a challenge because so many processed American foods are made from wheat, and gluten can hide in unexpected places, like soy sauce, licorice, and even over-the-counter and prescription drugs made with fillers that contain gluten. Gluten is also known as malt or malt flavorings and modified food starch.

Food Intolerance

Food intolerance is a much broader term and includes many types of reactions caused by foods. With a food intolerance, the body reacts in a variety of ways—from indigestion to headaches, skin blotches, diarrhea, or even an increased pulse rate. In one form of food intolerance, people lack the enzymes that digest the sugar in milk and other dairy products. This condition is known as lactose intolerance, and people who lack this enzyme may develop diarrhea and stomach pains after drinking milk. Some lactose-intolerant people can eat milk and dairy foods if they do so in small amounts such as a half a cup of milk at a sitting. Others can tolerate dairy foods in which the lactose is already broken down, like in yogurt with live, active cultures and aged cheeses. Ricotta, American, cream, and Neufchatel cheeses also contain smaller amounts of lactose, and they may be tolerated in small servings by someone intolerant of milk. The best way to test for lactose intolerance is to eliminate all lactose-containing foods. If symptoms improve, the patient can then eat small amounts of these foods to learn their individual tolerance level.

In fact, the most effective way to diagnose any specific food intolerance is to follow an exclusion diet. If, after excluding certain foods, your symptoms disappear or greatly improve, your physician can develop a diet that will reintroduce foods one at a time. The physician generally limits the most common allergic foods: wheat, oats, preserved meats, dairy products, caffeinated drinks, citrus fruits, chocolate, yeast, preservatives, and nuts. When the offending foods have been discovered, they can be excluded from your diet indefinitely, and in that way you can control the symptoms. It is also beneficial to discuss a nutrition plan with your doctor and a registered dietitian to make sure your nutritional needs are met.

DISEASES OF THE DIGESTIVE TRACT

The digestive tract includes the organs that turn food into fuel for the body. Diseases such as Crohn's disease, ulcerative colitis, hepatitis, cirrhosis, pancreatitis, gallbladder disease, and irritable bowel syndrome all affect the gastrointestinal tract. Understanding the path food takes as it is assimilated into the body may help you understand the need for a special diet when dealing with digestive diseases. When you eat, food is swallowed and goes down the esophagus into the stomach. There it is partially digested and changed into liquid. This liquid then passes into the small intestine where most of the nutrients are absorbed into the body. The small intestine is divided into three parts: the duodenum, the jejunum, and the ileum. The small intestine is also attached to the large intestine where nondigestible substances, such as fiber, are passed and stored until they are eliminated as waste. If you experience changes in bodily function it's important to see your doctor. Some digestive diseases are very serious so even if you have something as mundane as extended indigestion, see your doctor to make sure it isn't anything more serious. Here are brief descriptions of various diseases of the digestive tract and their symptoms.

Cancer

Cancer comes in many forms and attacks the body in many ways, but the American Cancer Society reports that a full third of the 563,000 cancer deaths in 1999 were nutrition-related. According to a 1997 report released by the Center for Science in the Public Interest (CSPI), of the 130,000 cases of colon cancer diagnosed each year, the majority, some

50% to 85%, have no major genetic component. The CSPI study was reported in the November 1997 *Nutrition Action Healthletter*, in an article titled, "Does one size fit all?" by Bonnie Liebman. This figure contradicts the public perception that most cancers are caused by genetics when, in fact, nutrition remains a large part of the equation. Noted English epidemiologists Sir Richard Doll, MD, D.Sc., and Richard Peto, MD, estimated that between 20% and 60% of cancer deaths were related to dietary factors. Those figures were reported in the article "Diet and Its Relationship to Cancer Prevention," published in the August 26, 1999 *American Cancer Society Research News*. Even though diet alone is not an adequate treatment for the disease, studies continue to link a high intake of plant foods to a low risk of cancer.

Cirrhosis

Cirrhosis occurs when liver cells are damaged and replaced by scar tissue that cannot act as normal liver tissue would. The disease can be caused by chronic alcoholism, malnutrition, hemachromatosis, iron overload, or prolonged biliary statis when the bile fails to flow normally and stagnates in the liver. Symptoms of cirrhosis include jaundice, nausea, vomiting, and loss of appetite. In advanced stages, fluid retention and liver failure may occur.

Crohn's Disease

This inflammation of the lower part of the small intestine usually affects children and young adults, and more women than men. Symptoms include diarrhea, abdominal pain, weight loss, and anemia. The bowel may become narrowed, or an obstruction may develop. Victims of Crohn's disease are treated with dietary changes since many show an intolerance to wheat.

Diverticulosis

This disease occurs when tiny sacs or diverticula develop in the large intestine. The problem comes when food waste gets caught in these pouches and inflammation develops. Symptoms of diverticulitis include persistent and often severe abdominal pain, fever, rectal bleeding, nausea, and cramping. Doctors use antibiotics to treat the infection and gradually switch their patients to a high-fiber diet as part of an overall treatment. Low-fiber foods have a greater chance of lingering in the large intestine, which can lead to infection. The best therapy for this condition is a diet high in fiber that will prevent the pouches from forming and will effectively move waste out of the large intestine.

Gallbladder Disease

This disease is diagnosed when stones formed in the gallbladder block the flow of bile, inflaming the gallbladder and causing pain, bloating, nausea, and vomiting. The gallbladder's main purpose is to concentrate and store bile, a bitter green liquid that is needed to digest fat. When high-fat foods are eaten, the gallbladder releases bile into the small intestine where it can break down the fat. If the chemical balance of bile is upset or changed, gallstones develop. Women are at higher risk for developing gallstones, and the disease is commonly linked with obesity.

Heartburn

Not a malfunction of the heart, heartburn is instead a burning sensation in the chest brought on by overindulgence in food or drink. The burning starts when the sufferer's belching brings stomach acids "back up." Since heartburn can be a symptom of stomach ulcers or gallbladder disease, it is important to see a doctor if you have persistent heartburn. Alkaline preparations relieve the symptoms by counteracting the excess stomach acidity. It can also occur late in pregnancy when the growing baby puts more pressure on the stomach. You can prevent heartburn by eating healthy foods, eating slowly, not exercising immediately after a meal, and avoiding spicy dishes.

Hepatitis

This is an inflammation of the liver, and there are several forms of the disease: viral hepatitis A, B, non-A and non-B, serum hepatitis, and post-transfusion hepatitis. The infectious type occurs sporadically or in epidemics when the virus is present, and it is passed through contaminated food or water. The best defense, especially for food service workers, is to wash hands properly. The incubation period for infectious hepatitis is only 2 to 6 weeks. Those exposed to the virus can be treated with injections of gamma globulin. Symptoms include fever, weakness, nausea, loss of appetite, and jaundice. Treatment is a combination of rest and adequate diet with recovery taking anywhere from 6 to 8 weeks.

Inflammatory Bowel Disease

This term includes two diseases of the intestines: Crohn's disease and ulcerative colitis. In colitis the mucous membranes of the colon become inflamed. Although its cause is unknown, symptoms include diarrhea, weight loss, dehydration, and anemia, as well as abdominal cramps and frequent urges to defecate.

Irritable Bowel Syndrome

Sometimes called spastic colon, this syndrome has various symptoms, including abdominal pain and distention, diarrhea, and changes in bowel habits. There is no inflammatory process as in inflammatory bowel disease, but sufferers experience significant discomfort and pain. Studies show that IBS symptoms improve with an allergy-elimination diet for products such as dairy and fat. This condition is more common among women than men.

Pancreatitis

Pancreatitis occurs when the flow of enzymes required to digest food cannot get into the intestine. Without the necessary enzymes, fat, protein, and carbohydrates cannot be broken down and absorbed by the body. The undigested fat interferes with the absorption of fat-soluble vitamins. Symptoms include diarrhea and nausea. A diet low in fat but high in protein and moderately high in carbohydrates is considered good nutritional therapy and can improve digestion and absorption of protein and carbohydrates.

KOSHER: A DIET WITH A HIGHER PURPOSE

Kosher foods may have their roots in the Bible, but they fit in with current trends of vegetarianism and rising concerns over food safety. A kosher diet is prepared and eaten according to specific Jewish dietary laws, known as kashruth. Why do observant Jews keep kosher? The 613 commandments contained in the Torah, the first five books of the Bible, make tradition and ritual an integral part of the Jewish religion. To religious Jews, a relationship with God is expressed and renewed dozens of times a day in many ordinary ways including the process of preparing and eating food. Health standards are not the primary reason for keeping kosher, but many non-Jews buy kosher foods for that reason. According to a 1999 article published in the *Wall Street Journal*, kosher food marketers are seeing an increase in non-Jewish customers for their products to the tune of $50 billion in sales in 1999. Vegetarians, Asian Americans, and those with lactose intolerance buy kosher to ensure a product is dairy free. Muslims, Hindus, and Seventh-Day Adventists share many of the Jewish dietary restrictions and purchase kosher foods for religious reasons.

Since kosher foods are produced under exacting, guaranteed controls, some people feel they are safer. The rules governing kosher products are still effective today, but modern Jews are increasingly deciding for themselves how closely they will adhere to the following guidelines.

• Meat and poultry: animals that have cloven hooves and chew their cud are considered kosher. When kosher animals are killed, Jewish law dictates they must be killed in a humane way.

• Fish: to be kosher, fish must have fins and removable scales; shellfish are not considered kosher.

• Dairy products: under Jewish dietary law, it is forbidden to combine meat products and dairy products, and cooks keep separate utensils and plates for them. After eating meat, Orthodox Jews must wait from one to six hours to consume any dairy products or vice versa.

• Bakery and packaged goods: products cannot contain mixtures of dairy and meat, and no un-kosher animal byproducts may be used.

• Fruits and vegetables: most fresh and unprocessed fruit is kosher. However, no fruit may be eaten from a tree for the first three years after it was planted.

• Only a rabbi is qualified to offer guidance and answer questions concerning any aspect of kashruth.

NUTRITION DURING PREGNANCY AND LACTATION

The teen birthrate in the United States has been decreasing—and public health specialists say that's a good thing. In 1998 nearly 485,000 babies were born to teenagers aged 15 to 19, or a birthrate of 51.1 live births per 1,000 women in that age group. That's 18% lower than in 1991, when the downward trend in teen births began. The decrease is even more striking among younger girls, ages 15 to 17, where the rate has dropped 21% during the same time frame.

The National Center for Health Statistics, which tracks these numbers, reported that "[t]eenage mothers are disadvantaged in several ways that affect their health and the health of their infants. Pregnant teenagers are far less likely to receive timely prenatal care in the first trimester of pregnancy and are more likely to smoke during pregnancy and to have a preterm or low birthweight infant." The agency released these numbers in an April 24, 2000, press release titled "State Data on Teen Births Now Available."

While those are huge improvements, the American Academy of Pediatrics (AAP) noted in a February 1, 1999, press release, "AAP Addresses Teen Pregnancy in New Policy Statement," that the United States still has the highest adolescent birthrate of developed countries and asserted that nearly 1 million teenagers become pregnant every year. "The incidence of an adolescent having a low birth weight baby is double the rate for adults and the neonatal death rate is also three times higher for babies born to adolescents. Adolescent pregnancy poses other health problems, including poor maternal weight gain, pregnancy induced hypertension, anemia and sexually transmitted diseases."

While the teenage birthrate is declining, the overall number of births rose about 2% between 1997 and 1998. The birthrate inched up as well, with much of this being driven by women in their twenties, according to a National Center for Health Statistics report issued in March 29, 2000, and reported in *The Washington Post*, "Number and Rate of U.S. Births Rise," p. A1.

Good nutrition for pregnant women is absolutely essential. Any woman who learns she is pregnant should seek prenatal care as soon as possible, certainly in the first trimester. Your doctor will guide you on specific nutritional requirements and whether you might need vitamin supplements. However, researchers have found that some fundamental guidelines apply.

• Calcium. The demands for calcium are highest during the second and third trimesters when the fetal skeleton is developing quickly. Pregnant and lactating women are apparently better able to absorb calcium during this phase, but the general recommendation is that calcium intake be increased by 400 milligrams per day.

• Folic acid or folate. The body's demand for folic acid doubles during pregnancy. Indeed, it's recommended that women trying to conceive a baby increase their folic acid intake. A deficiency in folic acid has been connected to some congenital conditions, such as spina bifida. Folic acid is found naturally in leafy vegetables, nuts, dark yellow fruits, and vegetables and broccoli.

- Fluids. Additional fluids are needed to help increase the blood volume and add continuously to the amniotic fluid supply. Fluids also reduce the likelihood of constipation during pregnancy. Avoid caffeine, for its diuretic qualities, and alcohol, because it is a diuretic and can damage the developing fetus.

Overall, a good diet is a factor in delivering a healthy baby. Poor prenatal nutrition has been associated with such conditions as low-birthweight babies, premature delivery, and developmental delays. A poor diet also affects the pregnant woman, who may develop anemia or toxemia, or feel fatigued or unwell for much of the pregnancy. Toxemia is a lay term referring to hypertensive disorders of pregnancy.

Weight gain during pregnancy is a given. Doctors often recommend a weight gain of from 25 to 35 pounds, but that's not a rule. For example, an underweight woman might benefit from gaining more; an overweight woman might be told to keep the weight gain lower. Discuss the appropriate range of weight gain with your doctor and realize that weight during pregnancy, just as during every other time in life, is dependent on two factors: the food you eat and the exercise you get. Pregnancy isn't the time to start training for a marathon, but fit women generally continue their exercise programs throughout the pregnancy. There are numerous books on exercises that are specifically designed for pregnant women. These exercises help tone muscles for a more comfortable pregnancy—muscles needed for delivery—and can help with a faster recovery.

The weight gained during pregnancy is more than the weight of the baby, who typically makes up from 25% to 35% of the mother's weight gain. Some of the additional weight is lost during or shortly after delivery with the shedding of the placenta and some additional blood and fluid. It takes longer to shed the fat stores that come along with pregnancy. How long it takes depends on many factors, including the mother's diet and her level of physical activity. It could be several months; it could be a year.

One of the reasons the body stores fat during pregnancy is to store energy for producing milk. In fact, breast-feeding can help a woman reach her prepregnancy weight and shape sooner. Breast-feeding demands extra calories from the mother. When babies reach between three and six months of age and have a high demand for breast milk, the weight loss is most noticeable for breast-feeding mothers.

There are numerous advantages to breast-feeding, mainly breast milk is the ideal nutrition for human babies. There are immunological and psychological benefits to breast-feeding, and it's free.

Good nutrition for a lactating mother is not much different from good nutrition during pregnancy. Many women have already taken steps to improve their diet during pregnancy, eating a wider variety of foods and substituting more natural foods for more processed ones. The few conditions a lactating woman should keep in mind, though, are that they will be more thirsty, will need more calcium than a mother who's not breast-feeding, and should avoid caffeine and alcohol and some medications. Ask your doctor for guidelines.

Particularly in the early weeks, breast-feeding mothers find they are particularly thirsty. Keep fluid levels high by drinking lots of water to reduce the likelihood of constipation promote comfort.

Breast-feeding mothers do lose some bone density while nursing their babies. However, bone density builds up again within about six months of weaning. Still, keeping dietary calcium intake up is a good idea. That doesn't necessarily mean drinking lots of milk. In fact, cow's milk is a fairly common allergen among babies. Other dietary sources of calcium include yogurt, cheese, tofu, and leafy green vegetables.

ADDITIONAL READING

Balch, James F. *Prescription for Nutritional Healing*. Garden City Park, N.Y.: Avery Publishing, 1997.

Barone, Jeanine. "A Lifesaving Diet." *Better Homes and Gardens*, June 1998, vol. 76, no. 6: 106.

Behan, Eileen. *Cooking Well for the Unwell*. New York: Hearst Books, 1996.

Bogo, Jennifer. "The Diet-Cancer Connection." *E*, May 1999, vol. 10, no. 3: 42.

Brody, Jane E. *New York Times Book of Health: How to Feel Fitter, Eat Better and Live Longer*. New York: Times Book, 1997.

Cowley, Geoffrey. "Cancer & Diet: Can You Eat to Beat Malignancy?" *Newsweek*, November 30, 1998, vol. 132, no. 22: 60.

D'Arrigo, Terri. "Drumroll, Please." Research results from American Diabetes Association 59th Annual Meeting. *Diabetes Forecast*, September 1999, vol. 52: 58.

Dreazen, Yochi. "Kosher Food Marketers Get Gentiles to Dig In." *Wall Street Journal*, July 30, 1999, s0, pB2 (W) pB2 (E) col. 3.

Food for Health & Healing. Des Moines, Iowa: Meredity, 1999.

Hunter, John, Virginia Alun Jones, and Elizabeth Workman. *Food Intolerance,* Tucson, Ariz.: Body Press, 1986.

Janowitz, Henry D. *Indigestion: Living Better with Upper Intestinal Problems from Heartburn to Ulcers and Gallstones.* New York: Oxford University Press, 1992.

La Leche League International. *The Womanly Art of Breastfeeding.* 6th ed. Schaumburg, Ill.: La Leche League International, 1997.

Levine, Joshua. "You Don't Have to Be Jewish: Can the Kosher Food Folk Convert the Masses to Matzos?" *Forbes,* April 24, 1995, vol. 155, no. 9: 154.

Liebman, Bonnie. "Does One Size Fit All? *Nutrition Action Healthletter,* November 1997, vol. 24, no. 9: 1.

Lipkowitz, Myron A. *Allergies A to Z.* New York: Facts on File, 1997.

O'Donnell, Sara Altshul. "Can Herbs Fight Cancer?" *Prevention,* September 1998, vol. 50, no. 9: 116.

Orenstein, Neil S. *Food Allergies: How to Tell If You Have Them, What to Do About Them If You Do.* New York: Putnam, 1987.

Rafinski, Karen. "Overweight Kids May Be Putting Themselves at Greater Risk for Diabetes." *Knight-Ridder/Tribune News Service,* August 27, 1999.

Roth, June. *Living Better with a Special Diet.* New York: Arco, 1983.

Sears, William, and Martha Sears with Linda Hughey Holt. *The Pregnancy Book: A Month-by-Month Guide.* Boston: Little Brown, 1997.

Whelan, Ann. "Getting Rid of Gluten." *Vegetarian Times,* April 1999, 24.

APPENDIX A
Glossary

Addiction: An addiction is a physical or emotional dependence on a substance, often alcohol or drugs. Increasing amounts of the substance are usually required to achieve the same effect over time.

Aerobic activity: Aerobic exercise, the process of using oxygen to break down carbohydrates and convert them into lasting energy, is in ideal exercise for burning fat. Good aerobic activities are repetitive, such as running, swimming, and aerobics classes, which combine fast-paced stretching, strength, and endurance exercises.

Al dente: This term describes the correct degree of doneness for pasta and vegetables (Italian for "to the bite"). Pasta should have a slight resistance when bitten into but not a hard center.

Allergy: An allergy is an exaggerated reaction to a substance or condition which is produced by the release of histamine or histamine-like substances in affected cells. Symptoms include rashes, nasal congestion, asthma, and in severe cases, shock.

Amino acids: Amino acids function as the building blocks of proteins. They are classified as essential, nonessential, and conditionally essential. Essential amino acids include leucine, isoleucine, valine, tryptophan, phenylalanine, methionine, threonine, lysine, histidine, and possibly arginine. Nonessential amino acids, which are synthesized by the body in adequate amounts, include alanine, aspartic acid, asparagine, glutamic acid, glutamine, glycine, proline, and serine. Conditionally essential amino acids are nonessential amino acids that become essential when certain diseases are present, like glutamine for some liver diseases.

Anabolic steroids: Properly known as "anabolic-androgenic" steroids for the two effects they create, these synthetic substances are related to the male sex hormones. They promote growth of skeletal muscle (anabolic) and the development of male sexual characteristics (androgenic).

Anaerobic activity: Anaerobic energy is created from burning carbohydrates, not oxygen. Anaerobic exercise is characterized by maximum bursts of energy, of short duration, to build muscle strength. Weight lifting and sprinting are examples.

Anemia: Anemia is a condition in which a deficiency in the size or number of red blood cells or the amount of hemoglobin they contain limits the exchange of oxygen and carbon dioxide between the blood and the tissue cells. It results from a variety of conditions, such as hemorrhage, genetic abnormalities, chronic disease states, and drug toxicity.

Anorexia nervosa: An eating disorder, anorexia is characterized by refusal to maintain a minimally normal weight for height and age. The condition includes weight loss, an intense fear of weight gain or becoming fat, a disturbance in the self-awareness of one's own body weight or shape, and in females, the absence of at least three consecutive menstrual cycles that would otherwise occur.

Antibiotics: These chemical substances, including penicillin and streptomycin, which are produced by microorganisms and fungi, are used in the treatment of infectious diseases.

Antibody: This protein, produced by the immune system, counteracts or eliminates foreign substances known as antigens.

Antigen: This foreign substance (almost always a protein), when introduced into the body, stimulates an immune response by causing antibodies to form.

Antioxidant: Antioxidants protect key cell components by neutralizing the damaging effects of free radicals, which are the natural byproducts of cell metabolism. Free radicals form when oxygen is metabolized, or burned by the body. They travel through cells, disrupting the structure of other molecules, causing cellular damage.

Aspartame: A low-calorie sweetener, aspartame is used in a variety of foods and beverages and as a tabletop sweetener, meaning it cannot be substituted for sugar in baked foods. It is about 200 times sweeter than sugar. It is made by joining the two protein components aspartic acid and phenylalanine.

Asthma: This chronic medical condition affects approximately 10 million Americans. Asthma results when irritants cause swelling of the tissues in the air passages of the lungs, making it difficult to breathe. Symptoms of asthma include wheezing, shortness of breath, and coughing.

Atherosclerosis: This condition exists when too much cholesterol builds up in the blood and accumulates in the walls of the blood vessels.

Attention Deficit Hyperactivity Disorder (ADHD): Commonly called hyperactivity, Attention Deficit Hyperactivity Disorder is a clinical diagnosis based on specific criteria. These include excessive motor activity, impulsiveness, short attention span, low tolerance to frustration, and onset before 7 years of age.

Baking powder: A leavening agent, baking powder combines an acid with bicarbonate of soda to form the gas carbon dioxide. The chemical reaction between the acid and soda enables baked products to rise.

Baking soda: This leavening agent is an essential ingredient in baking powder. When used alone as a leavener, recipes should include a type of acid such as yogurt, sour cream, buttermilk, or citrus juice to neutralize the sodium carbonate in the finished product.

Balsamic vinegar: This fragrant vinegar is made from grapes and aged in wooden barrels.

Beta-carotene: Found in plant and animal tissue, this nutrient is stored in the body and is transformed into Vitamin A, as the body requires it. It is also the main source of natural color in butter, carrots, and egg yolks.

Bidis: These small brown cigarettes, often flavored, consist of tobacco hand rolled in herbal leaves. They are not a safe alternative to cigarettes because they contain at least as much nicotine, more carbon monoxide, and more tar than cigarettes. They are also known as beedis or beedies.

Bioengineered foods: Also known as gene-altered foods, these foods have been altered to improve yields or disease resistance. In early 2000, the Food and Drug Administration stepped up some of its regulations on gene-altered, or GE, foods but was not requiring food producers to include that information on the label. However, GE Free labels can be placed on foods if producers can show no bioengineered products are included.

Biotechnology: Biotechnology is applied biology or the application of biological knowledge and techniques to develop products and modify the genetic materials of living cells so they will produce new substances or perform new functions.

Blanch: Blanching is the process of cooking foods in boiling water for a brief period of time.

Body mass index: This is a formula for determining ideal weight. See Chapter 2 "How's My Weight" for further information.

Bovine somatotropin (BST): The use of BST, a synthetic growth hormone used to stimulate higher milk production in cows, has been controversial. Some believe BST aggravates inflammation of the udder in cows; opponents believe this hormone naturally occurs in cow's milk and has little effect.

Bovine spongiform encephalopathy (BSE): Also known as mad cow disease, BSE is a rare, chronic degenerative disease affecting the brain and central nervous system of cattle. Cattle with BSE lose their coordination, develop abnormal posture, and experience changes in behavior. Clinical symptoms take 4 to 5 years to develop, but death follows in a period of from several weeks to months.

Bran: The outer husk of grains such as wheat, bran contains a great deal of fiber. White flours have the bran removed and contain little dietary fiber.

Bulimia nervosa: This eating disorder is characterized by the rapid consumption of a large amount of food in a short period of time. There are two forms of the condition, purging and nonpurging. The purging type regularly engages in purging through self-induced vomiting or the excessive use of laxatives or diuretics; the nonpurging type controls weight through strict dieting, fasting, or excessive exercise.

Caffeine: This natural substance is found in the leaves, seeds, or fruits of over 63 plant species worldwide and is part of a group of compounds known as methylxanthines. The most commonly known sources of caffeine are coffee and cocoa beans, cola nuts, and tea leaves.

Calcium: This mineral contributes to strong bones and teeth. It's found naturally in dairy products, leafy green vegetables, and tofu. Calcium requirements are highest for adolescents, whose bones are growing rapidly, and pregnant and lactating women.

Calorie: Calories measures the energy the body gets from food to perform all its functions such as breathing, circulating the blood, and performing physical activity. To determine the caloric content of foods, look at the Nutrition Facts label on the packaging. The body burns calories during exercise.

Carbohydrate: Carbohydrates are one of the three nutrients that supply calories (energy) to the body—specifically, the brain, the central nervous system, and the muscles. They are needed for normal body function. They are divided into three kinds: monosaccharides or simple sugars, such as glucose and fructose; disaccharides—composed of two monosaccharides—such as maltose, sucrose, and lactose; and polysaccharides, which are starches and glycogen.

Caries: *See* dental caries.

Celiac disease: This disease is characterized by an allergic reaction to any in-gested gluten. If it is not diagnosed, it can result in malnutrition.

Cellulose: This insoluble fiber is found in all plants. Food manufacturers chem-ically modify it to hold moisture and form gels. It appears on food labels as cellulose gel, microcrystalline cellulose, methylcellulose, or hydroxy-methylcellulose.

Centers for Disease Control and Prevention (CDC): The CDC, composed of 11 centers, institutes, and offices, is an agency of the U.S. Department of Health and Human Services. It was established to promote the health and quality of life of Americans by preventing and controlling disease, injury, and disability.

Chemotherapy: Chemotherapy is a drug therapy used to stop cancer cells from growing in size or number.

Cholesterol (blood serum): High blood cholesterol is a risk factor in the de-velopment of coronary heart disease. The body manufacturers most of the cholesterol that is found in the blood.

Cholesterol (blood types): Blood cholesterol is divided into three separate clas-ses of lipoproteins: very-low density lipoprotein (VLDL); low-density lipo-protein (LDL), which contains most of the cholesterol found in the blood; and high-density lipoprotein (HDL). LDL, popularly known as the bad cholesterol, seems to be the culprit in coronary heart disease. By contrast, HDL, known as the good cholesterol, is increasingly considered desirable.

Cholesterol (dietary): A fat-like substance classified as a lipid, dietary choles-terol is found in all cell membranes. It is necessary for the production of bile acids and steroid hormones. Dietary cholesterol is found only in animal foods. Abundant in organ meats and egg yolks, cholesterol is also contained in meats and poultry. Vegetable oils and shortenings are cholesterol free.

Chromosome: These thread-like components in the cell contain DNA and make proteins. Genes are carried on the chromosomes.

Clinical trials: Clinical trials undertake experimental study of human subjects. Trials may attempt to determine whether the findings of basic research are applicable to humans, or to confirm the results of epidemiological research.

Continuing Survey of Food Intake of Individuals (CSFII): This part of the National Nutrition Monitoring System, which was the first nationwide dietary intake survey, is designed to be conducted annually. The USDA conducts the survey.

Control group: This group of subjects in a study is the group to whom a com-parison is made in order to determine whether an observation or treatment has an effect. In an experimental study, it is the group that does not receive a treatment. Subjects are as similar as possible to those in the test or treatment group.

Corn syrup: Dextrose, maltose, and glucose are all products obtained by converting starch with acids. All are listed as corn syrup on ingredient labels.

Dehydration: Dehydration occurs when the body loses too much water or the intake of water is too low. Severe diarrhea or vomiting can cause dehydration. Fitness experts suggest drinking a cup of water about a half hour before exercising and immediately after a 20- to 30-minute workout to keep the body adequately hydrated.

Dental caries: Popularly known as cavities, dental caries occur when bacteria in the mouth feed on fermentable carbohydrates and produce acids that dissolve tooth enamel. Widespread use of fluoride in water supplies and oral health products are credited with the decline in dental caries among children and adults over the past 20 years. *See* fluoride.

Diabetes: This group of medical disorders is characterized by high blood sugar levels. Normally when people eat, food is digested and much of it is converted to glucose, a simple sugar the body uses for energy. The blood carries the glucose to cells where it is absorbed with the help of the hormone insulin. For a diabetic the body does not make enough insulin, or it cannot properly use the insulin it does make. Without insulin, glucose accumulates in the blood rather than moving into the cells. High blood sugar levels result.

Diet: A diet is the food you eat, including liquids and solids.

Dietary fat: This is one of the three nutrients that supply calories or energy to the body. Fat also helps the body absorb vitamins, and small amounts of fat are needed to maintain normal body function. *See* fats.

Diuretics: These drugs that help the body get rid of water and salt.

DNA: Also known as deoxyribonucleic acid, this is the molecule that carries the genetic information for most living systems.

E. coli: O157:H7: The bacteria *Escherichia coli: O157:H7* is a type of *E. coli* associated with food-borne illness. Healthy cattle and humans can carry the bacteria. It can be transferred from animal to animal and animal to human, and from animal to human on food. Symptoms of the disease include vomiting, high fever, and dehydration. It can result in death in severe cases.

Edema: Edema is the buildup of excess fluid within the tissues.

Electrolytes: This is a general term for the minerals needed by the body to retain proper fluid balance.

Emulsifiers: Fat substances, such as lecithin or mono- and diglycerides, emulsifiers are used in small amounts to keep mixtures mixed.

Environmental Protection Agency (EPA): This government agency was developed to protect human health and safeguard the natural environment—air, water, and land—upon which life depends. Through regulation, the EPA tries to protect the human population and the environment from environmental risks and exposure to toxic substances.

Epidemiology: Epidemiology is the study of the distribution and determinants of diseases or other health outcomes in human populations. Epidemiological studies may suggest relationships between two factors, but they do not provide the basis for conclusions about cause and effect.

Fats: Fats, composed of the same three elements as carbohydrates, carbon, hydrogen, and oxygen, are known chemically as triglycerides. Fats are a vital nutrient in a healthy diet. Fats help maintain healthy skin and regulate cholesterol metabolism, and they are needed to carry fat-soluble Vitamins A, D, E, and K and to aid in their absorption from the intestine. *See* dietary fats.

Fatty acid: Fatty acids are generally classified as saturated, monounsaturated, or polyunsaturated. These terms refer to the number of hydrogen atoms attached to the carbon atoms of the fat molecule. In general, fats that contain a majority of saturated fatty acids are solid at room temperature. Fats containing mostly unsaturated fatty acids are usually liquid at room temperature and are called oils. *See* fats; hydrogenation.

Fen-phen: A once popular prescription diet drug, combining fenfluramine and phenetermine, it was withdrawn from the market in 1997 after some users died and some developed serious side effects.

Fetal alcohol syndrome (FAS): One of the leading causes of mental retardation, FAS results from the exposure a developing fetus to alcohol. Because the level at which FAS is triggered is not known, pregnant women and those trying to conceive should avoid alcohol.

Fiber: Fiber is the part of fruits, vegetables, grains, nuts, and legumes that cannot be digested by humans. There are two basic types of fiber: insoluble and soluble. Insoluble fiber comes from grains; soluble fiber mostly comes from fruits and vegetables. Studies indicate that high-fiber diets can reduce the risks of heart disease and certain types of cancer.

Five-a-day: This phrase refers to the dietary recommendation to consume five servings of fruits and vegetables every day.

Flour: The term flour commonly refers to the finely ground grain of wheat, but it also includes corn, rice, oat, rye, or barley. Varieties of flour include all-purpose, bread flour, cake flour, pastry flour, whole-wheat flour, and semolina flour.

Fluoride: Fluoride is a natural component of minerals in rocks and soils. Widespread use of fluoride in water supplies and oral health products is credited with the decline in dental caries among children and adults in the United States. Fluoride also prevents the growth of harmful bacteria and interferes with converting fermentable carbohydrates to acids in the mouth. See dental caries.

Folic acid: This nutrient, an element of the Vitamin B complex, is found in leafy, dark green vegetables, legumes, citrus fruits and juices, peanuts, whole grains, and fortified breakfast cereals. Studies show a connection between birth defects of the brain and spinal cord and an inadequate intake of folic acid according to the U.S. Centers for Disease Control and Prevention.

Food and Drug Administration (FDA): The Food and Drug Administration is part of the Public Health Service of the U.S. Department of Health and Human Services. It is the regulatory agency responsible for ensuring the safety and wholesomeness of all foods sold in interstate commerce, except meat, poultry, and eggs (which are under the jurisdiction of the U.S. Department of Agriculture).

Food-borne disease: Food-borne disease, usually gastrointestinal, is caused by organisms or their toxins carried in ingested food. It is also commonly known as food poisoning.

Food guide pyramid: The food guide pyramid is a graphic design used to communicate the recommended daily food choices contained in the Dietary Guidelines for Americans developed by the U.S. Department of Agriculture and the U.S. Department of Health and Human Services.

Food irradiation: Food irradiation is the process of exposing food to sufficient radiant energy (gamma rays, x-rays, and electron beams) to destroy microorganisms and insects. Irradiation is used in food production and processing to promote food safety.

Fortified: A food is fortified with the addition of extra vitamins, minerals, or nutrients.

Fructose: A monosaccharide found naturally in fruits, fructose is also a component of high-fructose corn syrup. Along with glucose it is the fastest form of energy, passing directly into the blood stream unchanged.

Fruit: A fruit is the edible part of a plant. It usually has a sweet pulp.

Fruitarian: A fruitarian eats only foods that can be picked without killing the plants.

Functional foods: These foods provide health benefits beyond basic nutrition. An example includes tomatoes with lycopene, thought to help prevent the incidence of prostate and cervical cancers.

Gastrointestinal (GI): The gastrointestinal tract refers to the digestive tract, including the mouth, esophagus, stomach, and small and large intestines.

Gastronomy: Gastronomy is the study and appreciation of good food and good eating, as well as a culture's culinary customs, style, and lore.

Gelatin: A protein produced from animals in granular form, gelatin is used to gel liquids.

Genome: The total hereditary material of a cell, the genome contains the entire chromosomal set found in each nucleus of a given species.

Gestational diabetes: This temporary condition occurs during pregnancy when the body fails to produce the extra insulin needed. A woman diagnosed with gestational diabetes needs to monitor her food and blood sugar levels. Gestational diabetes typically ends after the pregnancy, but women who have it are at an increased risk of later developing Type 2 diabetes.

Glucose: This simple sugar comes from fruits, honey, and certain vegetables.

Glutamate: This amino acid, necessary for metabolism and brain function, is manufactured by the body. Glutamate is found in virtually every protein food. Foods especially rich in glutamate include tomatoes, mushrooms, Parmesan cheese, milk, and mackerel.

Gluten: Gluten is the protein found in wheat flours.

Glycerol: This colorless, odorless, syrupy liquid is obtained from fats and oils. Chemically an alcohol, it is used to retain moisture and add sweetness to foods.

Grains: Grains are the seeds or fruits of various food plants including wheat, corn, oats, barley, rye, and rice. Grain foods include such foods as bread, cereals, rice, and pasta.

GRAS (Generally Recognized as Safe): The regulatory status of food ingredients not evaluated by the FDA prescribed testing procedure, it includes common food ingredients that were already in use when the 1959 Food Additives Amendment to the Food, Drug and Cosmetic Act was enacted.

Herbicides: These specialty chemicals are used to control weeds on farms and in forests, as well as on golf courses and residential lawns.

Herbivore: A herbivore eats mainly grasses or plants.

Histamine: This is a chemical in the body present in tissue that is released by an allergic reaction. The histamine is released to combat a perceived invader.

Hydrogenation: Hydrogenation is the process of adding hydrogen molecules directly to an unsaturated fatty acid from sources such as vegetable oils to convert it to a semisolid form such as margarine or shortening.

Hyperactivity: *See* Attention Deficit Hyperactivity Disorder.

Hyperglycemia: High blood sugar, a condition characteristic of diabetes, can be treated with insulin or oral medications. Symptoms include unusual thirst, frequent urination, and unusual weight loss.

Hypertension: This disease is characterized by persistently elevated arterial blood pressure. It is the most common public health problem in developed countries. Diet can prevent and manage hypertension.

Hypoglycemia: Low blood sugar symptoms include hunger, sweating, dizziness, confusion, and irritability. It is caused by too much insulin or diabetes medication, or too little food.

Infection: An infection, which occurs when germs enter any part of the body, can often be defeated by the body's natural defense system. Antibiotics are prescribed for the treatment of various bacterial infections.

Insecticide: These specialty chemicals are used to control insects on farms and forests, as well as on residential lawns and golf courses.

Insulin: This hormone is required to convert sugars and starches contained in food into energy needed for everyday life.

Integrated pest management (IPM): IPM is the coordinated use of pest and environmental information along with available pest control methods, including cultural, biological, genetic, and chemical methods, to prevent pest damage to crops.

Intense sweeteners: *See* low-calorie sweetener.

Intolerance: A food intolerance, different from a food allergy, describes a broad range of reactions to foods eaten, from indigestion to headaches, skin blotches, diarrhea, or increased pulse rate. *See also* lactose intolerance.

Julienne: Julienne is a process of slicing foods into long, thin strips. It is usually associated with vegetables but may be applied to cooked meat or fish.

Kosher: These foods are prepared according to a set of Jewish dietary laws. Kosher foods are not necessarily vegan or vegetarian.

Lactation: Lactation is the production of breast milk.

Lacto-ovo-vegetarian: The diet of this type of vegetarian includes milk, cheese, yogurt, and eggs but no meat, fish, or poultry.

Lactose: This sugar, which naturally occurs in milk, is also known as milk sugar. It is the least sweet of all natural sugars and is used in baby formulas and candies.

Lactose intolerance: This intolerance is an inherited inability to digest dairy products properly. Symptoms of lactose intolerance include abdominal cramps, flatulence, and diarrhea. This intolerance can increase with age.

Lacto-vegetarian: The diet of a lacto-vegetarian includes dairy products but no eggs, meat, fish, or poultry.

Lasagna: In this dish, sheets of pasta are layered with sauce, cheese, and meat or vegetables.

Listeria: This food-borne illness is caused by bacteria associated with such foods as raw milk, soft-ripened cheeses, ice cream, raw vegetables, raw and cooked poultry, raw meat, and raw and smoked fish. An acute infection with listeria may result in flu-like symptoms including persistent fever, followed by septicemia, meningitis, encephalitis, and intrauterine or cervical infections in pregnant women. Gastrointestinal symptoms include nausea, vomiting, and diarrhea.

Low-calorie sweetener: These non-nutritive sweeteners are also referred to as intense sweeteners. Low-calorie sweeteners are used to lower the calorie content in foods. Examples of low-calorie sweeteners in use in the United States are saccharin, aspartame, and acesulfame K.

Lycopene: This carotenoid is related to the better-known beta-carotene. Lycopene gives tomatoes and some other fruits and vegetables their distinctive red color. Nutritionally, it functions as an antioxidant. *See* functional foods.

Mad Cow Disease: *See* bovine spongiform encephalopathy.

Magnesium: This mineral helps maintain muscle and nerve function, keeps heart rhythm steady, and metabolizes energy. It is found naturally in green leafy vegetables, seeds, nuts, and some whole grains. More refined foods, such as white bread, have less magnesium than less refined counterparts, such as whole wheat breads.

Malnutrition: Malnutrition occurs when the body receives too few of the essential nutrients and calories it needs as a result a poor diet, defective digestion, or defective assimilation of foods.

Margarine: This fatty solid butter substitute is used in cooking and baking. It consists of a blend of hydrogenated vegetable oils mixed with water, whey, yellow coloring, and vitamins.

Minerals: These nutrients are required by the body in small amounts. Examples include iron, calcium, and potassium.

Modified starches: These food starches from corn, potatoes, or tapioca are chemically modified to provide bulk with fewer calories than regular starch. Examples include polydextrose and maltodextrin.

MSG (monosodium glutamate): The sodium salt of the amino acid glutamic acid and a form of glutamate, found in wheat, beets, and soy bean products, is thought to help accentuate the flavors of foods. Some people suffer allergic reactions to it. *See* glutamate.

Morbid obesity: This is a state of adiposity or overweight, in which body weight is 100% above the ideal and the body mass index is 45 or greater.

National Health and Nutrition Examination Survey (NHANES): This series of surveys includes information from medical histories, physical measurements, biochemical evaluations, physical examinations, and dietary intake of population groups within the United States. The U.S. Department of Health and Human Services conducts the NHANES approximately every five years.

Nationwide Food Consumption Survey (NFCS): This survey is conducted by the USDA roughly every ten years to monitor the nutrient intake of a cross section of the U.S. public.

Neural tube defect: A neural tube defect (NTD) is a malformation of the brain or spinal cord (neurological system) during embryonic development. Infants born with spina bifida, in which the spinal cord is exposed, can grow to adulthood but usually suffer from paralysis or other disabilities. Babies born with anencephaly, in which most or all of the brain is missing, usually die shortly after birth. These NTDs make up about 5 percent of all U.S. birth defects each year. According to the CDC, the use of sufficient folic acid may eliminate the risk of NTDs. *See* folic acid.

Nicotine: This addictive substance is found in cigarettes. Nicotine withdrawal results in physical changes in body temperature, heart rate, digestion, muscle tone, and appetite. Psychological symptoms include irritability, anxiety, sleep disturbances, nervousness, headaches, fatigue, nausea, and cravings for tobacco.

Nitrite: This food additive is used to preserve meats, fish, and poultry. It also adds to the characteristic flavor, color, and texture of such processed meats as hot dogs.

Nutraceuticals: This term is used to describe substances in or parts of a food that may provide medical or health benefits beyond basic nutrition, including disease prevention.

Nutrient: When eaten this part of food helps the body grow, function, and stay healthy. Nutrients include proteins, carbohydrates, minerals, fats, and vitamins.

Nutrition: This process delivers nutrients the body needs. To get proper nutrition, a person must eat or drink enough of the foods that contain the correct amount of key nutrients.

Obesity or overweight: Overweight is defined as between 10% and 20% above an optimal weight for height derived from statistics. Obesity is defined as body weight of 20% above normal or a body mass index of more than 30.

Olestra: Also known as sucrose polyester, this compound is a nondigestible plastic created to replace fat in such high-calorie foods as potato chips, doughnuts, and French fries. Olestra can cause digestive disturbances from abdominal cramping and loose stools to diarrhea.

Olive oil: This distinctly flavored oil is made from olives. The acid content of the oil determines its grade from virgin to pure and cold pressed.

Organic: These agricultural products are grown using cultural, biological, and mechanical methods rather than pesticides and chemicals to control pests, improve soil quality, and enhance processing. Organic techniques include crop rotation, cultivation, mulching, soil enrichment, and the encouragement of predators and microorganisms to keep pests away.

Osteoporosis: Osteoporosis is a skeletal disease, in which bones lose mass and density, pores enlarge, and bones become fragile. The National Osteoporosis Foundation estimates the diseases is responsible for some 1.5 million bone fractures each year in the United States. The disease is four times more common in women than in men owing to differences in bone density. Lack of exercise and low calcium intake during childhood, adolescence, and early adulthood are all risk factors for the disease.

Ovo-vegetarian: This type of vegetarian eats eggs but no dairy products and no meat, fish, or poultry.

Pectins: Pectin is the soluble fiber from fruits, including citrus fruits, apples, prunes, dates, and pears. Pectin holds moisture and thickens, and is used in making jams and jellies.

Pesticide: This broad class of chemicals includes four major types: insecticides used to control insects, herbicides used to control weeds, rodenticides used to control rodents, and fungicides used to control mold, mildew, and fungi.

Phytochemical: These substances found in edible fruits and vegetables may be ingested by humans daily and may reduce the risk of cancer. *See* functional foods.

Placebo: Sometimes referred to as a sugar pill, a placebo is a fake treatment that appears identical to the real treatment. Placebo treatments are used to eliminate bias that arises from the expectation that a treatment could produce a certain effect.

Potassium: This mineral is needed by the body for fluid balance and other essential functions.

Prevalence: This term concerns the number of existing cases of a disease in a defined population at a specified time.

Prion: This rogue protein appears to cause bovine spongiform encephalopathy.

Protein: One of the many complex nitrogen-containing compounds, protein is composed of amino acids essential for the growth and repair of tissue.

Quince: This yellow-skinned fruit tastes like a combination apple and pear. It tastes better cooked than raw.

Quinoa: This grain was originally used by the Incas and is grown in South America.

Radiation therapy: This treatment uses high-energy x-rays designed to kill or damage cancer cells; it can be external or internal.

Rapid assays: These diagnostic tests use emerging technology to identify and remove impurities from foods before they reach the consumer. There are two major types of rapid assays. Antibody-based assays link a characteristic on a pathogen's surface (the antigen) to a substance known as an antibody. When this connection is made, the test registers success. Similarly, nucleic acid–based assays use the unique genetic materials of the cells to detect a pathogen.

Recombinant DNA (rDNA): Recombinant DNA is the DNA formed by combining segments of DNA from different organisms.

Registered dietitian: This professional plans diet programs based on proper nutrition.

Rennet: This extract from the stomach of lambs and calves is used in cheese making to coagulate milk. There are also vegetable rennets.

RNA: Also known as ribonucleic acid, RNA is a molecule similar to DNA in that it functions primarily to decode the instructions carried by genes for protein synthesis.

Saccharin: Saccharin is the oldest of the non-nutritive sweeteners. It is produced from purified, manufactured methyl anthranilate, a substance occurring naturally in grapes. Three hundred times sweeter than sucrose, it is heat stable and does not promote dental caries. Saccharin has a long shelf life, but a bitter aftertaste. It is not metabolized in the human digestive system, is excreted rapidly in the urine, and does not accumulate in the body.

SAD (Standard American Diet): This meat-based diet is centered on a main course of meat, fish, or poultry with side dishes of vegetables and starches.

Salmonellosis: This common type of food poisoning is often called salmonella because it results from infection by certain types of *Salmonella* bacteria. In the environment, *Salmonella* can be found in water, soil, insects, factory and kitchen surfaces, animal fecal matter, and raw meats, poultry (including eggs), and seafood. Symptoms include nausea, vomiting, diarrhea, abdominal cramps, headache, and fever.

Selenium: This trace mineral is part of the antioxidant enzymes. It also plays a role in immune system and thyroid gland function. The amount of selenium in the soil determines the amount of selenium that is in the crops and vegetables that grow in that soil, making plant foods a major source of dietary selenium. Animals that eat selenium-rich plants and grains also can provide dietary selenium.

Sodium: This mineral is required by the body to keep body fluids in balance. Too much sodium can cause a person to retain water.

Spina bifida: In this birth defect, the infant is born with the spinal cord exposed. These children can grow to adulthood although they often suffer from paralysis and other disabilities. *See* neural tube defect.

Sucralose: Sucralose is the only low-calorie sweetener that is made from sugar. Approximately 600 times sweeter than sugar, it does not contain any calories. Currently, sucralose is approved in more than 25 countries around the world for use in food and beverages. In 1998 the FDA approved its use in a variety of processed foods and as a tabletop sweetener in the United States.

Sucrose: This type of sugar is a diglyceride composed of glucose and fructose. *See* carbohydrate.

Sugar: There is a variety of sugars including sucrose, raw sugar, turbinado sugar, brown sugar, honey, and corn syrup. There is no significant difference in the nutritional content or energy each provides, and there is no advantage of one nutritionally over another.

Tahini: Tahini is a paste made from ground sesame seeds. It is used primarily in Middle Eastern cooking.

Target heart rate: This is a guide for the heart rate during exercise for maximum aerobic benefit. One ballpark formula is 220 − age = maximum heart rate. The target heart rate is about 80% of that number.

Tofu: A bean curd made by processing soybeans, tofu is high in protein. It comes in various textures and degrees of firmness.

Trans fats: These occur naturally in beef, butter, milk, and lamb fats and in commercially prepared, partially hydrogenated margarines, and solid cooking fats. The main sources of trans fats in the American diet today are margarine, shortening, commercial frying fats, and high-fat baked goods. Trans fats, like saturated fats, may raise blood LDL cholesterol levels and at high consumption, levels may also reduce the HDL or good cholesterol levels. *See* cholesterol (blood types).

Ugli: This citrus fruit hybrid is a grapefruit and tangerine cross. This fruit is native to Jamaica and is an excellent source of Vitamin C.

Umami: In addition to the four main taste components (sweet, sour, salty and bitter), there is the additional taste characteristic called umami or savory. One of the food components responsible for the umami flavor in foods is glutamate, an amino acid. *See* glutamate; MSG.

U.S. Department of Agriculture (USDA): The U.S. Department of Agriculture works to ensure a safe, affordable, nutritious, and accessible food supply for the American population by supporting production of agricultural products; caring for agricultural, forest, and range lands; supporting sound development of our rural communities; providing economic opportunities for farm and rural residents; expanding global markets for agricultural and forest products and services; and working to reduce hunger in America and throughout the world.

Vanilla: This plant native to Mexico is now common in other parts of the world. The plant pod is used to make liquid or powdered extracts for seasoning baked goods and other foods.

Variable: A variable is any characteristic that may vary in study subjects, including gender, age, body weight, diet, behavior, and attitude.

Vegan: This strict vegetarian eats a diet based on vegetables, fruits, grains, legumes, nuts, and seeds and excludes all animal-derived foods, even honey. Many vegans are also philosophically opposed to animal products such as wool, leather, and silk.

Vegetarian: A vegetarian eats a diet that omits meat, fish, and poultry and in some cases also excludes dairy foods and eggs. *See* lacto-ovo-vegetarian.

Veggie: Veggie is a nickname for a vegetarian. It is also used for "vegetable" or a non-meat dish, such as "veggie lasagna."

Vitamins: These key nutrients are needed by the body daily in small amounts to grow and stay strong. Vitamins are characterized as water soluble or fat soluble.

Water: Second to oxygen as essential for life, a person can survive only a few days without water. In addition, water plays a vital role in all bodily processes. It supplies the medium in which various chemical changes of the body occur, aiding in digestion, absorption, circulation, and lubrication of body joints.

Whole wheat: Flour and bread products made from the entire grain of wheat, including the bran.

WIC, or Special Supplemental Nutrition Program for Women, Infants, and Children: Established in 1972, the WIC program provides food and nutrition education to improve the nutritional status of medically high-risk pregnant and lactating women and children up to 5 years of age from low-income families. The U.S. Department of Agriculture administers the program.

Xanthan gum: Produced from the fermentation of corn sugar, xanthan gum is most commonly used as a stabilizer, emulsifier, and thickener in foods such as yogurt, sour cream, and salad dressings.

Xenobiotics: These synthetic chemicals are believed to be resistant to environmental degradation. A branch of biotechnology called bioremediation is seeking to develop biological methods to degrade such compounds.

Yeast: Yeast is a fungus used in the production of bread and beer. When mixed with sugar, yeast produces carbon dioxide and alcohol, a process called fermentation.

Zinc: An essential mineral, zinc is beneficial in triggering the release of many essential enzymes and is a component of insulin. Good sources include whole grains, pumpkin seeds, liver, eggs, meats, fish, poultry, soybeans, and brewer's yeast.

Zingerone: This compound, which is available naturally in ginger, is used as a synthetic flavoring in such foods as candy, bakery products, and chewing gum.

APPENDIX B
The Smart Snacker's Guide to Substitutions

Instead of . . .	Try . . .	To Save . . .	
Crunchies		*Calories*	*Fat*
			(gm)
Potato chips, regular, 17–22 (1 oz)	Pretzels, low salt, 6 (1 oz)	60	11
Potato chips, light, 17–20 (1 oz)	Raw vegetables, ½ cup	130	12
	Potato chips, baked, 28–30 (1 oz)	50	7
Popcorn, microwave reg., 2 cups	Popcorn, air popped, 2 cups	100	7
	Popcorn, mirowave light, 2 cups	80	5
Doritos tortilla chips, 15–16 (1 oz)	Tortilla chips, baked, 22–26 (1 oz)	30	6
Nachos made from tortilla chips with melted cheese, 8 pieces	Baked tortilla wedges with salsa, 8 pieces	40	7
Cheese crackers with peanut butter, 3 "sandwiches" (0.7 oz)	Ry Krisp crackers, 2 triple crackers (½ oz)	55	6
Ritz Bits crackers, 22 (½ oz)	Breadsticks, fat free, 2 (½ oz)	25	4
Wheat Thins crackers, 8 (½ oz)	Premium fat-free crackers, 5 (½ oz)	20	3
Sweets			
Snickers candy, 2-oz bar	Cocoa, from mix, regular, 6-oz cup	170	13
Oreo cookies, 3 (1 ½ oz)	Fig or apple bar, nonfat, 2 (1 ½ oz)	30	4

Chocolate chip cookies, 2 (1 oz)	oatmeal raisin cookie fat free, 1 large	20	4
Chips Ahoy cookies with chocolate chunks, 2 (1 oz)	Ginger Snaps, 3 (½ oz)	140	9
Granola bar, 1 (0.8–1 oz)	Frosted bite-size shredded wheat squares, ½ cup (1 oz)	30	6
Fun fruit, fruit roll-ups, and wrinkles, 1 pouch or 2 rolls	Fresh fruit, 1 piece, or	40	1
	dried fruit (raisins, apricots), ¼ cup	20	1
Pop-tarts, 1 pastry	Bagel, half with 2 tsp jelly	130	6
Double raspberry mocha	"Skinny" latte sprinkled with cinnamon (espresso and skim milk)	225	7

Frozen Snacks

Ice cream, regular, 1 cup	Frozen yogurt, nonfat, or low-fat ice cream, 1 cup	90	11
Ice cream, premium, 1 cup	Fruit sorbet, 1 cup	150	24
	Fudgesicle, 1 bar (1.75 oz)	280	24

Smooth Snacks

Yogurt, regular with fruit, 1 cup	Yogurt, low fat with fruit preserves	20	3
	Yogurt, plain nonfat, with ½ cup fresh strawberries, 1 cup	100	5
Dip, regular commercial, 2 Tbsp	Dip, from plain low-fat or nonfat yogurt with dab of lite mayonnaise	25	2
	Dip from nonfat cottage cheese, 2 Tbsp	30	5

Mini-meals

Pizza, pepperoni, 1 slice (5.25–5.5 oz)	English muffin or bagel pizza, low-fat cheese, 1 piece (4.25 oz)	25	4
Pizza, French bread, pepperoni, 1 piece (5.25–5.5 oz)	English muffin (see above)	245	15
Sandwich with 3 oz bologna, 1 oz regular cheese, 2 tsp regular mayo	Sandwich with 1 oz turkey, 1 oz lowfat cheese, 1 tsp mustard, lettuce, and tomato	320	36
Fast-food deluxe burger	Fast-food grilled chicken sandwich, plain	260	26
Hamburger (80% lean), 4 oz	Veggie burger	240	20
Fast-food French fries, large	Baked potato with 1 Tbsp low-fat sour cream with fresh chives	260	28
Mashed potatoes, 1 cup, with gravy	Baked potato (see above)	30	10
Regular hot dog (beef and pork)	Fat-free beef frank	109	13

Beverages

Soda, regular, 8 oz	Club soda or seltzer, with lime, 8 oz	120	0

Blended juice drinks, regular, 8 oz	Club soda with 2 oz juice	140	0
Wine cooler, 8 oz	Raspberry or peach iced tea, with 1 tsp sugar, lemon	140	0
Beer, 12 oz	Tomato or V-8 juice, 8 oz	100	0
2% milk, 8 oz	Nonfat (skim) milk, 8 oz	35	5

Source: Sneak Health Into Your Snacks, American Institute for Cancer Research, December 1998, pp. 10–15.

APPENDIX C
Recommended Dietary Intakes
for Young People

1989 Recommended Dietary Allowances (RDA)

	Males			Females		
	11–14	*15–18*	*19–24*	*11–14*	*15–18*	*19–24*
Energy (calories)	2500	3000	2900	2200	2200	2200
Protein (g)	45	59	58	46	44	46
Vitamin A (mcg)	1000	1000	1000	800	800	800
Vitamin E (mg)	10	10	10	8	8	8
Vitamin K (mcg)	45	65	70	45	55	60
Vitamin C (mg)	50	60	60	50	60	60
Thiamin (mg)	1.3	1.5	1.5	1.1	1.1	1.1
Riboflavin (mg)	1.5	1.8	1.7	1.3	1.3	1.3
Niacin (mg)	17	20	19	15	15	15
Vitamin B6 (mg)	1.7	2.0	2.0	1.4	1.5	1.6
Folate (mcg)	150	200	200	150	180	180
Vitamin B12 (mcg)	2.0	2.0	2.0	2.0	2.0	2.0
Iron (mg)	12	12	10	15	15	15
Zinc (mg)	15	15	15	12	12	12
Iodine (mcg)	150	150	150	150	150	150
Selenium (mcg)	40	50	70	45	50	55

In April 2000, a panel of the National Academy of Sciences recommended increasing the RDA of Vitamin E to 15 milligrams of alpha-tocopherol, increasing the Vitamin C RDA to 75 milligrams per day, and increasing the selenium recommendation to 55 micrograms per day.

1997 Dietary Reference Intakes for adolescents and young adults for Vitamin D are 5 micrograms per day. Calcium recommendations are 1,300 milligrams daily until age 19, when it drops to 1,000. Phosphorous recommendations are 1,250 milligrams until age 18, then 700. Magnesium requirements are slightly higher for men and pregnant women. Males aged 14 to 18 should have 410 milligrams; females in that age should have 360 milligrams. The requirement for young adult males decreases to 400, and for young females, 310.

APPENDIX D
Sample Five-Day Menu for 1,600, 2,200, and 2,800 Calories with Recipes

1,600-CALORIE MENUS

BREAKFAST

Day 1
Orange juice	3/4 c
Oatmeal	1/2 c
White toast	1 slice
Margarine	1 tsp
Jelly	1 tsp
Skim milk	1/2 c

Day 2
Grapefruit juice	3/4 c
*Breakfast pita	1 sandwich
Skim milk	1 c

Day 3
Grapefruit	1/2
Ready-to-eat cereal flakes	1 oz
Toasted English muffin with raisins	1/2
Jelly	1 tsp
Skim milk	1/2 c

Day 4
Fresh sliced strawberries	1/2 c
Whole-grain cereal flakes	1 oz
Toasted plain bagel	1/2
Cream cheese	1/2 Tbsp
2% fat milk	1 c

Day 5
Cantaloupe	1/4 melon
*Whole-wheat pancakes	2
*Blueberry sauce	1/4 c
Skim milk	1c

LUNCH

Day 1
*Split pea soup	1 c
*Quick tuna and sprouts sandwich	1
Mixed green salad	1 c
Reduced-calorie Italian dressing	1 Tbsp
*Chocolate mint pie 1 serving	

Day 2
*Turkey pasta salad	1–1/4 c
Tomato wedges on lettuce leaf	
	1 serving
Hard roll	1
Margarine	1 tsp
Skim milk	1 c

Day 3
*Taco salad greens	1 c
Chili	3/4 c
Sherbet	1/2 c

Day 4
Broiled chicken fillet sandwich	1
Mayonnaise	1 pkt
*Confetti coleslaw	1/2 c
2% fat milk	1 c

Day 5
*Chili-stuffed baked potato	1
*Spinach-orange salad	1 c
Wheat crackers	6

DINNER

Day 1
*Savory sirloin	3 oz
*Corn and zucchini combo	1/2 c
Tomato and lettuce salad	1 serv
Reduced-calorie French dressing	1 Tbsp
Whole-wheat roll	1
Margarine	1 tsp
*Yogurt-strawberry parfait	1 c

Day 2
*Creole fish fillet	3 oz
Small new potatoes with skin	2
Cooked green peas	1/2 c
with margarine	1 tsp
*Whole-wheat cornmeal muffin	1
Margarine	1 tsp
*Peach crisp	1/2 c

Day 3
*Pork and vegetable stir-fry	1 c
Rice	3/4 c
Cooked broccoli	1/2 c
White roll	1
Minted pineapple chunks	1/2 c

Day 4
*Lentil stroganoff mixture	1–1/2 c
Noodles	3/4 c
Cooked whole green beans	1/2 c
Tomato and cucumber salad	1 serv
Reduced-calorie vinaigrette dressing	1 Tbsp
Honeydew	1/8 melon

Day 5
*Apricot-glazed chicken	3 oz
*Rice-pasta pilaf	3/4 c
Tossed salad	1 c
Reduced-calorie Italian dressing	1 Tbsp
Hard roll	1
Vanilla ice milk	1/2 c

SNACKS

Day 1
Graham crackers	3 squares
Skim milk	1 c

Day 2
Bagel	1 medium
Margarine	1 tsp
Jelly	1 tsp

Day 3
Wheat crackers	6
Skim milk	1 c

Day 4
Roast beef sandwich	1/2

Day 5
Fig bar	1
Skim milk	3/4 c

2,200-CALORIE MENUS

BREAKFAST		
Day 1		
Orange juice	3/4 c	
Oatmeal	1/2 c	
White toast	2 slices	
Margarine	2 tsp	
Jelly	1 tsp	
2% fat milk	1/2 c	
Day 2		
Grapefruit juice	3/4 c	
*Breakfast pita	1 sandwich	
2% fat milk	1 c	
Day 3		
Grapefruit	1/2	
Banana	1 medium	
Ready-to-eat cereal flakes	1 oz	
Toasted English muffin with raisins	1	
Margarine	2 tsp	
Skim milk	1/2 c	
Day 4		
Fresh sliced strawberries	1/2 c	
Whole-grain cereal flakes	1 oz	
Toasted plain bagel	1 medium	
Cream cheese	1 Tbsp	
2% fat milk	1 c	
Day 5		
Cantaloupe	1/4 melon	
Turkey patty	1-1/2 oz	
*Whole-wheat pancakes	2	
*Blueberry sauce	1/4 c	
Margarine	1 tsp	
Skim milk	1 c	

LUNCH		
Day 1		
*Split pea soup	1 c	
*Quick tuna and sprouts sandwich	1	
Mixed green salad	1 c	
Reduced-calorie Italian dressing	1 Tbsp	
*Chocolate mint pie	1 serving	
Day 2		
*Turkey pasta salad	1-1/4 c	
Tomato wedges on lettuce leaf	1 serv	
Hard rolls	2	
Margarine	2 tsp	
Oatmeal cookies	4	
2% fat milk	1 c	
Day 3		
*Taco salad greens	1 c	
Chili	3/4 c	
Gingersnaps	2	
Day 4		
Broiled chicken fillet sandwich	1	
Mayonnaise	1 pkt	
*Confetti coleslaw	1/2 c	
Fresh orange	1	
2% fat milk	1 c	
Day 5		
*Chili-stuffed baked potato	1	
Low-fat low-sodium cheddar cheese	3 Tbsp	
*Spinach-orange salad	1 c	
Wheat crackers	6	
Skim milk	1 c	

DINNER

Day 1
*Savory sirloin	3 oz
*Corn and zucchini combo	3/4 c
Tomato and lettuce salad	1 serv
French dressing	1 Tbsp
Whole-wheat rolls	2
Margarine	1 tsp
*Yogurt-strawberry parfait	1 c

Day 2
*Creole fish fillet	4 oz
Small new potatoes with skin	2
Cooked green peas	1/2 c
with margarine	1 tsp
Whole-wheat cornmeal muffins	2
Margarine	2 tsp
*Peach crisp	1/2 c

Day 3
*Pork and vegetable stir-fry mixture	1 c
Rice	3/4 c
Cooked broccoli	1/2 c
White rolls	2
Margarine	2 tsp
Minted pineapple chunks	1/2 c

Day 4
*Lentil stroganoff mixture	1–1/2 c
Noodles	3/4 c
Cooked whole green beans	1/2 c
with margarine	1 tsp
Tomato and cucumber salad	1 serv
Reduced-calorie vinaigrette dressing	1 Tbsp
Pumpernickel roll	1
Margarine	1 tsp
Honeydew	1/8 melon

Day 5
*Apricot-glazed chicken	3 oz
*Rice-pasta pilaf	3/4 c
Tossed salad	1 c
Reduced-calorie Italian dressing	1 Tbsp
Hard rolls	2
Margarine	2 tsp
Vanilla ice milk	1/2 c

SNACKS

Day 1
Graham crackers	6 squares
2% fat milk	1 c
Peanut butter	2 Tbsp
Fresh peach	1
Carrot sticks	7–8 medium

Day 2
Bagel	1 medium
Margarine	2 tsp
Fresh pear	1

Day 3
Wheat crackers	6
Cheddar cheese	1–1/2 oz
Turkey sandwich	1/2
No-salt-added tomato juice	3/4 c

Day 4
No-salt-added vegetable juice	3/4 c
Roast beef sandwich	1
2% fat milk	1 c

Day 5
Soft pretzel	1 large
Fresh apple	1/2

2,800-CALORIE MENUS

BREAKFAST

Day 1

Orange juice	3/4 c
Oatmeal	1/2 c
White toast	2 slices
Margarine	2 tsp
Jelly	2 tsp
2% fat milk	1/2 c

Day 2

Grapefruit juice	3/4 c
*Breakfast pita	1 sandwich
Bran muffin	1 large
Margarine	1 tsp
2% fat milk	1 c

Day 3

Grapefruit	1/2
Banana	1 medium
Ready-to-eat cereal flakes	1 oz
Toasted English muffin with raisins	1
Margarine	2 tsp
Skim milk	1 c

Day 4

Fresh sliced strawberries	1/2 c
Hard-cooked egg	1
Whole-grain cereal flakes	1 oz
Toasted plain bagel	1 medium
Cream cheese	2 Tbsp
2% fat milk	1 c

Day 5

Cantaloupe	1/4 melon
*Turkey patty	1/2 oz
*Whole-wheat pancakes	3
*Blueberry sauce	6 Tbsp
Margarine	2 tsp
2% fat milk	1 c

LUNCH

Day 1

*Split pea soup	1 c
*Quick tuna and sprouts sandwich	1
Mixed green salad	1 c
Italian dressing	1 Tbsp
*Chocolate mint pie	1 serving
2% fat milk	1 c

Day 2

*Turkey pasta salad	1–1/4 c
Tomato wedges on lettuce leaf	1 serv
Hard rolls	2
Margarine	2 tsp
Tangerine	1
Oatmeal cookies	6
2% fat milk	1 c

Day 3

*Taco salad greens	1 c
Chili	3/4 c
Sherbet	1/2 c
Gingersnaps	3
Skim milk	1 c

Day 4

Broiled chicken fillet sandwich	1
Mayonnaise	1 pkt
*Confetti coleslaw	1/2 c
Fresh orange	1
*Lemon pound cake	1 slice
2% fat milk	1 c

Day 5

*Chili-stuffed baked potato	1
Low-fat low-sodium cheddar cheese	3 Tbsp
*Spinach-orange salad	1 c
Fresh grapes	12
Wheat crackers	6
Fig bars	2
2% fat milk	1 c

DINNER

Day 1

*Savory sirloin	4 oz
*Corn and zucchini combo	1 c
Tomato and lettuce salad	1 serv
Reduced-calorie French dressing	1 Tbsp
Whole-wheat rolls	2
Margarine	1 tsp
*Yogurt-strawberry parfait	1 c

Day 2

*Creole fish fillets	4 oz
Small new potatoes with skin	2
Cooked green peas	3/4 c
with margarine	1 tsp
*Whole-wheat cornmeal muffins	2
Margarine	2 tsp
*Peach crisp	1/2 c

Day 3

*Pork and vegetable stir-fry mixture	1 c
Rice	3/4 c
Cooked broccoli	1 c
White rolls	2
Margarine	2 tsp
Minted pineapple chunks	1/2 c

Day 4

*Lentil Stroganoff mixture	1–1/2 c
Noodles	3/4 c
Cooked whole green beans	1 c
with margarine	1 tsp
Tomato and cucumber salad	1 serv
Reduced-calorie vinaigrette dressing	1 Tbsp
Pumpernickel rolls	2
Margarine	2 tsp
Honeydew	1/4 melon

Day 5

*Apricot-glazed chicken	3 oz
*Rice-pasta pilaf	3/4 c
Steamed zucchini	1/2 c
Tossed salad	1 c
Italian dressing	1 Tbsp
Hard rolls	2
Margarine	2 tsp
Vanilla ice milk	1/2 c

SNACKS

Day 1

Graham crackers	6 squares
Peanut butter-banana sandwich	1
Fresh peach	1
Nonfat fruit-flavored yogurt	8 oz
Carrot sticks	7–8 medium

Day 2

Bagel	1 medium
Margarine	2 tsp
Jelly	2 tsp
Fresh pear	1
Low-fat fruit-flavored yogurt	1/2 c
Unsalted roasted peanuts	2–1/2 Tbsp
	(1/2 oz)

Day 3

Wheat crackers	6
Orange juice	3/4 c
Cheddar cheese	1–1/2 oz
Turkey sandwich	1
Raw vegetables	6 pcs
Spinach dip	2 Tbsp

Day 4

No-salt-added vegetable juice	3/4 c
Roast beef sandwich	1
2% fat milk	1 c
Lemonade	1 c

Day 5

Fresh apple	1/2
Soft pretzel	1 large
Lemonade	1 c
2% fat milk	1 c

The following recipes appear in same order as five days' menus on previous pages.

BREAKFAST MENU RECIPES

Breakfast Pita

4 servings, 1 pita each

PER SERVING:

Calories: 170

Total fat: 6 grams

Saturated fat: 2 grams

Cholesterol: 108 milligrams

Sodium: 400 milligrams

Margarine, 2 teaspoons

Mushroom pieces, drained 4-ounce can

Onion, chopped, ¼ cup

Green pepper, chopped, ¼ cup

Eggs, 2 large

Egg whites, 2 large

Low-fat cottage cheese, ¼ cup

Pepper, ⅛ teaspoon

Low-fat cheddar cheese, shredded, ¼ cup

Whole-wheat pita rounds, 4 inch, 4

1. Melt margarine in nonstick frying pan. Add mushrooms, onion, and green pepper; cook until onion and green pepper are tender, stirring often.
2. Combine eggs, egg whites, cottage cheese, and pepper; mix well. Pour over mushroom mixture.
3. Cook over medium heat, stirring frequently, until eggs are firm but still moist. Stir in cheddar cheese.
4. Using a sharp knife, split edge of pita open about 3 inches to make a pocket. Spoon ¼ of mixture, about ½ cup, into each pita. Serve immediately.

EACH SERVING PROVIDES:

Meat alternate equal to ½ ounce from meat group

1 serving from bread group

¼ serving from vegetable group

Turkey Patties

4 servings, 1 patty each

PER SERVING:

Calories: 125

Total fat: 6 grams

Saturated fat: 2 grams

Cholesterol: 46 milligrams

Sodium: 200 milligrams

Ground turkey, 8 ounces (½ pound)

Ground sage, ½ to ¾ teaspoon

Marjoram leaves, ¼ teaspoon

Pepper, ¼ teaspoon

Salt, ⅛ teaspoon

Vegetable oil, ½ teaspoon

1. Mix all ingredients except oil thoroughly.

2. Shape into 4 patties about 3 inches in diameter.

3. Heat oil in nonstick frying pan.

4. Cook patties in hot frying pan about 4 minutes turning once to brown other side.

EACH SERVING PROVIDES:

1-½ ounces from meat group

Whole-Wheat Pancakes

4 servings, 2 4-inch pancakes each

PER SERVING:

Calories: 170

Total fat: 4 grams

Saturated fat: 1 gram

Cholesterol: 54 milligrams

Sodium: 230 milligrams

Whole-wheat flour, 1 cup

Brown sugar, packed, 2 teaspoons

Baking powder, 1-½ teaspoons

Salt, ⅛ teaspoon

Egg, 1

Skim milk, 1 cup

Vegetable oil, 2 teaspoons

1. Preheat griddle.

2. Mix dry ingredients.

3. Beat egg, milk, and oil together.

4. Add milk mixture to dry ingredients; stir until dry ingredients are barely moistened. Batter will be lumpy.

5. For each pancake, pour ¼ cup of batter onto hot griddle.

6. Cook until surface is covered with bubbles; turn, cook other side until lightly browned.

EACH SERVING PROVIDES:

2 servings from bread group

Blueberry Sauce

4 servings, ¼ cup each

PER SERVING:

Calories: 35

Total fat: Trace

Saturated fat: Trace

Cholesterol: 0

Sodium: 1 milligram

Cornstarch, 1 tablespoon

Sugar, 1 tablespoon

Water, ⅔ cup

Frozen blueberries, unsweetened, ⅔ cup

Lemon juice, 2 teaspoons

1. Mix cornstarch and sugar in a small saucepan.

2. Add water and stir until smooth. Add blueberries.

3. Bring to boil over medium heat, stirring constantly. Cook until thickened.

4. Remove from heat. Stir in lemon juice.

5. Serve warm over whole-wheat pancakes.

EACH SERVING PROVIDES:

⅓ serving from fruit group

LUNCH MENU RECIPES

Split Pea Soup

6 servings, 1 cup each

PER SERVING:

Calories: 220

Total fat: 2 grams

Saturated fat: 1 gram

Cholesterol: 5 milligrams

Sodium: 190 milligrams

Boneless smoked pork chop, 1 small (about 3 ounces)

Dry green split peas, 1-½ cups

Onion, chopped, ½ cup

Carrot, shredded, ½ cup

Pepper, ⅛ teaspoon

Water, 2-½ cups

Low-sodium chicken broth, 3-½ cups

1. Cut fat from smoked pork chop; discard. Chop or dice meat.
2. Mix ingredients in a large saucepan. Bring to a boil, cover, reduce heat, and simmer 1-½ hours. Stir occasionally.

EACH SERVING PROVIDES:

Meat alternate equal to 1-¼ ounces from meat group

½ serving from vegetable group

Quick Tuna and Sprouts Sandwich

4 servings, 1 sandwich each

PER SERVING:

Calories: 200

Total fat: 4 grams

Saturated fat: 1 gram

Cholesterol: 10 milligrams

Sodium: 320 milligrams

Mayonnaise-type salad dressing, 2 tablespoons

Celery seed, ¼ teaspoon

Onion powder, ¼ teaspoon

No-salt-added water-pack tuna, 1 can undrained (6-½ ounces)

Alfalfa sprouts, ½ cup

Whole-wheat hamburger rolls, 4

1. Mix salad dressing and seasonings in a bowl. Add tuna and sprouts; mix well.

2. Use ¼ of filling per sandwich.

EACH SERVING PROVIDES:

1-½ ounces from meat group

2 servings from bread group

Chocolate Mint Pie

8-inch pie, 8 servings

PER SERVING:

Calories: 175

Total fat: 6 grams

Saturated fat: 1 gram

Cholesterol: 1 milligram

Sodium: 175 milligrams

Graham Cracker Crust

Graham crackers, crushed, 1-¼ cups

Margarine, softened, 3 tablespoons

Filling

Unflavored gelatin, 1 envelope (about 1 tablespoon)

Cold water, ¼ cup

Sugar, ½ cup

Cocoa, ¼ cup

Cornstarch, 2 tablespoons

Skim milk, 2 cups

Peppermint extract, 4 drops

To Make Crust

1. Mix graham cracker crumbs and margarine thoroughly. Reserve ¼ cup of crumb mixture for top of pie.

2. Press remaining crumb mixture into 8-inch pie pan so the bottom and sides are completely covered.

To Make Filling

1. Soften gelatin in cold water.

2. Mix sugar, cocoa, and cornstarch in saucepan. Add milk. Cook, stirring constantly, until thickened.

3. Stir softened gelatin into hot mixture and cool 20 minutes, stirring occasionally. Stir in extract. Cool an additional 20 minutes.

4. Pour filling into crust.

5. Sprinkle reserved crumb mixture over top of filling.

6. Chill until set. Keep in refrigerator until served.

EACH SERVING PROVIDES:

¼ serving from milk group

½ serving from bread group

Turkey Pasta Salad

4 servings, 1-¼ cups each

PER SERVING:

Calories: 265

Total fat: 6 grams

Saturated fat: 1 gram

Cholesterol: 47 milligrams

Sodium: 225 milligrams

Elbow macaroni, uncooked, 1 cup

Dried chives, 1-½ teaspoons

Salad dressing, mayonnaise-type, light, ¼ cup

Cooked turkey, diced, 1-⅔ cups

Seedless red grapes, halved, 1 cup

Celery, thinly sliced, ⅓ cup

Salad greens, 4 leaves

1. Cook macaroni according to package directions. Drain.

2. Stir chives into salad dressing.

3. Mix macaroni, turkey, grapes, and celery together lightly.

4. Stir in salad dressing.

5. Chill well. Serve on salad greens.

EACH SERVING PROVIDES:

2 ounces from meat group

1 serving from bread group

½ serving from fruit group

Taco Salad

4 servings, 1 cup greens, ¾ cup chili each

PER SERVING:

Calories: 455

Total fat: 19 grams

Saturated fat: 6 grams

Cholesterol: 43 milligrams

Sodium: 545 milligrams

Lean ground beef, ½ pound

Kidney beans, undrained, 15-½-ounce can

No-salt-added tomato puree, 1 cup

Chili powder, 1-½ tablespoons

Instant minced onion, 1 tablespoon

Iceberg lettuce, broken, 2 cups

Spinach leaves, broken, 2 cups

Low-fat low-sodium cheddar cheese, shredded ¾ cup (3 ounces)

Unsalted tortilla chips, 40 chips (about 2-½ ounces)

1. Cook beef in hot frying pan until lightly browned. Drain off fat.
2. Add beans, tomato puree, chili powder, and onion.
3. Bring to a boil, reduce heat, cover, and simmer 10 minutes. Stir as needed.
4. Place ½ cup of lettuce and ½ cup of spinach in a salad dish. Top with ¾ cup chili and ¼ of the cheese. Place 10 chips around each salad.

EACH SERVING PROVIDES:

Meat and meat alternate equal to 2-½ ounces from meat group

¾ serving from bread group

½ serving from milk group

1-½ servings from vegetable group

Confetti Coleslaw

4 servings, about ½ cup each

PER SERVING:

Calories: 35

Total fat: Trace

Saturated fat: Trace

Cholesterol: 0

Sodium: 10 milligrams

Green cabbage, finely chopped, 2 cups

Green pepper, finely chopped, ¼ cup

Red pepper, finely chopped, ¼ cup

Onion, finely chopped, 1 tablespoon

Vinegar, 2 tablespoons

Water, 1 tablespoon

Sugar, 1-½ tablespoons

Celery seed, ⅛ teaspoon

Pepper, ⅛ teaspoon

1. Mix vegetables together lightly.

2. Mix remaining ingredients together for dressing.

3. Stir dressing into vegetables. Chill well.

NOTE: *This salad keeps well in the refrigerator for one or two days. Green peppers may be used in place of red peppers. Add color by adding a small amount of shredded carrot.*

EACH SERVING PROVIDES:

1 serving from vegetable group

Lemon Pound Cake

18 servings, 1 slice, about ½-inch thick

PER SLICE:

Calories: 195

Total fat: 8 grams

Saturated fat: 2 grams

Cholesterol: 48 milligrams

Sodium: 120 milligrams

Margarine, softened, ⅔ cup

Sugar, 1-⅓ cups

Eggs, 4

Vanilla, 1 teaspoon

Flour, 2 cups

Baking powder, ¼ teaspoon

Baking soda, ¼ teaspoon

Low-fat lemon yogurt, ⅔ cup

Lemon juice, 3 tablespoons

Lemon peel, grated, 1 teaspoon

1. Preheat oven to 325° F. Grease and flour 9" × 5" loaf pan.
2. Cream margarine in large mixing bowl. Gradually add sugar; beat until light and fluffy.
3. Add eggs one at a time, beating well after each addition. Add vanilla.
4. Mix dry ingredients.
5. Mix yogurt, lemon juice, and lemon peel.
6. Add dry ingredients and lemon mixture alternately to egg mixture, mixing until dry ingredients are just moistened.
7. Pour batter into pan.
8. Bake 1-¼ hours until lightly browned.
9. Cool 10 minutes in pan on a rack before removing from pan.

EACH SERVING PROVIDES:

¾ serving from bread group

Chili-Stuffed Baked Potato

Variation for Taco Salad

4 servings, 1 potato each

PER SERVING:

Calories: 395

Total fat: 9 grams

Saturated fat: 3 grams

Cholesterol: 38 milligrams

Sodium: 460 milligrams

1. Omit lettuce, spinach, cheese, and tortilla chips from salad recipe. Prepare chili mixture as directed in the Taco Salad recipe.
2. Wash and bake 4 medium baking potatoes (in oven or microwave). Cut a slit in top of each potato. Top potatoes with chili, using about ¾ cup for each. Shredded cheddar cheese can be added as a garnish.

EACH SERVING PROVIDES:

Meat and meat alternate equal to 2-½ ounces from meat group

1-½ servings from vegetable group

Spinach-Orange Salad

4 servings, about 1 cup each

PER SERVING:

Calories: 110

Total fat: 7 grams

Saturated fat: 1 gram

Cholesterol: 0

Sodium: 25 milligrams

Spinach, torn into pieces, 4 cups

Orange, sectioned, 2 medium

Fresh mushrooms, sliced, ⅔ cup

Red onion, sliced, ½ cup

Vegetable oil, 2 tablespoons

Vinegar, 2 tablespoons

Orange juice (from sectioning of orange), ¼ cup

Ground ginger, ½ teaspoon

Pepper, ¼ teaspoon

1. Place spinach in bowl. Add orange sections, mushrooms, and onion. Toss lightly to mix.
2. Mix oil, vinegar, orange juice, ginger, and pepper well. Pour over spinach mixture. Toss to mix.
3. Chill.

EACH SERVING PROVIDES:

1-½ servings from vegetable group

½ serving from fruit group

DINNER MENU RECIPES

Savory Sirloin

4 servings, about 3 ounces meat each

PER SERVING:

Calories: 130

Total fat: 5 grams

Saturated fat: 2 grams

Cholesterol: 52 milligrams

Sodium: 155 milligrams

Boneless sirloin steak, lean, 1 pound

Garlic, minced, 1 clove

Rosemary, crushed, ¼ teaspoon

Thyme leaves, ¼ teaspoon

Margarine, 1 teaspoon

Plain low-fat yogurt, 1 tablespoon

Prepared mustard, 1 tablespoon

Worcestershire sauce, 1 tablespoon

Parsley, chopped, 1 tablespoon

1. Trim fat from meat.

2. Combine garlic and spices. Sprinkle over meat.

3. Melt margarine in a nonstick frying pan. Add meat and cook over medium heat 6 minutes on each side, or to desired doneness.

4. Place meat on serving platter and keep warm.

5. Combine yogurt, mustard, and Worcestershire sauce in a small microwave-safe bowl. Cover and microwave on high power for 1 minute. Spread mixture over warm meat.

6. Garnish with parsley.

7. To serve, slice meat on diagonal into thin slices.

NOTE: *Sauce may also be heated in a small saucepan over low heat; stir constantly until warm.*

EACH SERVING PROVIDES:

3 ounces from meat group

Corn and Zucchini Combo

4 servings, about ½ cup each

PER SERVING:

Calories: 75

Total fat: 2 grams

Saturated fat: Trace

Cholesterol: 0

Sodium: 15 milligrams

Margarine, 1 teaspoon

Onion, diced, ½ cup

Zucchini squash, sliced ⅛-inch thick, 1-½ cups

Frozen whole kernel corn, 1-½ cups

Basil leaves, ¼ teaspoon

Oregano leaves, ⅛ teaspoon

Pepper, ⅛ teaspoon

1. Melt margarine in frying pan over low heat.
2. Add onion; cook 2 minutes.
3. Add zucchini, cover and cook 5 minutes. Stir occasionally.
4. Add corn and seasonings. Cover and cook over low heat 5 minutes or until corn is done. Stir as needed.

EACH SERVING PROVIDES:

1 serving from vegetable group

Yogurt-Strawberry Parfait

4 servings, ½ cup frozen yogurt and ½ cup fruit each

PER SERVING:

Calories: 130

Total fat: 2 grams

Saturated fat: 1 gram

Cholesterol: 5 milligrams

Sodium: 60 milligrams

Frozen low-fat vanilla yogurt, 1 pint

Strawberries, sliced, 2 cups

Mint leaves (optional), 8

1. Layer yogurt and berries in parfait glass.
2. Garnish with mint leaves and serve.

NOTE: *For variety, use other berries or sliced fresh fruit in season.*

EACH SERVING PROVIDES:

½ serving from milk group

1 serving from fruit group

Creole Fish Fillets

4 servings, 3 ounces fish and ½ cup sauce each

PER SERVING:

Calories: 130

Total fat: 1 gram

Saturated fat: Trace

Cholesterol: 49 milligrams

Sodium: 155 milligrams

No-salt-added tomatoes, cut up, 16-ounce can

Celery, chopped, ½ cup

Onion, chopped, ½ cup

Green pepper, chopped, ¼ cup

Garlic, minced, 1 clove

Bay leaf, 1

Thyme leaves, ½ teaspoon

Red pepper flakes, ¼ teaspoon

Salt, ⅛ teaspoon

Fresh cod fillets, 1 pound

1. Preheat oven to 400° F.
2. Combine all ingredients, except fillets, in a saucepan. Bring to a boil. Cover; reduce heat and simmer 25 minutes, stirring occasionally. Remove bay leaf.
3. Place fillets in a baking dish. Bake, uncovered, for 15 minutes or until fish flakes easily when tested with a fork.
4. Pour sauce over fish and serve.

EACH SERVING PROVIDES:

3 ounces from meat group

1 serving from vegetable group

Whole-Wheat Cornmeal Muffins

8 muffins

PER MUFFIN:

Calories: 130

Total fat: 4 grams

Saturated fat: 1 gram

Cholesterol: 27 milligrams

Sodium: 130 milligrams

Yellow degerminated cornmeal, ⅔ cup

Whole-wheat flour, ⅔ cup

Sugar, 1 tablespoon

Baking powder, 2 teaspoons

Salt, ⅛ teaspoon

Skim milk, ⅔ cup

Egg, beaten, 1

Vegetable oil, 2 tablespoons

1. Preheat oven to 400° F.
2. Grease 8 muffin tins or use paper liners.

3. Mix dry ingredients thoroughly.

4. Mix milk, egg, and oil. Add to dry ingredients. Stir until dry ingredients are barely moistened. Batter will be lumpy.

5. Fill muffin tins ⅔ full.

6. Bake until lightly browned, about 20 minutes.

EACH SERVING PROVIDES:

2 servings from bread group

Pork and Vegetable Stir-fry

4 servings, 1 cup meat mixture, ¼ cup sauce and ¾ cup rice each

PER SERVING:

Calories: 370

Total fat: 9 grams

Saturated fat: 3 grams

Cholesterol: 69 milligrams

Sodium: 240 milligrams

Boneless pork loin, lean, 1 pound

Tarragon leaves, ½ teaspoon

Pepper, ¼ teaspoon

Garlic powder, ¼ teaspoon

Salt, ¼ teaspoon

Cornstarch, 2 teaspoons

Water, 1 cup

Lemon juice, ¼ cup

Carrots, sliced, 1 cup

Fresh mushrooms, sliced, 1 cup

Celery, sliced, 1 cup

Onions, chopped, ½ cup

Rice, cooked, 3 cups

1. Partially freeze meat. Trim fat and slice meat across the grain into ¼ inch-thick slices.

2. Combine seasonings. Sprinkle mixture over meat.

3. Combine cornstarch, water, and lemon juice. Set aside.

4. Heat nonstick frying pan. Add meat and stir-fry until brown, about 5 minutes. Drain meat, remove to another container, and cover to keep warm.

5. In same frying pan, stir-fry carrots 5 minutes or until tender crisp. Add

remaining vegetables and stir-fry 2 minutes. Add meat and cornstarch mixture. Bring to a boil. Cook, stirring constantly, until thickened.

6. Serve over rice.

EACH SERVING PROVIDES:

3 ounces from meat group

1 serving from vegetable group

1-½ servings from bread group

Lentil Stroganoff

4 servings, 1-½ cups stroganoff and ¾ cup noodles each

PER SERVING:

Calories: 520

Total fat: 5 grams

Saturated fat: 1 gram

Cholesterol: 48 milligrams

Sodium: 340 milligrams

Lentils, dry, 1-½ cups

Water, 4-½ cups

Salt, ¼ teaspoon

Vegetable oil, 1 teaspoon

Fresh mushrooms, sliced, 1-½ cups

Red or green pepper, cut in strips, 1 cup

Onion, chopped, ½ cup

Flour, 3 tablespoons

Dry mustard, 2 teaspoons

Black pepper, ¼ teaspoon

Plain low-fat yogurt, 8-ounce container

Egg noodles, cooked, 3 cups

Green onion, sliced, 2 tablespoons

1. Combine lentils, water, and salt in a large saucepan. Bring to a boil; cover, reduce heat, and cook until lentils are tender, about 30 minutes. Drain; set lentils aside and keep warm. Save liquid; add water to make 1-½ cups.

2. Heat oil in a large frying pan. Add mushrooms, peppers, and onion. Cook until vegetables are just tender.

3. Mix flour and seasonings. Stir evenly into vegetable mixture. Add saved

liquid, stirring constantly; cook over medium heat until mixture is smooth and thickened.

4. Add lentils; mix well. Heat to serving temperature.

5. Just before serving, stir in yogurt.

6. Cook noodles according to package directions.

7. Serve stroganoff over noodles. Garnish with green onion slices.

EACH SERVING PROVIDES:

Meat alternate equal to 2 ounces from meat group

1-½ servings from bread group

1-¼ servings from vegetable group

¼ serving from milk group

Apricot-Glazed Chicken

4 servings, about 3 ounces chicken each

PER SERVING:

Calories: 210

Total fat: 2 grams

Saturated fat: Trace

Cholesterol: 68 milligrams

Sodium: 155 milligrams

Lemon juice, 2 tablespoons

Garlic, minced, 1 clove

Pepper, ¼ teaspoon

Boneless skinless chicken breast halves, 4

Orange juice, ¾ cup

Dried apricots, 12 halves

Vinegar, 1 tablespoon

Brown sugar, packed, 1 teaspoon

Prepared mustard, 1 teaspoon

Ground ginger, ¼ teaspoon

Salt, ⅛ teaspoon

Raisins, ¼ cup

1. Preheat oven to 400° F.

2. Combine lemon juice, garlic, and pepper. Brush chicken with the mixture.

3. Arrange chicken on a rack in a baking dish. Cover and bake 45 minutes.

4. Combine orange juice and apricots in a small saucepan. Simmer, uncovered, for 10 minutes until apricots are tender. Stir in vinegar, sugar, mustard, ginger, and salt. Simmer 2 minutes longer. Remove from heat and pour into blender jar. Puree apricots about 15 seconds. Add raisins.

5. Spread half of the glaze on one side of the chicken; bake 3 minutes longer. Turn chicken and spread with remaining glaze. Return to oven for 3 more minutes or until chicken is tender.

EACH SERVING PROVIDES:

3 ounces from meat group

½ serving from fruit group

Rice-Pasta Pilaf

4 servings, about ¾ cup each

PER SERVING:

Calories: 205

Total fat: 5 grams

Saturated fat: 1 gram

Cholesterol: 0

Sodium: 225 milligrams

Brown rice, uncooked, ½ cup

Chicken broth, unsalted, 2-¼ cups

Thin spaghetti, broken into ½- to 1-inch pieces, ½ cup

Margarine, 1 tablespoon

Green onions, chopped, 3 tablespoons

Green pepper, chopped, 3 tablespoons

Fresh mushrooms, chopped, 3 tablespoons

Garlic, minced, 1 small clove

Savory, ¾ teaspoon

Salt, ¼ teaspoon

Pepper, ⅛ teaspoon

1. Cook rice in 1-¾ cups of the broth in a covered saucepan until almost tender, about 35 minutes.

2. Cook spaghetti in margarine in heavy pan over low heat until golden brown, about 2 minutes. Stir frequently; watch carefully.

3. Add browned spaghetti, vegetables, remaining ½ cup of chicken broth, and seasonings to rice.

4. Bring to boil, reduce heat, cover, and cook over medium heat until liquid is absorbed, about 10 minutes.

5. Remove from heat; let stand 2 minutes.

EACH SERVING PROVIDES:

1-½ servings from bread group

¼ serving from vegetable group

Peach Crisp

10 servings, about ½ cup each

PER SERVING:

Calories: 155

Total fat: 4 grams

Saturated fat: 1 gram

Cholesterol: 0

Sodium: 40 milligrams

Frozen unsweetened peaches, 2 16-ounce bags

Cornstarch, 2 tablespoons

Lemon juice, 2 teaspoons

Flour, ½ cup

Sugar, ½ cup

Ground cinnamon, ½ teaspoon

Ground cloves, ¼ teaspoon

Margarine, softened, 3 tablespoons

Quick rolled oats, ½ cup

1. Preheat oven to 375° F.

2. Place peaches in an 8" × 8" baking dish. Add cornstarch; toss to mix evenly.

3. Sprinkle lemon juice over peaches.

4. Mix flour, sugar, and spices.

5. Stir margarine into oats; add flour mixture. Mix until crumbly.

6. Sprinkle crumb mixture evenly over peaches.

7. Bake 45 minutes or until peaches are tender and top is lightly browned.

EACH SERVING PROVIDES:

¾ serving from fruit group

½ serving from bread group

Source: Using the Food Guide Pyramid: A Resource for Nutrition Educators, edited by Anne Shaw, Lois Fulton, Carole Davis, and Myrtle Hogbin, Washington, D.C.: U.S. Department of Agriculture, Food, Nutrition, and Consumer Services, Center for Nutrition Policy and Promotion, pp. 86–88, 58–82. The booklet is only available through the USDA web site, www.usda.gov, and it continues to be updated by the USDA.

APPENDIX E
A Well-Stocked Pantry

You're ready to move into your own place and anxious to start cooking good meals. To avoid the Old Mother Hubbard syndrome, of finding your cupboard bare, use this list of essential ingredients. There are many mix-and-match meals contained in this list, enough to guarantee that you won't be left scratching your head wondering what's for dinner.

The list itself comes from the USDA.

Grains and Pastas
cornmeal, yellow, degerminated
fig bars
flour, white, enriched
flour, whole wheat
graham crackers
macaroni, enriched
noodles, enriched
ready-to-eat cereal (whole grain flakes)
rice, brown
rice, enriched
rolled oats, quick

spaghetti, enriched
wheat crackers

Oils and Dressing
French dressing, regular
French dressing, reduced calorie
Italian dressing, regular
Italian dressing, reduced calorie
salad dressing, mayonnaise type, regular
salad dressing, mayonnaise type, reduced calorie
vegetable oil
vinaigrette dressing, reduced calorie

Broth/Vegetables

low-sodium chicken broth

no-salt-added tomatoes, puree, vegetable juice

Seasonings and Spices

basil leaves

bay leaves

black pepper

celery seed

chili powder

dried chives

dry mustard

garlic, fresh

garlic powder

ground cinnamon

ground cloves

ground ginger

ground sage

marjoram leaves

minced onion

onion powder

oregano leaves

peppermint extract

red pepper flakes

rosemary

salt

savory

tarragon leaves

thyme leaves

vanilla

worcestershire sauce

Leavening basics

baking powder

baking soda

Other basics

cocoa

cornstarch

dry beans and peas (kidney, lentils, split peas)

jelly

peanut butter

prepared mustard

raisins

sugar, brown

sugar, granulated

unflavored gelatin

unsalted roasted peanuts

vinegar

Refrigerator

eggs, large

lemonade

lemon juice, bottled

margarine (soft or hard)

milk (skim or 2% fat)

onions

yogurt, low fat and plain

Freezer

corn

grapefruit juice, concentrate

ice milk, vanilla

orange juice, concentrate

peas

sherbet

yogurt, frozen, low fat, vanilla

APPENDIX F
Pesticides

How do pesticides and other chemicals in food affect my risk for cancer?
According to the expert report from the American Institute for Cancer Research, *Food, Nutrition and the Prevention of Cancer: A Global Perspective* (1998), there is no convincing evidence that eating foods containing trace amounts of chemicals such as fertilizers, pesticides, herbicides, and drugs used on farm animals changes cancer risk. Exposure to all manufactured chemicals in air, water, soil, and food is believed to cause less than 1% of all cancers.

Should I avoid vegetables and fruits so I'm not exposed to pesticides?
Definitely not. The benefits of eating a diet based on vegetables, fruits, and grains far outweigh any potential harm from exposure to food additives, pesticide residues, and other chemicals in these foods. There is convincing evidence that diets high in vegetables and fruits protect against cancers of the colon, rectum, stomach, lung, mouth, pharynx, and esophagus. Eating plenty of produce probably also results in lower rates of cancers of the breast, bladder, pancreas, and larynx. Eating five or more servings of vegetables and fruits a day could cut cancer risk by as much as 20%. It is always a good idea to take the usual safety precautions. Scrub vegetables and fruits before eating them to remove any residues, along with any dirt or bacteria. Other tips are listed below.

Are vegetables and fruits the only foods that contain pesticide residues?
Pesticides can enter our diets through meat and dairy products, too. Organ meats like liver, and fatty meat, fish, and dairy products may have higher residue levels than low-fat choices. This is because residues accumulate in the liver and in the fat of animals. Grain products have little residue because crops are often treated soon after planting, long before edible plant parts have grown. Additionally, grinding and milling grains removes much of the residues present.

How are limits on pesticide use set?
From animal studies, the U.S. Environmental Protection Agency (EPA) projects the maximum amount of a pesticide residue a person could take in daily during a 70-year life span without suffering harm. It then sets the legal limit at a small fraction of that amount—generally 100 times lower. In 1996 Congress passed the Food Quality Protection Act which requires the EPA to reassess all existing tolerances over a period of 10 years, starting with those believed to be most dangerous.

Are children protected by pesticide limits too?
Yes, the Food Quality Protection Act requires that a pesticide must be shown to be safe for infants and children before it is used on crops. When the effects on children are not known, only one-tenth of the amount that is considered safe for adults is used, as added protection.

Are imported fruits and vegetables safe to eat?
In 1996, 38% of fruits and 12% of vegetables consumed in the United States were imported. Imports must meet the same standards as produce grown in this country, but inspection is often less than stringent. Take the same precautions with imported fruits and vegetables that you would with those grown domestically.

AICR'S RECOMMENDATIONS REGARDING ADDITIVES AND RESIDUES

When levels of additives, contaminants, and other residues are properly regulated, their presence in food and drink is not known to be harmful. However, unregulated or improper use can be a health hazard, and this applies particularly in economically developing countries.

An international expert panel of 15 scientists analyzed more than 4,500 scientific research studies about diet and cancer from around the world. Their analysis is published in the report *Food, Nutrition and the Prevention of Cancer: A Global Perspective*. From this report, the panel developed recommendations on the best ways to prevent cancer. All the recommendations are summed up in the Diet and Health Guidelines for Cancer Prevention. One of their 14 recommendations is to reduce the chemical residues in food:

• Choose produce free of holes; wash well using running water; remove outer leaves.
• Consider buying certified organic food.
• Eat a variety of foods to lower exposure to any one pesticide.

ORGANIC PRODUCE

Do organic products have any pesticide residues?
Organic farming restricts or eliminates the use of chemical pesticides, fertilizers, herbicides, and fungicides, resulting in lower pesticide residue levels in products and released into the environment. However, even crops grown by organic farming methods may contain some chemical residues.

Foods may be exposed to contaminated rain water, irrigation water, soil, or chemicals carried from farm to farm by wind. In a recent test of over 1,000 pounds of produce, 25% of organic vegetables and fruits contained residues, compared with 77% of conventionally grown produce.

Are organic vegetables and fruits healthier?
Both organic and conventionally grown vegetables and fruits are healthy. The chemicals used to treat a vegetable or fruit don't change its nutritional value.

Nutrient content depends mostly on the plant's variety—its genetic makeup. It also depends on the season it is planted, the soil it is grown in, the amount of rain and sun it gets, and how it is harvested, handled, and stored before it gets to the store and, eventually, to you.

It is important to eat at least five servings of organic or conventional vegetables and fruits a day to prevent cancer.

Source: American Institute for Cancer Research, *Pesticides: Facts on Preventing Cancer*, *American Institute for Cancer Research*, 1998.

APPENDIX G
What's on the Web

American Academy of Allergy Asthma and Immunology (AAAAI)
Address: 611 East Wells Street, Milwaukee, WI 53202
Phone: 414-272-6071 / 800-822-2762
Web address: www.aaaai.org
Web site: The AAAAI is a large professional medical specialty organization that represents allergists, clinical immunologists, physicians, and other health professionals in the country. Established in 1943, it works to improve the knowledge and practice of allergy, asthma, and immunology. The web site offers a physical referral directory plus a resource center for patients and for professionals. There are also links to other professional organizations. Geared for health care workers and other professionals, the information may be of interest to allergy sufferers or those seeking nutritional facts on these topics.

American Anorexia/Bulimia Association (AABA)
Address: 165 West 46th Street, Suite 1108, New York, NY 10036
Phone: 212-575-6200
Web address: www.aabainc.org
Web site: The AABA is a national, nonprofit organization comprised of health care professionals and others dedicated to the prevention and treatment of eating disorders. This site is geared toward the general public with information, articles, and lists of risk factors for sufferers as well as help lines, referral

networks, public information, support groups, and prevention programs. Articles and information work to expose and change the idealization of thinness. This site provides information for all ages.

American Association for the Advancement of Science (AAAS)
Address: 1200 New York Avenue, NW, Washington, DC 20005
Phone: 202-326-6400
Web address: www.aaas.org
Web site: The AAAS is a nonprofit, professional association working to educate the public on issues of science and technology. Founded in 1848, the group has a worldwide membership of more than 143,000 scientists, engineers, science educators, policy makers, and others. The site provides education and human resource programs plus science online and EurekAlert!, a section devoted to the latest research from journals and institutions covering all aspects of science, medicine, and technology. Although not an attractive site, the information it contains is solid and useful.

American Cancer Society
Address: 1599 Clifton Road, NE, Atlanta, GA 30329–4251
Phone: 404-320-3333 / 800-ACS-2345 / Fax: 404-329-7530
Web address: www.cancer.org
Web site: This site is designed for easy access to information. The navigator section provides entry to cancer information while the Cancer Resource Center focuses on the major concerns of cancer patients. The resource center also provides fast access to news, publications, and links to other organizations. Users can correspond with specially trained cancer information specialists and nurses. There is a glossary of cancer terms and definitions. The site provides information on support groups and patient service programs. This is a quick way for newly diagnosed cancer patients to gather reliable information written in understandable language.

American Council on Science and Health (ACSH)
Address: 1995 Broadway, Second Floor, New York, NY 10023-5860
Phone: 212-362-7044 / Fax: 212-362-4919
Web address: www.acsh.org
Web site: The ACSH is a consumer-education consortium made up of scientists, physicians, and policy advisors. The council tracks the accuracy of nutrition articles in popular magazines and publishes its survey online. This site, geared for the general public, offers a useful, conservative interpretation of current health information from product safety to food labeling to safety of "natural" products.

American Culinary Federation (ACF)

Address: 10 San Bartula Drive, St. Augustine, FL 32086
Phone: 904-824-4468 / 800-624-9458 / Fax: 904-825-4758
Web address: www.acfchefs.org
Web site: The ACF, founded in New York City in 1929, is a professional, not-for-profit organization for chefs working to promote a professional image of the American chef worldwide through education. The site includes a job bank, directories of accredited culinary programs and apprenticeship programs, and information on receiving certification and a calendar of culinary events. The section titled Chef and Child provides a look at a culinary-education program designed to teach nutrition and cooking to youngsters. The site also includes material appropriate for high school vocational educators.

American Diabetes Association (ADA)

Address: 1701 North Beauregard Street, Alexandria, VA 22311
Phone: 800-342-2383
Web address: www.diabetes.org
Web site: The ADA works to prevent and cure diabetes and to improve the lives of all people affected by diabetes. This easy-to-use web site contains information about the disease, risk factors, complications, and the warning signs of diabetes. There are also sections on nutrition, exercise, tips, and recipes, as well as general information. Users can request an information packet, but the association cautions that representatives cannot perform diagnosis or recommend medical treatment. There are links to other Internet resources and to magazines and journals dealing with diabetes and related health issues.

American Dietetic Association (ADA)

Address: 216 W. Jackson Boulevard, Chicago, IL 60606
Phone: 312-899-0040 / 800-366-1655
Web address: www.eatright.org
Web site: The number-one feature of this attractive and easy-to-use site is its ability to link to many other nutrition-related sites. Categories include consumer education and public policy, dietetic practice groups, medical and health professionals, and dietetic associations. This fact-filled site includes a "tip of the day," as well as an in-depth look at monthly features. Users can find information on the food guide pyramid, fact sheets, and a nutrition reading list. This site also provides a link to the ADA's journal and a function to help people "find a dietitian," plus an 800 hotline for professional advice on improving your diet.

American Heart Association (AHA)
Address: 7272 Greenville Avenue, Dallas, TX 75231
Phone: 214-373-6300 / 800-242-8721
Web address: www.americanheart.org
Web site: This colorful, user-friendly association web site has an easy-to-use A–Z guide that provides clear, concise information on heart disease and stroke-related illness. Sections deal with nutrition, exercise, professional publications, and a news bureau. Users can link to a special site for women who want heart health information or link to an additional site titled Living with Heart Failure designed for caregivers and patients. Visitors can send a message to Congress about various biomedical issues and other health care initiatives.

American Institute for Cancer Research (AICR)
Address: 1759 R. Street, NW, Washington, DC 20009
Phone: 202-328-7744 / 800-843-8114
Web address: www.aicr.org
Web site: This national cancer charity has created a web site that offers information on food, nutrition, and the prevention of cancer; news updates; critiques of fad diets and diet books; and a helpful resource that answers common questions of newly diagnosed cancer patients and their families. It features recipes as well as a nutrition hotline and kids' newsletter. Users can also link to other cancer and nutrition sites.

American Medical Association (AMA)
Address: 515 North State Street, Chicago, IL 60610
Phone: 312-464-5000
Web address: www.ama-assn.org
Web site: Although this site is clearly geared toward physicians, there are useful resources for the lay person, including a section on consumer health information. There is a members-only portion to this site with an AMA staff directory. Journals and the *American Medical News* are available as well as JAMA (*Journal of the American Medical Association*) and its related links on HIV/AIDS, asthma, migraines, and women's health.

Animal Rights Resource Site (ARRS) EnviroLink Network
Address: EnviroLink Network, 5808 Forbes Avenue, Second Floor, Pittsburgh, PA 15217
Phone: 412-420-6400 / Fax: 412-420-6404
Web address: http://arrs.envirolink.org
Web site: EnviroLink created this ARRS site to serve as a clearinghouse of information and data on a wide variety of animal rights topics. AARS is a project of the EnviroLink Network, a nonprofit organization that provides

web site hosting, automated mailing lists, interactive bulletin boards, and chat rooms to environmental organizations. This page offers one of the largest listings of environmental organizations on the web with good search capabilities for finding specific information.

Ask the Dietitian
Web address: http://www.dietitian.com
Web site: This site, developed by nutritionist Joanne Larsen, has a cool feature, the Healthy Body Calculator, found at http://www.dietitian.com/ibw/ibw. html. Have a tape measure handy and know your weight. This interactive tool creates a dietary recommendation as well as graphics to show you where you fall in the ideal health and body-mass-index ranges.

Burger King Corporation
Address: 17777 Old Cutler Road, Miami, Fl 33157-6347
Phone: 305-378-7011 / Fax: 305-379-7262
Web address: www.burgerking.com
Web site: This colorful site is filled with feel-good information about Burger King, but it also gets high marks for better than average nutritional information. Unlike sites that bury their numbers on fats and calories, Burger King provides an Interactive Nutritional Information Wizard, where users can select menu items, theoretically eat a reasonable amount of calories, and limit their fat intake if they choose. But advertising is still the most important part of this site with entry to the Kids Club filled with toys, games, and a clubhouse plus a What's Hot section that highlights the latest toy giveaway. Franchise locations are listed as well as the company information.

Center for Food Safety
Address: 666 Pennsylvania Avenue, SE, Suite 302, Washington DC 20003
Phone: 202-547-9359 / Fax: 202-547-9429
Web address: www.centerforfoodsafety.org
Web site: The Center for Food Safety is a public interest and environmental advocacy organization which addresses the impacts of the food-production system on human health, animal welfare, and the environment. The site contains legislative alerts and information on food safety issues such as genetically modified organisms (bioengineered foods), irradiation, sludge, and methyl bromid. New is www.foodsafetynow.org—an interactive tool for the public to use in submitting food safety comments to government officials, agencies, and members of Congress.

Center for Science in the Public Interest (CSPI)
Address: 1875 Connecticut Avenue, NW, Suite 300, Washington, DC 20009
Phone: 202-332-9110 / Fax: 202-265-4954
Web address: www.cspi.net

Web site: The CSPI is a nonprofit education and advocacy organization which works to improve the safety and nutritional quality of food. The organization promotes health education about nutrition and alcohol and represents the public's interests in the legislative, regulatory, and judicial arenas. The site offers excellent links to both private and government nutrition sources as well as access to CSPI's *Nutrition Action Healthletter*. An interesting nutrition quiz and a document library add to the wealth of information on this site. Special reports, such as *Liquid Candy*, spell out the facts on soft drinks and health.

Centers for Disease Control and Prevention (CDC)
Address: 1600 Clifton Road, NE, Atlanta, GA 30333
Phone: 404-639-3311 / 800-311-3435
Web address: www.cdc.gov
Web site: The Centers for Disease Control and Prevention is an agency of the Department of Health and Human Services. The web site is designed to answer a multitude of questions from the general public, and Health Topics A–Z or Frequently Asked Questions are filled with updated documents for that purpose. Categories of Frequently Asked Questions range from diabetes or *E. coli* to hanta virus and listeriosis. The site includes access to data and statistics, training and employment information, and links to other sites. It is a useful first stop for anyone with concerns about a medical condition. Keep in mind, however, that the CDC strongly recommends against self-diagnosis or self-management without the involvement of health care professionals.

Consumer Information Center (CIC)
Address: Pueblo, CO 81009
Phone: 888-878-3256
Web address: www.pueblo.gsa.gov
Web site: The CIC, part of the General Services Administration (GSA), has a large catalog of some 200 consumer publications currently in print. The Health and Food sections cover everything from fitness and medications to food safety, nutrition, and food preservatives. The site receives high marks for the access to highly accurate information it provides to consumers. Order a free catalog by calling 1-888-878-3256.

Council for Responsible Nutrition (CRN)
Address: 1875 Eye Street, NW, Suite 400, Washington, DC 20006-5409
Phone: 202-872-1488 / Fax: 202-872-9594
Web address: www.crnusa.org
Web site: The CRN is a trade association which represents companies that make nutritional supplements. This site offers comprehensive links to many government sites that deal with nutrition, legislation, and regulation of dietary

supplements. Other useful information includes the section on Scientific Affairs with current scientific articles on dietary supplements.

Earthsave International
Address: 600 Distillery Commons, Louisville, KY 40204-1922
Phone: 502-589-7676 / 800-DNA-DOIT
Web address: www.earthsave.org
Web site: This site features information on how a vegetarian diet helps the planet. The organization, founded by John Robbins, author of *Diet for America*, states its purpose as creating a better world and encouraging the benefits of healthy and life-sustaining food choices. Funding is provided by memberships and contributions from foundations, corporations, and private individuals.

Ethnic Grocer
Address: 1033 University Place #350, Evanston, IL 60201
Phone: 800-523-1961 / Fax: 847-475-7717
Web address: www.EthnicGrocer.com
Web site: This site makes ethnic cooking and eating as easy as possible for the average family. With choices like Chef Chat, Comfort Foods, and Select a Dish, users can choose by region or by meal parts like entrée, salad, dessert, and soup. For each type of ethnic eating, such as Japanese, Swedish or Greek, you pick from a list of choices. Ingredient lists are provided as well as step-by-step directions. There is also a culinary world tour and history of each region's foods plus featured products. Visitors can also fill up grocery carts with specials like raspberry champagne vinegar, maple syrup, or grape leaves.

Five-a-day
Address: 5301 Limestone Road, Suite 101, Wilmington, DE 19808-1249
Phone: 302-235-ADAY/Fax: 302-235-5555
Web address: www.5aday.gov
Web site: This site was created by the National Cancer Institute and the Centers for Disease Control and Prevention. Users can find a health chart that rates health habits along with how-to ideas and recommended portion sizes. Information is provided on the basics of eating 5 or more servings of fruits and vegetables per day plus recipes and tips on physical activity for optimum health. There is also a direct link to the USDA Dietary Guidelines for Americans.

Food Allergy Network
Address: 10400 Eaton Place, Suite 107, Fairfax, VA 22030-2209
Phone: 703-691-3179
Web address: www.foodallergy.org

Web site: This helpful site offers facts on food allergies with sections that answer common questions, dispel myths, and offer the latest research on food allergies. Users can also sign-up for "Product Alerts," a free service via email.

Food and Drug Administration/U.S. Department of Health and Human Services
Address: 200 Independence Avenue, SW, Washington, DC 20201
Phone: 888-463-6332
Web address: www.fda.gov
Web site: This user-friendly government site includes information on a wide range of topics from cosmetics to articles on acne, sports, asthma, and eating disorders. There is a special section titled For Kids, Teens & Educators that has a wealth of information in formats from crossword puzzles to a food safety word match and food safety quiz. There are also links to many nutrition sites and a useful resource list.

Food and Nutrition Board (FNB) Institute of Medicine
Address: Institute of Medicine, 2101 Constitution, Avenue, NW, Washington, DC 20418
Phone: 202-334-1601 / Fax: 202-334-2419
Web address: www4.nas.edu/IOM/IOMHome.nsf
Web site: The Food and Nutrition Board is part of the National Academy of Sciences (NAS). The NAS is a private, nonprofit corporation created by Congress and made up of biomedical scientists with expertise in nutrition and food science. The FNB makes recommendations to improve food quality and to promote public health and prevent diet-related diseases. This web site provides access to ongoing FNB studies, upcoming events, and links to related food and nutrition sites and to the IOM and NAS. Not for the casual user, this site is difficult to navigate, and the information appears in highly technical terms.

Food Finder/Olen Publishing
Phone: 415-383-4280 / 800-424-6536
Web address: www.olen.com
Web site: This site is based on the book *Fast Food Facts* published in 1998 by the Minnesota Attorney General's Office. The site allows users to search by individual fast-food restaurants or by different fields, including fat, cholesterol, and sodium. For example, you can find all fast-food restaurants that offer items with less than 10 grams of fat by putting 10 in the maximum fat field and leaving all other fields empty. This is a great way to compare and make better fast-food choices.

Good Karma Café
Web address: www.goodkarmacafe.com
Web site: This vegetarian-oriented site provides practical how-to advice for new vegetarians. Users can also purchase books, locate restaurants, find recipes, or link to an eclectic variety of other web sites. The recipe section also offers vegetarian versions of familiar foods. The Teen Veggie Forum offers information on how other teens cope with friends and family when they go veg or chat about getting healthy and exchange recipes.

Grain Nutrition Information Center
Address: 10841 South Parker Road, Suite 105, Parker, CO 80134
Phone: 303-840-8787 / Fax: 303-840-6877
Web address: www.wheatfoods.org
Web site: Sponsored by the Wheat Foods Council, this site is filled with information that lets you know that all kinds of grains are an important part of a well-balanced diet. There are special sections including Grain Food Trends, Healthy Lifestyles, Medical/Health, and Kids and Teens. The Education Resources section offers fact sheets that have been used by health professionals as client handouts. Users can also e-mail two registered dietitians with questions. The site includes recipes with nutrient analysis.

Harvard Eating Disorders Center
Address: 356 Boylston Street, Boston, MA 02116
Phone: 617-236-7776 / 888-236-1188 / Fax: 617-236-2068
Web address: www.hedc.org
Web site: This national, nonprofit organization is dedicated to research and education about eating disorders and their treatment. The site includes excellent resources, a question-and-answer section entitled Do I Have a Problem?, and lots of facts about eating disorders. There is also a list of events and programs and referrals for help and support for anyone dealing with an eating disorder.

Healthfinder/U.S. Department of Health and Human Services
Address: 200 Independence Avenue, SW, Washington, DC 20201
Phone: 202-619-0257 / Toll free: 877-696-6775
Web address: www.healthfinder.gov
Web site: The Department of Health and Human Services site covers everything from current topics like breast-feeding and folic acid to nutrition information from federal and state agencies. There is also a list of online medical journals, a database of toll-free numbers, a medical dictionary, a library locator, and information about support and self-help groups. There is a search engine for

subject searches or for browsing by topics. This easy-to-navigate site is filled with understandable and useful information.

Health Mall
Address: 2051 Springdale Road, Cherry Hill, NJ 08003
Phone: 800-204-1902
Web address: www.healthmall.com
Web site: With a database of some 4,800 health food stores, Health Mall calls itself the most comprehensive source for information concerning health, nutrition, and alternative medicine. The site has a handy Health Food Store Directory, a way to check for drug interactions between prescription drugs and vitamins. There is a database of chiropractors and a page of health-related links plus more alternative features like a directory of herbal remedies and a naturopath search, as well as a list of massage therapists. The section on symptoms and remedies is heavily visited. The monthly newsletter contains an alternative medicine update, which focuses on nutrition and herbal remedies.

Healthy People 2010
Web address: http://www.health.gov/healthypeople/default.htm
Web site: This site details the goals of the Healthy People 2010 initiative of the U.S. Department of Health and Human Services. It contains progress reports and reviews, links to community Healthy People initiatives, and information on how Americans' health compares with that of people in other countries. The 10 Leading Health Indicators, for which there are updated statistics, are physical activity, overweight and obesity, tobacco use, substance abuse, responsible sexual behavior, mental health, injury and violence, environmental quality, immunization, and access to health care.

Images of Health—the Nutrition Link
Address: Department of Family Medicine, East Carolina University, Greenville, NC 27858
Phone: 252-816-5459
Web address: www.preventivenutrition.com
Web site: Sponsored by the East Carolina University School of Medicine, this site was originally designed as a tutorial for students in the medical program. Each section links to assessment tools for use in clinical settings where students learn to teach patients the relationship between disease and diet. The four areas of information on the site are the U.S. Dietary Guidelines, the Natural History of Cancer, physician interventions research, and case studies.

International Food Information Council (IFIC)
Address: 1100 Connecticut Avenue, NW, Suite 430, Washington, DC 20036
Phone: 202-296-6540 / 202-296-6547
Web address: http://ificino.health.org

Web site: The IFIC collects and disseminates scientific information on food safety and nutritional health to nutritional professionals and educators plus government officials, journalists, and consumers. The IFIC, founded in 1985, is a nonprofit organization. Information for educators is included along with sections on general nutrition facts, current nutrition developments, and additional resources. A lengthy glossary plus the variety of food safety and nutritional information makes this site better than average.

La Leche League International
Address: PO Box 4079, Schaumburg, IL 60168-4079
Phone: 847-519-7730
Web address: http//www.lalecheleague.org
Web site: Provides information on breast-feeding, nutrition during breast-feeding, and parenting topics. Allows women to post questions and find a local breast-feeding support group or volunteer counselor.

Mayo Health Oasis/Mayo Foundation for Medical Education and Research
Address: 200 First Street, SW, Rochester, MN 55905
Phone: 507-266-4057
Web address: www.mayohealth.org
Web site: Put out by the famous Mayo Health Clinic, this site is rated among the best by the Tufts University Nutrition Navigator. The user-friendly format offers information on anything from past articles concerning nutritional topics to a virtual cookbook where readers send recipes to be "made over" into a healthier version. Ask the Mayo Dietitian is in a question-and-answer format, and there are quizzes and tests, some interactive, for users to test their nutrition knowledge.

McDonald's Corporation
Address: 1 McDonalds Plaza, Oak Brook, IL 60523-1928
Phone: 630-623-3000
Web address: www.McDonalds.com
Web site: This is an attractive and easy-to-use site, but business comes first as it features all the promotional products McDonalds has to offer consumers. However, there is good nutritional information to be had if you click on menu choices like Nutrition Facts and Nutrient Card. Consumers can find the breakdown on all McDonalds food products as well as fat grams and calories of each. The information gives interested consumers the opportunity to make informed menu selections—something that chains like Mrs. Fields Cookies and Cinnabon lack.

Meals for You (My Menus)/Point of Choice
Address: P.O. Box 2309, Fairfield, IA 52556
Phone: 515-472-3434 / 800-446-3687

Web address: www.MealsForYou.com
Web site: Welcome to a web site that is free, fast, and easy to use, where it's possible to find thousands of recipes by type, ingredients, or nutrient content. This site is sponsored by My Menus/Point of Choice, a small independent company founded in 1991. Users can search by categories of menus for diabetics, vegetarians, and dieters. The site offers menu plans complete with nutrient analysis and a shopping list, which can be organized, based on the floor plans of participating stores. Meals for You/Point of Choice has tested in-store interactive recipe centers in several U.S. grocery store chains.

National Academy of Sciences (NAS) (Institute of Medicine/Food Nutrition Board)
Address: 2101 Constitution Avenue, NW, Washington, DC 20418
Phone: 202-334-2587
Web address: www4.nas.edu
Web site: The NAS is a private, nonprofit corporation made up of biomedical scientists with expertise in nutrition, food science, food safety, and other areas. They provide independent advice on scientific issues to government. The site sections include news, current projects, publications, reports, books, articles, and a subject index for searching. This site offers important information, but it is difficult for the casual browser.

National Association of Anorexia Nervosa and Associated Disorders (ANAD)
Address: P.O. Box 7, Highland Park, IL 60035
Phone: (Hotline) 847-831-3438 / Fax: 847-433-4632
Web address: www.anad.org
Web site: The ANAD, founded in 1976, is among the oldest national, nonprofit organizations to help eating disorder victims and their families. The site offers access to free hotline counseling, an international network of support groups for sufferers and their families, and it provides referrals to health care professionals. There are sections on insurance discrimination and legislative news. The association also provides educational speakers, programs, and presentations for schools, colleges, public health agencies, and community groups. There is an online form to request information or to volunteer.

National Cancer Institute (NCI)
Address: 9000 Rockville Pike, Building 31, Room 10A19 (Press Office), Bethesda, MD 20892-2582
Phone: 301-496-6641
Web address: www.nci.nih.gov
Web site: This web site is designed to help users locate answers to cancer-related questions. There are also statistics on cancer mortality in the United States

as well as information on medical research related to cancer. CancerTrials is a comprehensive list of clinical trials, and CancerNet is a section devoted to information on the treatment, prevention, and detection of cancer and coping with the effects of cancer. This site also links to the National Institute of Health as well as other sites that deal with cancer and health issues.

National Center for Health Statistics (NCHS)
Address: 6525 Belcrest Road, Hyattsville, MD 20782-2003
Phone: 301-458-4636
Web address: www.cdc.gov/nchs
Web site: This center is affiliated with the Centers for Disease Control and Prevention (CDC), under the U.S. Department of Health and Human Services. Health topics A–Z is a list of disease and health subjects found on the CDC web site. Those are divided by categories from teens to environmental health and women's health. This site links to vital records for the entire United States and also links to the U.S. State Department.

National Institutes of Health (NIH)
Address: Building 1, Room B156, 1 Center Drive, MSC 0122, Bethesda, MD 20892-0148
Phone: 301-496-4000
Web address: www.nih.gov
Web site: This government site offers a very comprehensive list of hotline resources on any imaginable health problem from ADHD to Z. There are sections about the NIH, news and events, scientific resources from journals to research labs, and health information in the form of publications as well as access to resources like MEDLINEplus. Information is also provided in Spanish. The NIH is part of the U.S. Department of Health and Human Services.

New York Online Access to Health (NOAH)
Web address: www.noah.cuny.edu/wellness.nutrition/nutrition.html
Web site: NOAH is a consumer health web site of quality filtered materials in English or Spanish. The volunteer staff receives the information from medical librarians working in academic, special, hospital, and public libraries throughout New York. Page editors organize and arrange the full-text consumer information, which is available through an effective keyword search.

Nutrition on the Web—for Teens/ThinkQuest
Address: 200 Business Park Drive, Armonk, NY 10504
Phone: 914-273-1700
Web address: http://library.thinkquest.org
Web site: The ThinkQuest site was developed by students, and it is written especially for that audience. Informative sections include Exercises, Myths,

Case Files, Teen Health, and Recipes, among others, and interactive sites allow users to take a Nutri-Quiz, to ask fellow users questions, to find the number of calories in common foods, and to logon to the diet planner for healthy meal planning. There is also access to a chat room, and users can choose the language in which they want to view the web site.

Oldways Preservation and Exchange Trust
Address: 25 First Street, Cambridge, MA 02141
Phone: 617-621-3000/Fax: 617-621-1230
Web address: www.oldwayspt.org
Web site: This nonprofit education organization promotes healthy eating based on the "old ways" or traditional cuisines from around the world. They have created four food pyramids; Asian, Latin, Mediterranean, and vegetarian. The Oldways site also offers educational programs, nutritional news, and a bookstore. Users can browse an assortment of health issues by searching their archive of articles.

People for the Ethical Treatment of Animals (PETA)
Address: 501 Front Street, Norfolk, VA 23510
Phone: 757-622-PETA
Web address: www.peta-online.org
Web site: This site offers information on subjects from vegetarians to animals in entertainment and animal experimentation. There are fact sheets, videos, and photographs available. When they concern controversial topics, they are not for the squeamish. PETA also has a special kids' section, a store, and action alerts. Those interested can also join PETA and make donations via the Internet.

Physicians Committee for Responsible Medicine (PCRM)
Address: 5100 Washington Avenue, NW, Suite 404, Washington, DC 20016
Phone: 202-686-2210
Web address: www.pcrm.org
Web site: PCRM promotes preventive medicine and a nutrition program, the New Four Food Groups that includes a nutrition curriculum for schools. They support research programs in diabetes, cancer, and other health care issues and have developed a program for healthful eating for businesses, hospitals, and schools called the Gold Plan. A keyword search can locate topics like restaurant reviews and physician referrals, and special resources are available for medical students and educators.

President's Council on Food Safety
Address: 200 Independence Avenue, SW, Washington, DC 20201
Phone: 888-SAFEFOOD

Web address: www.foodsafety.gov

Web site: The President's Council on Food Safety was established in August 1998 to coordinate the nation's food safety policy and resources. This site, a gateway to government food safety information, is jointly sponsored by the Department of Commerce, the Environmental Protection Agency, the Department of Health and Human Services, and the U.S. Department of Agriculture. It is maintained by the FDA's Center for Food Safety and Applied Nutrition. Sections include Consumer Advice; Kids, Teens and Educators; Report Illnesses; and Product Complaints. There is also quick access to current government publications on safety topics and links to federal and state government agencies.

Shape Up America

Address: 6707 Democracy Boulevard, Suite 306, Bethesda, MD 20817

Web address: www.shapeup.org

Web site: Shape Up America is a national initiative to promote healthy weight, nutrition, and increased physical activity across America. Made up of a large coalition of industry, physical fitness, medical, health, and nutritional experts, Shape Up America works to promote the importance of a healthy weight, works to educate people about the ways in which to achieve appropriate body weight, and cooperates with other organizations to advance a healthy lifestyle. The site offers a support center for practical tips on weight loss. It also offers an interactive weight loss program, a cyber kitchen, and a center to help you determine your body mass index (BMI).

Simple Living Network

Address: P.O. Box 233, Trout Lake, WA 98650

Phone: 800-318-5725

Web address: http://www.simpleliving.net

Web site: Relax, make yourself a cup of tea, and plan to stay a while according to this site whose stated goal is to provide information and the tools to live a simple and restorative lifestyle. Users can chat live with others, look at past newsletter archives or current issues, or follow the step-by-step guide into the Web of Simplicity. The focus is on free community services and resources with lots of food for thought.

Snack Food Association

Address: 1711 King Street, Suite 1, Alexandria, VA 22314

Phone: 703-836-4500 / 800-628-1334

Web address: http://www.sfa.org

Web site: Ever thought of snacking across America? This site provides regional recipes using every possible snack food from chocolate-covered potato chips to spicy Santa Fe trail mix. The association, founded in 1937, continues to grow just like the industry it supports. Users can find information on the state of the snack-food industry, consumer snacking behavior, and an interesting timeline and history of snack food. If you want to know who invented the potato chip, the information is easily available.

Taco Bell/Trigon Global Restaurants
Address: 17901 Von Karman Avenue, Irvine, CA 92614
Phone: 949-863-4500
Web address: http://www.tacobell.com
Web site: This fast-food restaurant site offers easy-to-find nutritional information plus the usual company information about franchise locations, employment information, and even an online gift shop. Though not as interactive as the McDonald's site, this is still a colorful and informative tool. It links to Kentucky Fried Chicken (KFC) and Pizza Hut, both under the Trigon corporate umbrella.

Teenage Research Unlimited (TRU)
Address: 707 Skokie Boulevard, Suite 450, Northbrook, IL 60062
Phone: 847-564-3440
Web address: www.teenresearch.com
Web site: Teenage Research Unlimited, founded in 1982, calls itself the first marketing-research firm to specialize exclusively in the teenage market. From this site, users can subscribe to a syndicated teen study and access news releases and descriptions of their marketing strategy and company officials. Although much of the information must be purchased, the news released has current facts useful to teens and educators.

U.S. Department of Agriculture (USDA)
Address: 14th and Independence Avenue, SW, Washington, DC 20250
Phone: 202-720-2791
Web address: www.usda.gov / www.usda.gov/cnpp
Web site: The USDA site has a wealth of government information, starting with a message from the secretary, and including a history of American agriculture. One cool feature is the interactive Healthy Eating Index. Plug in what you've eaten in recent days, and the site produces a score on how healthy your overall diet is. There is also access to the Code of Federal Regulations for agriculture, animals, and forests and a link to the USDA Fraud Hotline. The site also links to the USDA Center for Nutrition Policy and Promotion. That site offers professionals who work on nutrition and hunger issues access to USDA documents, but it is not for the casual browser.

U.S. Department of Agriculture Food and Nutrition Information Center
Address: 10301 Baltimore Avenue, Beltsville, MD 20705-2351

Phone: 301-504-5719
Web address: www.nal.usda.gov/fnic
Web site: Sponsored by the USDA National Agricultural Library, this site con-
nects users to the resources of the National Agricultural Library, which contains educational materials, research briefs, and food composition data. This
site is geared toward professionals looking for technical information; however,
some information is aimed at consumers.

U.S. Department of Health and Human Services
Address: 200 Independence Avenue, SW, Washington, DC 20201
Phone: 202-619-0257 / Toll free: 877-696-6775
Web address: www.hhs.gov
Web site: The Department of Health and Human Services (HHS) is the U.S.
government's principal agency overseeing all aspects of American health with
more than 300 programs on everything from food and drug safety to Medicare
and Medicaid. The site links to other HHS agencies and sponsored sites, such
as News and Public Affairs, What's New, and a calendar of events and health
observances. It also links to YouthInfo, a web site developed to provide the
latest information about America's adolescents. That site contains a profile
of youth, resources for parents, and speeches on topics of interest to youth.

University of Illinois Office of Extension and Outreach
Address: 214 Mumford Hall, 1301 West Gregory Drive, Urbana, IL 61801
Phone: 217-333-5900
Web address: www.ag.uiuc.edu/~VISTA/foodnutr.html
Web site: With a focus on nutrition education, this University of Illinois–sponsored site covers the usual range of topics from making good food choices to
reducing dietary fat and cholesterol. Although many topics are devoted to
the concerns of senior citizens, other unique choices include the preparation
of food during a power failure, a guide to reusing food packaging, and using
cooking substitution to decrease sugar and fat and increase nutrition.

University of Missouri Food and Nutrition
Address: 225 University Hall, Columbia, MO 65211
Phone: 573-882-2428
Web address: http://outreach.missouri.edu/hes/food.htm
Web site: Sponsored by the University of Missouri in partnership with Columbia
Extension Service, this site is designed to help consumers of all ages improve
their health by selecting nutritious foods. Consumer tip sheets and the *Food
and Nutrition Resource Newsletters* are consumer friendly and easy to search,
and they answer questions from the latest diet and sports supplements to food
safety and educational resources. A Resource Network Hotline links to different categories of companies, organizations, and web sites. Educators will

find information divided by grade level with activities and links. A nice addition is a health days calendar.

Vegetarian Pages
Web address: www.veg.org/veg
Web site: This online guide for vegetarians and vegans contains a vast collection of information geared toward anyone interested in becoming a vegetarian or anyone who wants to stop eating a lot of meat. Sections range from Frequently Asked Questions, to the Mega Index of Everything Vegetarian, plus recipes, nutrition, a list of famous vegetarians, and contacts with many organizations.

Vegetarian Resource Group (VRG)
Address: P.O. Box 1343, Baltimore, MD 21203
Phone: 410-366-VEGE
Web address: www.veg.org
Web site: The VRG, a nonprofit group, works to educate the public on vegetarian and related issues such as health, ecology, world hunger, and nutrition. Financial support comes largely from membership, contributions, and book sales. The site provides news, recipes, and a huge list of nutrition and related links. There is a lengthy section on vegetarian nutrition, geared for anyone interested in meatless eating. Although developed for students and consumers, health care professionals as well may find useful information here.

Vegetarian Society of the UK
Address: Parkdale, Dunham Road, Altrincham, Cheshire, WA144QG
Phone: 0161-925-2000
Web address: www.vegsoc.org
Web site: For new vegetarians, this resource offers a glimpse into the lifestyle of the British vegetarian. Geared for student users who can find anything from tips on stumbling blocks to being vegetarian to a section for matching up with a vegetarian pen pal. For those who want to know more about the Paul McCartney Fame School, otherwise known as the Liverpool Institute for the Performing Arts, there is information and a picture of the institute.

Wake Forest University—Baptist Medical Center
Address: School of Medicine, Medical Center Boulevard, Winston-Salem, NC 27157
Phone: 336-716-2011
Web address: www.bgsm.edu/nutrition
Web site: Run by Wake Forest University's Bowman Gray School of Medicine and its Center for Research on Human Nutrition and Chronic Disease Prevention, this site gives a nutritional breakdown of common foods including

fast food and offers quizzes on diet and fitness. The school's research center devised this site to promote preventative health care. It also offers a calorie calculator to estimate calories and fat, cholesterol, and sodium levels in a variety of common foods and beverages. Unsure you're eating a balanced diet? Take the "How's your Diet?" quiz. Eating habits are compared to the U.S. Dietary Guidelines put out by the USDA.

Wendy's/Wendy's International
Address: 4288 West Dublin-Granville Road, Dublin, OH 43017
Phone: 614-764-3100
Web address: www.wendys.com
Web site: This site prominently features Wendy's founder Dave Thomas and includes sections called Dave's Favorites, Meet Dave, and Wendy's Story in an attempt to humanize the company. There is adequate nutritional information and also a place for comments and information about company-sponsored programs.

World Health Organization (WHO)
Address: (Liaison office) 1775 K Street, NW, Suite 430, Washington, DC 20006
Phone: 202-331-9081
Web address: www.who.org
Web site: With an obvious emphasis on international health issues, this site offers reports and research information on issues from eradicating polio to making advances in tuberculosis medications. It is not for the casual browser, but a great deal of information about the state of the world's health is made available here.

Yale Center for Eating and Weight Disorders
Address: Yale University Department of Psychology, P.O. Box 208205, New Haven, CT 06520-8205
Phone: 203-432-4610
Web address: www.yale.edu/ycewd
Web site: This no-nonsense web site is clear and concise. The home page includes a short introduction to the center and its services, fees, and location. There is a brief description of various eating disorders, but the obvious purpose of the site is to connect anyone with a suspected eating disorder with the appropriate treatment.

INDEX

About the Authors

MARJOLIJN BIJLEFELD is a freelance writer and editor. She is the author of *The Gun Control Debate: A Documentary History* (Greenwood, 1997), *People For and Against Gun Control* (Greenwood, 1999), and *Teen Guide to Personal Financial Management* (Greenwood, 2000).

SHARON K. ZOUMBARIS is a professional librarian, freelance writer and storyteller. She is the author of *Teen Guide to Personal Financial Management* (Greenwood, 2000).